Foundations
of First Peoples'
Sovereignty

PETER LANG
New York • Washington, D.C./Baltimore • Bern
Frankfurt am Main • Berlin • Brussels • Vienna • Oxford

Foundations of First Peoples' Sovereignty

HISTORY, EDUCATION & CULTURE

Edited by Ulrike Wiethaus

PETER LANG
New York • Washington, D.C./Baltimore • Bern
Frankfurt am Main • Berlin • Brussels • Vienna • Oxford

Library of Congress Cataloging-in-Publication Data

Foundations of First Peoples' sovereignty: history, education and culture /
edited by Ulrike Wiethaus.
p. cm.
Includes bibliographical references and index.
1. Indians of North America—Government relations. 2. Indians of North America—History.
3. Indians of North America—Social life and customs. 4. Self-determination, National—
North America. 5. Mayas—Government relations. 6. Mayas—History. 7. Mayas—
Social life and customs. 8. Self-determination, National—Mexico. I. Wiethaus, Ulrike.
E93.F68   323.1197—dc22   2007051197
ISBN 978-0-8204-8169-2

Bibliographic information published by **Die Deutsche Bibliothek**.
Die Deutsche Bibliothek lists this publication in the "Deutsche
Nationalbibliografie"; detailed bibliographic data is available
on the Internet at http://dnb.ddb.de/.

Cover design and photograph by Duncan Lewis,
based on a design concept by Orrie Charger.

The paper in this book meets the guidelines for permanence and durability
of the Committee on Production Guidelines for Book Longevity
of the Council of Library Resources.

© 2008 Peter Lang Publishing, Inc., New York
29 Broadway, 18th floor, New York, NY 10006
www.peterlang.com

Printed in the United States of America

Dedicated to Lydia and Willie French Lowery, and David DeHorse

CONTENTS

IN THE PLACE OF A FOREWORD:
STILL CODE TALKING

LeAnne Howe

We are stronger when the words of our ancestors are heard. Our stories travel through communities and into art and scholarship. They code talk along the way. This volume tracks some of our stories, and the art and scholarship that contain them across multiple boundaries, across academic disciplines, across geographies, across time. These codes are no less vital and no less global than those used by the Choctaw Code Talkers of World War I and World War II.[1] In the brief moment of a contemporary academic "now," the authors of *Foundations of First Peoples' Sovereignty* make an effort to remain faithful to the words as spoken in our communities, especially those spoken by our elders. In the place of a fore/word, I offer such words from my community, once and now again, in code, spoken by Choctaw Chief Cobb. The story sustains historical memory, offers focus and depth to the vision of this volume. Chief Cobb's words carry the urgency of this book's theme: first peoples' sovereignty in historical perspective, in education, and the arts.

In 1843, Chief Cobb addressed Captain McRea in the Choctaw Council as follows:

> "Brother, when you were young, we were strong; we fought by your side; but our arms are now broken. You have grown large. My people have become small. Brother, my voice is weak; you can scarcely hear me; it is not the shout of a warrior, but the wail of an infant. I have lost it in mourning over the misfortunes of my people.
>
> There are their graves, and in those aged pines you hear the ghosts of the departed.—Their ashes are here and we have been left to protect them. Our warriors are nearly all gone to the far country west; but here are our dead. Shall we go, too, and give their bones to the wolves? Brother, our hearts are full. Twelve winters ago our chiefs sold our country. Every warrior that you see here was opposed to the treaty.
>
> If the dead could have counted, it would never have been made, but alas, though they stood around, they could not be seen or heard. Their tears came in raindrops, and their voices in the wailing wind, but the pale faces knew it not, and our land was taken away. . . . When you took our country, you promised us land. There is your promise in the book. Twelve times have the trees dropped their leaves and yet, we have received no land. Our houses have been taken from us. The white man's plough turns up the bones of our fathers. We dare not kindle our fires; and yet you said we might remain and you would give us land."[2]

In these brief paragraphs, Chief Cobb is invoking the story, or the history of an event on the Choctaw land. He reminds Captain McRea and the United States government what has transpired there and what promises were made to the Choctaw people.

I have long argued that stories are a foundational principle of sovereignty. Native stories, no matter what form they take—history, oral story, drama, memoir, poem—seem to pull all the elements together of the storyteller's tribe, meaning the people, the land, multiple characters—immigrants, friends, enemies—and connect these in past, present, and future milieus. This *tribalography* comes from the Native propensity for bringing things together, for creating consensus, and for symbiotically connecting one thing to another.

Stories nurture and sustain First Peoples' scholarship, strengthen and sustain it. In this volume, stories are woven into academic discourse, sometimes more hidden and submerged, sometimes interrupting academic reflection to the point of truth coalescing as *tribalography*: stories about tobacco, about family, about ceremony, about diplomacy, about words.

In the following pages, Native and non-Native scholars, educators, and artists make an effort to re-kindle our fires. They code talk in a new hybridity, and through academic discourse interrupted by story and image, connecting one event with another—from tribal peoples to show that our histories and Native sovereignties are still alive—though under duress. How shall we continue then? Together! However, this togetherness means that we must attend to the past, as well as the future, globally, now.

> "Everything is alive
> Everything is past
> Present
> Future
> Something endures.
> And I tell you now
> I dreamed the vision that is you.
> And I wait."[3]

NOTES

1 In World War I, during the Meuse-Argonne campaign, Choctaw Code Talkers led to the capture of one hundred seventy-one Germans; in World War II, Choctaw Code Talkers worked in campaigns from Africa, Sicily, Italy, and Germany. I honor and acknowledge their work, literally and symbolically, in LeAnne Howe, *Evidence of Red* (Cambridge, UK: Salt Publishing, 2005), 1.

2 These words were transcribed in the *Niles Register* LXIV, 1843, 131–32. Excerpted from LeAnne Howe, *Evidence of Red*, 89.

3 LeAnne Howe, "The Unknown Women," in LeAnne Howe, *Evidence of Red*, 15.

BIBLIOGRAPHY

Howe, LeAnne. *Evidence of Red.* Cambridge, UK: Salt Publishing, 2005.

ACKNOWLEDGMENTS

My greatest debt of gratitude belongs to my contributors, whose patience knows no bounds. I am deeply indebted to Rosa Revels Winfree, Barbara Locklear, Ruth Revels, Ruth Woods, and Helen Maynor Scheirbeck for their knowledge, wisdom and passion as this project found its way from inspiration and need into print. A big thank you goes to my scholar activist colleagues in the 2004 Lannan Summer Institute "Teaching American Indian Sovereignty" at the D'Arcy McNickle Center for American Indian History at the Newberry Library, to David Wilkins for inviting me, and to Brian Hosmer and Clara Sue Kidwell for their gracious hospitality; to the participants of the NIEA post-convention symposium on sovereignty, especially to Lionel Bordeaux, Floyd Westerman *in memoriam*, and Willie French Lowery; to my colleagues in Lakota Studies at Sinte Gleska University, especially to Sylvan Whitehat and Francis Cutt; always, *pilamayaye* to Harry Charger, to Danny Bell, Roseanna Belt, Keith Brown, and Arnold Richardson. I am grateful to Wake Forest University's generous financial and administrative support, and to Wake Forest University colleagues who strengthened this project in ways subtle and robust, especially to Wanda Balzano, Sally Barbour, Debbie Best, Steve Boyd, Mary DeShazer, Mary Friedman, Alice Goodman, Billy Hamilton, Toby Hale, Candide Jones, Candyce Leonard, Linda Nielsen, Barbee Oakes, Mary Scanlon, Gillian Overing, Gale Sigal, Donna Simmons, Olga Valbuena, Robert Vidrine, and Steve Whittington. My research assistants added enthusiasm and expertise along the journey. A heartfelt thank you goes to Mary Bowden, Dustin Frye, and Sarah Pirovitz, and to Joey Boylan, Elizabeth Burke, Stacie McGeever, Michael Marks, Matthew Newell, and Kaitlyn Oschwald. I am immensely grateful to Amy Gormley for her supple translation of *Soledad y Esperanza*; to Orrie Charger and Duncan G. Lewis for the poignant cover concept and art; to Jessica Koman for taking the manuscript into her own competent hands at the right time. I thank Nancy Netzer, Director of the McMullen Museum of Art at Boston College, for graciously granting permission to reprint an earlier version of Eva Garroutte's essay; Jaune Quick-to-See Smith for granting permission to print *Modern Times*; Hulleah Tsinhnahjinnie for granting permission to reprint *Nobody's Pet Indian* and *Grandchildren*; and Muriel Antoine for granting permission to reprint *I Dreamt I was an Aztec Goddess in my Maidenform Bra*. Heidi Burns at Peter Lang will always be connected to this volume's community of scholars and teachers.

INTRODUCTION

Ulrike Wiethaus

Foundations of First Peoples' Sovereignty is a methodologically diverse collection of essays. It introduces educational initiatives and scholarship in the humanities and social sciences on behalf of Indigenous freedom in four geographical regions in the Americas: Hawai'i, Chiapas, the Great Plains, and the Southeastern United States. Unlike mono-methodological academic analyses of sovereignty, the individual chapters and case studies affirm and explore the give and take between tribal community action and academic reflection, the possibility of a bridge between the philosophical and spiritual force of Native community responsibilities and language protocol and Western academic discourse and intellectual work.[1] By bringing together work from four different geographical regions, it acknowledges the commonalities shared by Indigenous nations across this hemisphere.[2]

The ethnocentricity of traditional academic discourse about Indigenous issues has been labeled "Euro-forming" by Haudenosaunee scholar Barbara Mann, who asserts that Euro-centric "bias at the base of the humanities tends to drive non-Europeans from the field."[3] Several essays in this volume analyze the uniqueness of Indigenous approaches to the contentious issue of sovereignty, a concept that in its increasingly popular usage "masks its own ideological origins in colonial legal-religious discourses as well as the heterogeneity of its contemporary histories, meanings, and identities for Indigenous peoples."[4] By doing so, the authors allow other equally complex systems of knowledge and logic shape our understanding of Indigenous freedom, of the complexity of traditional political decision-making processes, and of an Indigenous protocol of nation-to-nation relationships of exchange and world-building. We thus move gradually toward healing past and present in this hemisphere. An early template for such work is the Haudenosaunee contribution to the creation of the United States constitution. A *locus classicus* for the argument on behalf of a continuity of shared values on both sides, despite all efforts to destroy First Peoples' autonomy might well be Felix Cohen's statement in 1952 that

> . . . it is out of a rich Indian democratic tradition that the distinctive political ideals of American life emerged. Universal suffrage for women as well as for men, the pattern of states within a state that we call federalism, the habit of treating chiefs as servants of people instead of their masters, the insistence that the community must respect the diversity of men and the diversity of their dreams—all these things were part of the American way of life before Columbus landed.[5]

This volume asserts that the foundation of Indigenous freedom has always been transmitted and formed in lived relationships—to each other, to the natural and spiritual world—and communicated and reflected upon beyond European-style political and philosophical academic discourse. Indigenous sovereignty has been practiced in language, art, pedagogy, and ceremony. The collection's authors thus contribute to a growing global effort to support and protect Indigenous sovereignty and autonomy not only in the political arena of state and federal governmental activities, but in all areas of public life, whether economic, cultural, intellectual, or spiritual.[6] The authors, almost exclusively American Indian and Native Hawaiian, are trained in anthropology, political science and critical race theory, law, history, education, sociology, public health, and religious studies, and have worked as community educators and administrators, ceremonial leaders, scholars, and artists.

Their shared premises can be summarized briefly. The authors affirm the tribally specific existence of an Indigenous understanding of freedom and sovereignty equal to any Western European notion of political independence. The current difficulty in communicating this fact effectively is that public Euro-American records chronicling and analyzing the assault on, the defense or the affirmation of Indigenous sovereignty have largely been determined by the epistemologies, discursive practices, and hermeneutics of Western legal traditions.[7] Still, First Nations' practices of self-determination and politico-philosophical thought have remained in continuous, autonomously defined existence, even if hidden from Euro-American view or not fully understood by Euro-Americans. Sovereignty is being fought for in the courts, but equally important, it is being kept alive and vibrant in daily practices, teachings, and traditions. To underscore this point, the collection includes contributions by elders and artists. The concept of sovereignty, problematical as it is from a historical perspective,[8] as employed by the authors of this volume, covers a diversity of social, economic, and cultural practices that extends well beyond legal discourse and political governance. Such diversity, the authors posit, constitute the basis and legitimacy of all legal efforts. It has carried the heart and breath of Indigenous self-determination.

Living, broadly shared expressions of art, education, literature, theatre, local community action, and ceremony as the foundation of political life have in the past been either rendered invisible or delegated in a fragmented way to the academic domain of the humanities and social sciences, often perceived as "soft knowledge," polemically gendered as "feminine" rather than "virile," and deemed of lower political capital.[9] This dangerous misperception is not rooted in any Indigenous paradigm, but in the Western ("Euro-formed") construction of the rational political subject, gendered as male and, through the heavily masculinized social discipline of rationality and individuality, isolated from counter-hegemonic alternative networks, discursive practices, and relationships that could sustain a critique of the hegemonic and homogenizing claims of the state and creatively imagine political alternatives to nation state democracies. The economic, social, and cultural consequences of such a construction of political identity seem self-evident, especially given the worsening gaps in economic well-being and ethnic disparities in the United States.[10]

However, this rift between public (Euro-centric) and internal (Indigenous) approaches to Indigenous sovereignty is beginning to be challenged. A careful observer may witness a shift at the margins of mainstream public transcripts, gated and guarded as they are as a divided and divisive discourse of sovereignty. As part of the growing impact of Indigenous activists and intellectuals who work toward a paradigm shift in scholarship and policy making, Rennard Strickland noted the emerging trend in sovereignty studies to contextualize legal issues and key law cases by emphasizing existing sovereign practices within an Indigenous nation. In his essay, "The Eagle's Empire: Sovereignty, Survival, and Self-Governance in Native American Law and Constitutionalism,"[11] Strickland asserts that "we need scholars who step beyond the theory of sovereignty and explore it in practice."[12]

Indigenist critiques of mainstream political knowledge and practices are used to reveal domains of relationships otherwise hidden. Scholar Joely De La Torre articulates this point for her own discipline, political science. In her view, "power and politics analyzed under an interpretive [post-positivist] approach become expressions of meanings and an understanding of experiences and shared values; political reality is created or constituted symbolically through language."[13]

The list of academic monographs redefining the field of sovereignty studies is steadily growing. Indigenist projects of reclaiming the complexity of First Nations sovereignty globally include Robert Allen Warrior, *Tribal Secrets: Recovering American Indian Intellectual Traditions,* Taiaiake Alfred, *Peace, Power, Righteousness: An Indigenous Manifesto,* and Haunani-Kay Trask, *From a Native Daughter: Colonialism and Sovereignty in Hawai'i.* Jacob K. Olupona's edited collection of essays, *Beyond Primitivism: Indigenous Religious Traditions and Modernity* brings together scholars reflecting on the global emergence of Indigenist alternatives to Western imperial methodologies and a critique of their ideological gatekeepers.[14]

In terms of recognizing the importance of previously neglected sources in constructing an Indigenous nation's own sense of sovereignty and the practice of sovereignty in everyday life, a study by Native Hawaiian author Noenoe K. Silva, entitled *Aloha Betrayed: Native Hawaiian Resistance to American Colonialism (American Encounters/Global Interactions)* is highly instructive.[15] Silva recovered a stunning example of Native Hawaiian people's exercise of sovereign power at the end of the nineteenth century through a careful sifting of letters, books, and newspapers written in Native

Hawaiian—all overlooked by mainstream historians precisely because the sources were created by Native Hawaiians for Native Hawaiians.

This volume is the outcome of a meeting of scholars and community leaders at a 2003 conference entitled "Native American Indian Sovereignty: An Interdisciplinary and Cross-Cultural Symposium." The gathering was co-sponsored by the National Indian Education Association, the Lilly Endowment, and Wake Forest University. Part One brings together theoretical positions (Wilkins and Herman), case studies (Clark, Maynor, and Sanders), and social ramifications often overlooked in political debates (Shorty) in the fields of historical and political studies.

David E. Wilkins offers a nuanced survey of global political initiatives on behalf of Indigenous sovereignty and underscores the need to strengthen international exchange and collaboration. Matthew D. Herman presents an analysis of the conceptual spectrum of sovereignty in literary studies by both First Nation and Western Euro-American scholars. Kauila Clark weighs the impact of traditional practices, as they are expressed in spirituality, ceremony, and art on Hawaiian autonomy. Malinda M. Maynor demonstrates the vigorous and sophisticated Lumbee community strategies to gain federal recognition for the Lumbee tribe in the early 1930s. The essay authored by E. Fred Sanders and Thomas J. Blumer offers a window into the difficult history of Catawba Sovereignty in the twentieth century. Lawrence Shorty links American Indian health issues to the impact of colonization, and he describes culturally appropriate strategies to reclaim health as an act of sovereignty.

Part Two of *Foundations of First Peoples' Sovereignty* focuses on education, art, and cultural topics. David Kekaulike Sing presents the principle of *Ike Pono* as used within a Native Hawaiian school system throughout all levels of instructions and in all subjects.

Lakota elders Harry Charger and Ione V. Quigley discuss traditional Lakota values and principles that have shaped Lakota political identity and are being reactivated in conjunction with United Nations definitions of nationhood. J. T. Garrett invokes sovereignty through a combination of psychological and spiritual categories as a life in balance and harmony written from a Cherokee perspective. Thomas Belt and Margaret Bender highlight the crucial role of revitalizing Cherokee language in the reclamation of tribal sovereignty, an issue also touched upon by Ione V. Quigley and others. Jeanne Simonelli contextualizes two very different artistic reflections by women on the Mayan struggle for autonomy in Chiapas, theater and spiritual autobiography. As Josefa Hernandez Perez stresses in her autobiographical reflections, no understanding of the lives of the Mayan people of Chiapas is complete without acknowledging the continuity of their pre-Hispanic worldviews to the current meaning of Mayan life. Hernandez Perez's personal story parallels the larger struggle in Chiapas for dignity, voice, and equal participation in society. The women of LA FOMMA (Forteleza de la Mujer Maya) continue the story, using theater as a way of compelling the conquerors to truly see Maya life, while empowering Mayan women to take their rightful place in a gradually changing society. They argue for the success of community theater as a fluid and joyous form of autonomous exercise in self-determination and as a provocative alternative to armed conflict in the creation of full autonomy. Eva Marie Garroutte completes the volume describing how contemporary Indigenous artists claim intellectual sovereignty as defined by Robert Warrior by unmasking stereotypes about First Nation peoples and by employing tribal values, viewpoints, and philosophies in their art.

NOTES

1 See, for example, Thomas W. Cooper, *A Time Before Deception: Truth in Communication, Culture, and Ethics* (Santa Fe, NM: Clear Light Publishers, 1998).

2 Donald L. Fixico describes an Indigenous intellectual paradigm as grounded in the understanding that "'Indian thinking' is 'seeing' things from a perspective emphasizing that circles and cycles are central to the world and that all things are related within the universe." Donald L. Fixico, *The American Indian Mind in a Linear World: American Indian Studies and Traditional Knowledge* (London and New York: Routledge, 2003), 1.

3 Barbara A. Mann, "Epilogue: Euro-Forming the Data," in Bruce E. Johansen, *Debating Democracy: Native American Legacy of Freedom* (Santa Fe, NM: Clear Light Publishing, 1998), 177.

4 Joanne Barker, "For Whom Sovereignty Matters," in *Sovereignty Matters: Locations of Contestation and Possibility in Indigenous Struggles for Self-Determination,* edited by Joanne Barker (Lincoln: University of Nebraska Press, 2005), 1.

5 Felix Cohen, "Americanizing the White Man," *The American Scholar* 21.2 (Spring 1952): 179–80. Quoted in Johansen, *Debating Democracy,* 24.

6 For an overview of the history of the concept of Indigenism and its growing global significance, see Ronald Niezen, *The Origins of Indigenism: Human Rights and the Politics of Identity* (Berkeley: University of California Press, 2003). I agree with Niezen's summary statement that "the category 'indigenous people' has thus flourished through the combination of a broad legal definition of a nondominant form of society with global patterns (or their historical residues) of invasion, occupation, imposed cultural change, and political marginalization," (93), but would add, as this volume demonstrates, that Indigenism also denotes feats of trenchant analysis and resistance to colonization efforts.

7 Chronicled, e.g., in Robert A. Williams, Jr. *The American Indian in Western Legal Thought: The Discourses of Conquest* (New York: Oxford University Press, 1990).

8 To quote Joanne Barker, "[The concept of] Sovereignty carries the horrible stench of colonialism. It is incomplete, inaccurate, and troubled. But it has also been rearticulated to mean altogether different things by indigenous peoples," in "For Whom Sovereignty Matters," in Joanne Barker, ed., *Sovereignty Matters: Locations of Contestation and Possibility in Indigenous Struggles for Self-Determination* (Lincoln and London: University of Nebraska Press, 2005), 26. See David Wilkins with K. Tsianina Lomawaima, *Uneven Ground: American Indian Sovereignty and Federal Law* (Norman: University of Oklahoma Press, 2001), for an overview of federal stances toward Indigenous sovereignty. For the rich global possibili-

ties that extend far beyond this volume, see, for example, Alexander Ewen, ed., *Voice of Indigenous Peoples: Native People Address the United Nations* (Santa Fe, NM: Clear Light Publishers, 1994).

9 See Andrea Smith, *Conquest: Sexual Violence and American Indian Genocide* (Cambridge: South End Press, 2005) for an effort in unearthing some of the links between gender coding, sexism and state dominance in U.S. policies toward American Indian nations.

10 For a comparative analytical grasp of the situation in the United States, study of other post-colonial nation structures and their gendering process are instructive. See, e.g., the incisive analysis by Rajeswari Sunder Rajan, *The Scandal of the State: Women, Law, and Citizenship in Postcolonial India* (Durham and London: Duke University Press, 2003).

11 See Rennard Strickland, "The Eagle's Empire: Sovereignty, Survival, and Self-Governance in Native American Law and Constitutionalism," in *Studying Native America: Problems and Prospects*, edited by Russell Thornton (Madison: The University of Wisconsin Press, 1998), 247–71.

12 Strickland, 267.

13 Joely De la Torre, "In the Trenches: A Critical Look at the Isolation of American Indian Political Practices in the Nonempirical Social Science of Political Science," in *Indigenizing the Academy: Transforming Scholarship and Empowering Communities*, edited by Devon Abbott Mihesuah and Angela Cavender Wilson (Lincoln and London: University of Nebraska Press, 2004), 180. In contrast, historian John R. Wunder, for example, has published several impressive volumes with an interdisciplinary focus on legal issues, but the collections remain firmly situated in academic discourse with a strong emphasis on the application of federal law. See, for example, his edited volume, *Native American Cultural and Religious Freedoms,* Native Americans and the Law Series: Contemporary and Historical Perspectives on American Indian Rights, Freedoms, and Sovereignty (New York: Garland Publishing, 1996).

14 Robert Allen Warrior, *Tribal Secrets: Recovering American Indian Intellectual Traditions* (Minneapolis: University of Minnesota Press, 1994); Taiaiake Alfred, *Peace, Power, Righteousness: An Indigenous Manifesto* (Don Mills, Ontario: Oxford University Press, 1999); Haunani-Kay Trask, *From a Native Daughter: Colonialism and Sovereignty in Hawai'i,* rev. ed. (Honolulu: University of Hawai'i Press, 1999); Jacob K. Olupona, ed., *Beyond Primitivism: Indigenous Religious Traditions and Modernity* (New York and London: Routledge, 2004).

15 Noenoe K. Silva, *Aloha Betrayed: Native Hawaiian Resistance to American Colonialism*, American Encounters/Global Interactions (Durham, NC: Duke University Press, 2004).

BIBLIOGRAPHY

Alfred, Taiaiake. *Peace, Power, Righteousness: An Indigenous Manifesto.* Don Mills, Ontario: Oxford University Press, 1999.

Barker, Joanne. "For Whom Sovereignty Matters." In *Sovereignty Matters: Locations of Contestation and Possibility in Indigenous Struggles for Self-Determination,* edited by Joanne Barker. Lincoln: University of Nebraska Press, 2005.

Cohen, Felix. "Americanizing the White Man." *The American Scholar* 21.2 (Spring 1952): 179–80.

Cooper, Thomas W. *A Time Before Deception: Truth in Communication, Culture, and Ethics.* Santa Fe, NM: Clear Light, 1998.

De la Torre, Joely. "In the Trenches: A Critical Look at the Isolation of American Indian Political Practices in the Nonempirical Social Science of Political Science." In *Indigenizing the Academy: Transforming Scholarship and Empowering Communities*, edited by Devon Abbott Mihesuah and Angela Cavender Wilson. Lincoln and London: University of Nebraska Press, 2004.

Ewen, Alexander, ed. *Voice of Indigenous Peoples: Native People Address the United Nations*. Santa Fe, NM: Clear Light, 1994.

Fixico, Donald L. *The American Indian Mind in a Linear World: American Indian Studies and Traditional Knowledge*. London and New York: Routledge, 2003.

Johansen, Bruce E. *Debating Democracy: Native American Legacy of Freedom*. Santa Fe, NM: Clear Light, 1998.

Mann, Barbara A. "Epilogue: Euro-Forming the Data." In *Debating Democracy: Native American Legacy of Freedom,* edited by Bruce E. Johansen. Santa Fe, NM: Clear Light, 1998.

Niezen, Ronald. *The Origins of Indigenism: Human Rights and the Politics of Identity*. Berkeley: University of California Press, 2003.

Olupona, Jacob K., ed., *Beyond Primitivism: Indigenous Religious Traditions and Modernity*. New York and London: Routledge, 2004.

Rajan, Rajeswari Sunder. *The Scandal of the State: Women, Law, and Citizenship in Postcolonial India*. Durham and London: Duke University Press, 2003.

Silva, Noenoe K. *Aloha Betrayed: Native Hawaiian Resistance to American Colonialism*. American Encounters/Global Interactions. Durham, NC: Duke University Press, 2004.

Smith, Andrea. *Conquest: Sexual Violence and American Indian Genocide*. Cambridge: South End Press, 2005.

Strickland, Rennard. "The Eagle's Empire: Sovereignty, Survival, and Self-Governance in Native American Law and Constitutionalism." In *Studying Native America: Problems and Prospects*, edited by Russell Thornton. Madison: The University of Wisconsin Press, 1998.

Trask, Haunani-Kay. *From a Native Daughter: Colonialism and Sovereignty in Hawai'i*. Rev. ed. Honolulu: University of Hawai'i Press, 1999.

Warrior, Robert Allen. *Tribal Secrets: Recovering American Indian Intellectual Traditions*. Minneapolis: University of Minnesota Press, 1994.

Wilkins, David, with K. Tsianina Lomawaima. *Uneven Ground: American Indian Sovereignty and Federal Law*. Norman: University of Oklahoma Press, 2001.

Williams, Robert A., Jr. *The American Indian in Western Legal Thought: The Discourses of Conquest*. New York: Oxford University Press, 1990.

Wunder, John R., ed. *Native American Cultural and Religious Freedoms.* Native Americans and the Law Series: Contemporary and Historical Perspectives on American Indian Rights, Freedoms, and Sovereignty. New York: Garland, 1996.

I. HISTORICAL AND POLITICAL PERSPECTIVES

1 INDIGENOUS SELF-DETERMINATION: A GLOBAL PERSPECTIVE

David E. Wilkins

The concepts of self-determination and sovereignty, from an Indigenous perspective, embrace values, attitudes, perspectives, and actions. Of course, as a result of the historical phenomenon known as colonialism, in which expansive European states sought to dominate the rights, resources, and lands of aboriginal peoples worldwide, one cannot discuss Indigenous self-determination and sovereignty without some corresponding discussion of how states and their policy makers understand these politically charged terms as well.

I have been thinking, acting, researching, and writing on these two vital concepts, intergovernmental relations, critical legal theory, and comparative Indigenous politics for nearly two decades. Along with this, I have also been interested in how the American states and the federal government, and international states and non-governmental organizations and the various political actors and social, economic, geographical, and cultural forces active in those polities have set about defining themselves and how their understanding of their own institutional identities have affected Native peoples.

Since I am trained in comparative politics, I have also long been interested in exploring the linkages, similarities, and differences in the experiences aboriginal peoples have to one another and in the relations that exist between First Nations and the various states of the world that these distinct congregations of humanity inhabit.

This bird's eye or Fourth World perspective, or what I refer to as a "thinking outside the reservation" perspective, is critical and should and must be balanced with what Gunnar Myrdal once referred to as a "frog's eye perspective," in which analysts must also maintain a deep focus on each of the local Indigenous homelands, governments, and peoples. In fact, I suggest that we need to be able to navigate and critically examine both the "frog's eye perspective" and "thinking outside the rez" perspective if we are to be effective advocates of Indigenous rights.

With this said, it is that last area—the "thinking outside the rez" view—that I want to concentrate on for the balance of this essay. Suffice it to say, there is a remarkable level of diversity in the global Indigenous world. Although there are 191 formally recognized "states" in the United Nations, there are, at a minimum, over 5,000 distinctive Indigenous peoples in the world, with an estimated population of 350 million.[1] In the United States alone there are over 562 federally recognized First Nations, fifty or so state-recognized tribal groups, and a number of bona fide Native communities that have neither federal nor state recognition. Hawaiian Natives constitute yet another distinct category of aboriginal peoples under U.S. federal law. Such staggering diversity has made it difficult for researchers to engage in comprehensive analysis, although there are numerous quality works that aim at such a comparison, either at the hemispheric or the global level.[2]

Some years ago, while I was still at the University of Arizona, I inherited a course titled "Indigenous Peoples: A Global Perspective." I embraced the chance to learn more about First Nations in other parts of the world—who they were, how they defined themselves, how they governed their communities, how they had been treated by invasive European powers, and, once these Europeans had settled permanently in Native lands, what kinds of laws, policies, and attitudes they carried with them or developed toward Native nations. More importantly, I wanted to know how Indigenous peoples had responded to these profound state and societal pressures.

The course focused on the colonial origins, internal, neocolonial, and dependency policies of states, and other policies of a more enlightened nature proposed by those states, and their relations to and the reactions of Native nations in the United States, the First Nations, Métis, and Inuit peoples in Canada, Native peoples in parts of Latin America, the Saami of Europe, the Ainu of Japan, the Maori of New Zealand, and the Aborigines of Australia.

When I teach the course at the undergraduate level, we begin by defining the key term *colonialism* and all its variants—internal, captive, neo, dependency, and imperialism. We then focus on why European states decided to expand from the 1400s forward and how their engulfment and subsequent attempts to incorporate, assimilate, exterminate, isolate, among other policies, affected Native peoples, and we engage in significant discussion on how First Nations have strategically responded to these various forces.

Next, we engage in some broad reading on the pre-invasion status of First Nations before moving into a long section on the advent and expansion of colonialism and discuss how the states and their agents used pathological germs and weapons and how they relied on specific attitudes of racism, ethnocentrism, and arrogance to cause remarkable destruction in aboriginal societies. The succeeding section focuses on the profound psychological impact that colonialism has had on aboriginal peoples. Here, the students read either Frantz Fanon's *The Wretched of the Earth* or Rigoberta Menchú's *I, Rigoberta Menchú: An Indian Woman in Guatemala*.[3] Both of these powerful and compelling books contain detailed analyses and descriptions about the ways in which colonizers seek to dehumanize Indigenous peoples.

In one telling passage, Fanon says that "because it is a systematic negation of the other person and a furious determination to deny the other person all attributes of humanity, colonialism forces the people it dominates to ask themselves the question constantly: In reality, who am I?"[4] This sentence is pregnant with meaning and helps explain the ongoing psychological damage that First Nations peoples continue to endure given their ongoing and seemingly perpetual internal colonial situation.

Fanon also has a comment on the content of African sovereignty that I also find quite telling à propos to the situation of First Nations in the United States. He says, "The African peoples were quick to realize that dignity and sovereignty were exact equivalents, and in fact, a free people living in dignity is a sovereign people."[5] This is a splendid definition of the substantive meaning of sovereignty. Importantly, both Fanon and Menchú discuss strategies and attitudinal variables that have enabled them to surmount the ravages of colonialism.

Once all this information has been discussed and critically evaluated, we move into our case studies—beginning with the United States, Latin America, and so on. I conclude the course with a section titled "Indigenous Peoples and Future Directions." In this final part we discuss the internationalization of Indigenous peoples and the increasingly important role of the United Nations in its difficult task of addressing the complicated and diverse conditions still bedeviling aboriginal peoples in their political, economic, and cultural relations with states.

Throughout the course, I insist that the students think and experience comparatively. The three broad questions investigated in the course are:

1. How and why did each settler state seek to incorporate or not incorporate the First Nations they encountered and with whom they now live permanently?
2. How have the First Nations responded to these policies?
3. What are the long-term cultural, economic, legal, and political goals of the various aboriginal peoples, and what are the opportunities and constraints affecting their choices?

According to Richard Perry, author of a comparative study featuring Mexico, the United States, Canada, and Australian policies toward the aboriginal peoples located in the borders now controlled by these polities, states, in a general way, have acted thus toward Native peoples:

1. States, rather than First Nations, have been far more likely to expand into other peoples' lands.
2. The early stages of state expansion have typically involved violence.
3. After initial expansion, states have sought to consolidate their holdings, both internally and externally.

4. Internal consolidation has often involved attempts to exterminate Indigenous peoples (e.g., Tasmania and Newfoundland, where the state was successful; California and Texas, which nearly succeeded in eradicating aboriginal peoples).

5. These attempts at early eradication of First Nations have involved genocidal policies (e.g., labor practices, sterilization, defining who is or is not aboriginal or legal status, boarding or residential schools, and so on).

6. Genocide has usually failed, and efforts at assimilation, acculturation, or absorption of the Indigenous population have followed, frequently coupled with displacement or relegation to reserved areas (e.g., reservation or reserve confinement, forced Christianity, denial of traditional religious expressions).

7. Finally, assimilation policies have also generally failed. Many states eventually, however grudgingly, have arrived at the realization that Indigenous peoples have a right to exist and are sometimes entitled to exercise a measure of internal sovereignty or self-determination.[6]

Keeping with his broadly generalized framework, Perry also summarized the ways in which Indigenous peoples have generally reacted to these intrusive polities:

1. Indigenous peoples have often met their intruders with peaceful reactions, unless violent behavior was previously endemic to the community.

2. Violent Indigenous resistance typically followed after more aggressive intrusions, although this was usually limited to "the parameters of existing Indigenous affiliations."

3. Coalitions for violent resistance that reach beyond local tribal allegiances (Tecumseh, the Great Pueblo Revolt, and so on) have occasionally arisen among Native peoples during the process of state expansion.

4. After state consolidation, many Indigenous peoples have sought to retrench, negotiating treaties or other diplomatic arrangements, or simply looking for refuge.

5. Many Indigenous peoples have pursued economic incorporation in the state's system, especially when it appears they have little alternative.

6. If economic rewards are not forthcoming, some Native peoples have pursued political solutions, including attempts to initiate inter-tribal alliances and coalitions.[7]

As good as the Perry book is, generalizing about Indigenous/state relations is a difficult task, but it is a most fruitful endeavor, given the understandings that one can glean from comparative analysis. First, it facilitates the sorting out and categorization of data. Second, it assists in the defining of key concepts. Third, it provides an additional perspective on one's own context from the knowledge of what occurs elsewhere—thus serving to limit bias and ethnocentrism. Fourth, it helps us to evaluate the utility of treaty making and other forms of diplomacy in different contexts. Finally, it improves researchers' chances of identifying and isolating factors that might explain the success or failure of policy making in Indigenous affairs.

While the course seeks to balance why various states have engaged in the kinds of policies they have and discusses how First Nations have coped and continue to evolve and struggle with their unique situations, the question that is most interesting to the students and me is: How do First Nations understand their self-identity, sovereignty, and self-determination? Are their governments and their peoples looking to remain in a semi-independent position apart from the state; are they seeking a deeper form of accommodation that reflects their unique identities while still leading to a measure of economic and political incorporation; or are they pursuing cultural, political, and economic sovereignty or autonomy?

The short yet unsatisfactory answer to these critical questions is "It depends." Indeed, much of it depends on how each Native community defines its core identity and how it will be manifested in its members' understanding of what it means to be a self-determined community wielding the inherent power of sovereignty. Such decisions, be they social, political, intergovernmental, religious, economic, legal, or cultural, will depend on the First Nation involved—the extant values, lands, traditions, religious beliefs, languages, and so on, that distinguish one First Nation from another. The decisions further depend on the settler state that has inserted itself and that today has the dominant economic, political, and military position in or surrounding a given aboriginal peoples' community.

I have learned in the course of my global pursuit of Indigenous understanding and perspective that we must be careful about making categorical generalizations about "what Natives want," what constitutes an "Indigenous" people, and what exactly does "self-determination" means for First Nations.

One could safely argue that in the broadest sense Indigenous peoples around the world are seeking as much independent control over their own affairs as possible and demand a comparable amount of control over their remaining lands and natural resources. However, beyond these goals, there are many ideological, strategic, and tactical differences in evidence that deny a uniform Indigenous thrust.

This revelation is not a surprise to most aboriginal peoples, although it is often shocking to non-Indigenous persons or governments who assume a cultural and political homogeneity among aboriginal peoples that has never, in fact, existed. Interestingly, many of those same individuals and governing bodies would never assume uniformity among states or non-Native governing bodies or organizations.

Russell L. Barsh, in "Political Diversification of the International Indigenous Movement,"[8] evaluated and critiqued the complexities of Indigenous diversity, the different goals and orientations of Native peoples in pursuit of self-determination, and pointed out the pitfalls of trying to merge the remarkably diverse array of Native peoples and their ever increasing organizations into one unified front.

He noted, for example, that Indigenous organizations and peoples in the United States and Australia, where Native peoples constitute less than two percent of the national population and occupy less than five percent of the territory, are fundamentally different from aboriginal nations and their political organizations in Guatemala, Bolivia, and other Latin American states where Indigenous peoples form a majority of the population and inhabit, even if they do not own, more of the land than non-Natives. In those Latin American countries, where Native peoples are or are beginning to exercise a considerable political and economic clout, Indigenous organizations tend to focus their efforts on "direct representation in the national government and to seek political linkages with a broad range of other disaffected sectors of society."[9] Even so, in the United States and Australia, where Native peoples comprise a very small minority of the overall population, Indigenous groups are more likely to insist on the inherent right of sovereignty or as strong a measure of independence as is possible, and they tend to also want to remain at least semi-isolated politically.

Geography and demography, therefore, play impressive roles in the status and expectations of Native peoples and the states they must interact with. In the United States and Australia, Indigenous numbers are very slight and will most likely remain so compared to the rest of the state's population. However, in many Latin American states and in the former Northwest Territories of Canada, especially the circumpolar region, home of the Inuit; and the Nordic countries of Europe, home to the Saami, where Native peoples form a larger bloc of the population, if not a majority, the aboriginal population has more significant political and economic influence. This reality helps explain the 1999 birth of Canada's newest territory, Nunavut,[10] that was established largely to benefit the majority Inuit population, and the fact that the Saami of Norway, Sweden, and Finland, while fewer in number, now have their own parliaments that coexist alongside the regular parliaments of those states. These parliaments are largely advisory or consultative bodies, but they provide the Saami with a structural opportunity to officially voice their concerns and grievances.[11]   Russia, which is also home to several thousand Saami, has not yet acted to establish a Saami parliament but is said to be considering it.

The Saami, like the vast majority of Native communities throughout Latin America, are not pursuing secession or separation as sovereign entities, but they do desire clear title to their original lands, veto power over state-sponsored resource extraction, and greater input into state policy decisions that directly affect their peoples and lands and resources.

Additionally, in major parts of Latin America, New Zealand, and much of South Asia, aboriginal peoples form ten or more percent of the national population, and this gives these First Nations a much greater opportunity to influence or gain a substantial foothold in the state's governing apparatus.[12]

Thus, according to Barsh, in international aboriginal affairs there appears to be a U.S.-Australian axis, and a Latin-Asian Axis, with Canadian, Maori, and circumpolar peoples leaning toward the Latin-Asian side. Barsh believes this alignment is "reinforced by more North-South considerations, including the wealth, mobility, and aggressiveness of the North Americans and Australians."[13]

While American Indian nations frequently invoke the term tribal sovereignty and have been using the term "self-determination" since the late 1960s, Native peoples throughout Latin America rarely speak of tribal sovereignty. They are far more likely to discuss their desire for local and regional autonomy, respect for traditional forms of authority and government, recognition of customary alternative legal systems, and, only more recently, of a collective right of self-determination.

These are profoundly important terms that carry significant political and legal weight at both the domestic and international levels. The fact that Indigenous peoples worldwide have substantially different views on the use and meaning of these terms is a reflection of the inherent diversity among Native peoples, as well as the distinctive geo-political positions in which various First Nations are situated in specific international states.

Here we see some profound differences among aboriginal peoples. First, many Latin American Indigenous organizations insist that their goal is to transform the state, and armed struggles are not an irregular activity in some states. Second, the Maori of New Zealand are in a situation where their language is now officially recognized and their one treaty—the 1840 Treaty of Waitangi—is considered a foundational document by both Maori and the state. Third, most North American Indigenous nations assert varying degrees of self-determination, with many still said to be "domestic-dependent nations" in an alleged government-to-government relationship with the United States based on treaties and the trust doctrine, though always subject to federal plenary power.

Fourth, the Aborigines of Australia are pushing for a clear recognition of their long denied self-determination and have hopes that a treaty might someday be negotiated with the state; or at the least that a preamble might be added to the Australian Constitution that makes explicit reference to the aboriginal peoples, or that a Bill of Rights might be enacted to aid in the protection of Indigenous civil and political rights.

CONCLUSION

While First Nations in the United States seem enamored of the term sovereignty because it provides, in our deeply legalistic and litigious society, some common ground by which tribal nations can speak to the constituent states and the federal government. It is not generally a term that is widely used by aboriginal peoples elsewhere who, while sharing a common Anglo/British heritage, find that their goal of self-determination or political autonomy, although still difficult to achieve in their host states because of the fear of political dismemberment, is more palatable than the European-based and hierarchically oriented term sovereignty.[14]

Sovereignty, however, means different things to different peoples, polities, and First Nations. If we define it as Fanon did, as the equivalent of "dignity" and "freedom," who would dispute that? Vine Deloria, Jr., building upon Fanon's definition, said that "sovereignty, in the final instance, can be said to consist more of continued cultural integrity than of political powers and to the degree that a nation loses its sense of cultural identity, to that degree it suffers a loss of sovereignty."[15] Both of these definitions hint at a much broader, morally and culturally based definition that resonates comfortably for many First Nations in the United States and Canada, if not elsewhere. In a global sense, sovereignty certainly no longer means absolute or supreme authority, given the interconnectedness and interdependence of all peoples and states in our globalized world.

Even the United States, as powerful as it is militarily, has learned during its actions in Iraq and Afghanistan that it, too, does not wield absolute power. It is, in fact, denied that power by the Constitution itself. U.S. sovereignty is further divided between the three coordinate branches of government; it is shared with the fifty constituent states, and it is also limited by the treaties the United States signed with First Nations and continues to sign with other governments as well. States, by explicit constitutional design, are denied full sovereignty and exist as clipped or limited sovereign polities.

Indigenous nations in the United States and abroad are societies whose histories long predate the settler states that were established in their midst. They retain a land base, however diminished; exhibit distinctive cultural identities, despite horrendous assimilative campaigns; retain control over variable amounts of natural resources; have their own citizens/members; and wield political leaders who exercise differing amounts of jurisdictional authority over their remaining territories and citizens and those non-Natives who travel through their lands. This is what sovereign or self-determined peoples and their governments do.

NOTES

1 John H. Bodley, *Victims of Progress,* 4th ed. (Mountain View, CA: Mayfield Publishing Co., 1999), 201.

2 See, e.g., Bodley, *Victims of Progress;* Franke Wilmer, *The Indigenous Voice in World Politics* (Newbury Park, CA: Sage, 1993); Richard J. Perry, *From Time Immemorial: Indigenous Peoples and State Systems* (Austin: University of Texas Press, 1996); Marie Leger, ed., *Aboriginal Peoples: Toward Self-Government* (Montreal: Black Rose Books, 1994); Paul Havemann, ed., *Indigenous Peoples' Rights in Australia, Canada, & New Zealand* (Auckland: Oxford University Press, 1999); and Bruce Granville Miller, *Invisible Indigenes: The Politics of Nonrecognition* (Lincoln: University of Nebraska Press, 2003).

3 Frantz Fanon, *The Wretched of the Earth* (New York: Grove Weidenfeld, 1991); Rigoberta Menchú, *I, Rigoberta Menchú: An Indian Woman in Guatemala* (New York: Verso, 1987).

4 Fanon, *The Wretched of the Earth,* 250.

5 Fanon, *The Wretched of the Earth,* 198.

6 Perry, *From Time Immemorial,* 226.

7 Perry, *From Time Immemorial,* 226–27.

8 Russell Barsh, "Political Diversification of the International Indigenous Movement," *Native American Studies* 5.1 (1991): 7–10.

9 Barsh, "Political Diversification," 8.

10 Patrick Macklem, *Indigenous Difference and the Constitution of Canada* (Toronto: University of Toronto Press, 2001), 270.

11 Mervyn Jones, "The Sami of Lapland," Report No. 55 (London: Minority Rights Group, 1982), 13–14.

12 Barsh, "Political Diversification," 8.

13 Barsh, "Political Diversification," 8.

14 See Taiaiake Alfred's, "Sovereignty," in *A Companion to American Indian History,* edited by Philip J. Deloria and Neal Salisbury (Malden, MA: Blackwell, 2002), 460–74.

15 Vine Deloria, Jr. "Self-Determination and the Concept of Sovereignty," in *Economic Development in American Indian Reservations,* edited by Roxanne Dunbar Ortiz (Albuquerque, NM: Native American Studies, 1979), 27.

BIBLIOGRAPHY

Alfred, Taiaiake. "Sovereignty." In *A Companion to American Indian History*, edited by Philip J. Deloria and Neal Salisbury. Malden, MA: Blackwell, 2002.

Barsh, Russell. "Political Diversification of the International Indigenous Movement." *Native American Studies* 5.1 (1991): 7–10.

Bodley, John H. *Victims of Progress.* 4th ed. Mountain View, CA: Mayfield Publishing Co., 1999.

Deloria, Vine, Jr. "Self-Determination and the Concept of Sovereignty." In *Economic Development in American Indian Reservations,* edited by Roxanne Dunbar Ortiz. Albuquerque, NM: Native American Studies, 1979.

Fanon, Frantz. *The Wretched of the Earth.* New York: Grove Weidenfeld, 1991.

Havemann, Paul, ed. *Indigenous Peoples' Rights in Australia, Canada, & New Zealand.* Auckland: Oxford University Press, 1999.

Jones, Mervyn. "The Saami of Lapland." Report No. 55. London: Minority Rights Group, 1982.

Leger, Marie, ed. *Aboriginal Peoples: Toward Self-Government.* Montreal: Black Rose Books, 1994.

Macklem, Patrick. *Indigenous Difference and the Constitution of Canada.* Toronto: University of Toronto Press, 2001.

Menchú, Rigoberta. *I, Rigoberta Menchú: An Indian Woman in Guatemala.* New York: Verso, 1987.

Miller, Bruce Granville. *Invisible Indigenes: The Politics of Nonrecognition.* Lincoln: University of Nebraska Press, 2003.

Perry, Richard J. *From Time Immemorial: Indigenous Peoples and State Systems.* Austin: University of Texas Press, 1996.

Wilmer, Franke. *The Indigenous Voice in World Politics.* Newbury Park, CA: Sage, 1993.

2 "THE MAKING OF RELATIVES": SOVEREIGNTY AND COSMOPOLITAN DEMOCRACIES

Matthew D. Herman

The concept of cosmopolitanism enjoys a long, rich history of associations. The concept is so versatile, in fact, that even a grossly incomplete catalog of its meanings over time—meanings, for example, that have ranged from "absolute homelessness" to "worldwide distribution" to "a density of overlapping allegiances"—can convey a full sense of its nearly inexhaustible mutability.[1] Cosmopolitanism emerges again today largely to herald the trends and tendencies collectively reckoned as "globalization," that "set of processes in which capital, technology, people, goods, and information move relentlessly across the inherited map of political boundaries, and through which the interdependence of societies over vast distances and ever-shortening time frames has been intensified."[2] Within the context of this worldwide "compression of time and space," many commentators see this new cosmopolitanism as merely globalization's ideological shadow, a public relations prop that gives aid and comfort to a suspect system of global economic liberalization by championing the post-nationalist ethic to which such a system gives rise.[3] As a congratulatory nod to the transnational movements and cultural blending embraced by this ethic, cosmopolitanism today appears to offer very little to the theorization of North American Indigenous culture and politics, both of which align closely with the nationalist ethic of tribal sovereignty.

Incompatibilities of this kind begin to fade, however, within particular academic contexts where cosmopolitanism is not uniformly synonymous with post-nationalism. Recent research programs in the humanities and social sciences variously describe cosmopolitanism as situated and idiosyncratic, and, in more specific formulations, as "actually existing," "comparative," "rooted," amenable to "patriotism," and, "discrepant."[4] These reconceptualizations remind us that, as is sometimes forgotten in the heady blur of today's fresh global outlooks, cosmopolitanism offers more than a single either-or proposition on the global future. More than just a binary political alternative to nationalism, cosmopolitanism, we learn, articulates a wide range of practices and "habits of thought and feeling" that "sometimes works together with nationalism."[5] On this definition, cosmopolitanism functions as a mediating filter rather than as a strict opposition between the universal and particular poles of culture, embodying modes of attachment, allegiance, and identity that inhere simultaneously between the local and the global. Cosmopolitanism is thus not wholly inclusive, a total renunciation of the boundedness of culture, nation, and self that follows the triumphalist rhetoric of global capital, or what Pheng Cheah calls "imperializing cosmopolitanism."[6] In other incarnations, cosmopolitanism recognizes that the bounded spaces comprising culture, nation, and self are fluid, provisional, capable of overlapping, and open to change. This discrepancy is not necessarily a contradiction. As Pheng Cheah observes, "from a historical perspective, it is evident that the relationship between cosmopolitanism and nationalism has fluctuated between varying degrees of alliance and opposition and that both discourses have progressive as well as reactionary dimensions."[7]   Given such historical alliances between nationalism and cosmopolitanism, it thus becomes possible to treat the matter of compatibility between cosmopolitanism and tribal sovereignty as an open question. Although this fact is not widely recognized, cosmopolitanism's importance to Indigenous political philosophies should not be disregarded, for it functions—with an ironic echo of Arif Dirlik's phrase—both as legacy and as project.

One place to look for answers is the tribal historical record. The kinds of social, cultural, and political arrangements imagined by cosmopolitanism's "progressive dimensions" have been in practice for centuries among the indigenous peoples of North America. There is, in fact, no shortage of examples that could qualify for consideration as Indigenous cosmopolitanisms, and this would include versions that fall in line with the present-day ethics and habits associated with tribal sovereignty. One of the more historically prominent examples can be found in the political traditions of the Haudenosaunee, or Iroquois Confederacy, which, according to Onondaga historian Oren R. Lyons, deserve credit and recognition for the development of long-standing democratic international institutions based on participation, peace, non-coercion, and mutual respect among its member polities. As such, Haudenosaunee democratic political philosophy matches up well as a form of cosmopolitanism, generally defined. Defined more particularly, it also matches up well as a form of non-post-nationalist cosmopolitanism. As Lyons adds,

> in these [Haudenosaunee] traditions, there is recognition that peoples are distinct from each other. However, since the beginning of our memory this distinctiveness has been seen as a foundation for mutual respect; and we have therefore always honored the fundamental right of peoples and their societies to be different. This is a profoundly important principle, and one which, even in the twentieth century, humans continue to struggle to realize.[8]

As Lyons reminds us here, it is these traditions, initiated centuries ago by the Iroquois prophet Peacemaker and his followers to bring peace among nations at a time "when humans had cast aside the rules of coexistence, a period when bloodlust and vengeance overshadowed the goodness in human beings," that created the alliances making up the great Iroquois Confederacy, dictated the negotiation of treaties and other arrangements made later with the Europeans, and persists to this day as a guiding politico-spiritual philosophy among the Haudenosaunee.[9]

Thus, to those wedded to the idea that cosmopolitanism is post-nationalism, Haudenosaunee political philosophy, with its strong internationalist bent, probably makes little sense as cosmopolitanism. However, to those persuaded by the abundant but underappreciated historical record of cosmopolitanism's compatibility with nationalism, Haudenosaunee political philosophy—and North American Indigenous political philosophy, in general—probably makes good sense as cosmopolitanism, another example, perhaps, in the growing list of what James Clifford calls "discrepant cosmopolitanisms." In what follows, I pursue the possibility of "actually existing" Indigenous cosmopolitanisms, examining how such forms relate to the principles and practices of tribal sovereignty today. Part one below takes a brief detour through current cosmopolitan political theory outside the Indigenous context to assess two specific theoretical challenges to sovereignty-specific cosmopolitanism. In part two, I examine Black Elk's famous account of Hunkapi, or "the making of relatives," as a possible expression of Indigenous cosmopolitanism. In part three, I examine current cosmopolitan strands in contemporary Native American literary criticism where nationalism versus cosmopolitanism debates now hold that field's center stage. Then, in part four, I explore Indigenous cosmopolitanism within the context of current debates over tribal sovereignty within Native American political theory.

COSMOPOLITANISM AND THE STATE

On the broader terrain of contemporary political theory outside the immediate indigenous context, global outlooks cast doubt on the viability of both nation and state. Cosmopolitanism is being called upon to meet such questions, and the implications for tribal sovereignty are dire given the wide-ranging antagonism toward such forms as modes of political redress. One model of cosmopolitanism that addresses existing social and political inequities is Daniele Archibugi's "cosmopolitan democracy." As Archibugi describes it in the essay "Principles of Cosmopolitan Democracy," "cosmopolitan democracy is an ambitious project whose aim is to achieve a world order based on the rule of law and democracy."[10] Archibugi follows David Beetham when defining democracy as "a mode of decision-making about collectively binding rules and policies over which the people exercise control, and the most democratic arrangement to be that where all members of the collectivity enjoy effective equal rights to take part in such decision-making directly."[11] When defining "cosmopolitanism," Archibugi follows Mary Kaldor:

the term cosmopolitanism, when applied to political institutions, implies a layer of governance that constitutes a limitation on the sovereignty of states and yet does not itself constitute
a state. In other words, a cosmopolitan institution would coexist with a system of states but
would override states in certain clearly defined spheres of activity.[12]

When combined into a single concept, "cosmopolitan democracy" thus constitutes an admittedly open-ended and utopian political project that endeavors to give
life to global democracy by striking a balance between the rights of individuals and the
rights of states within an integrative network of "transnational" organizations whose
function it would be "to develop democracy within nations, among states and at the
global level."[13]

So just how utopian is cosmopolitan democracy, and does it hold out promise to
Indigenous peoples in their quest for self-determination? When it comes to the question of indigenous political status on the global scale, blind spots within cosmopolitan
democracy begin to emerge, the most glaring being the ambivalence with which it
regards the political contexts embodying the aspirations of embedded indigenous nations. Cosmopolitan democracy's focus on rights as state rights and individual rights
leaves out the question of national rights. As we have known at least as early as the
publication of Vine Deloria Jr.'s *Custer Died for Your Sins: An Indian Manifesto,* Native
groups embedded within settler states (what Deloria would later term "nations within
nations") are not national minorities. They are nations—historically, politically, and
culturally—whose sovereignty has been compromised during the contact period but
whose sense of themselves as distinct peoples—as sovereign nations—has never diminished.

On this important discrepancy, Timothy Brennan's recent rejoinder to Archibugi, "Cosmopolitanism and Internationalism," is instructive, for it points out how
cosmopolitan democracy, while noble in purpose, ultimately fails to address issues
like Indigenous sovereignty. First, Brennan associates Archibugi's cosmopolitical democracy with "the cultural dominant to which his [Archibugi's] political theory is still
unwittingly suspect." In Brennan's view, the rush to embrace contemporary cosmopolitanism's utopian promise ought to be more tempered given the easy confu-
sions and complicities between formulations such as Archibugi's and "culturally
dominant" neoliberal ideologies and policies yoked to global capital. Given existing
international relations, proposals for a "world state" ironically risk playing into the
interests of the most powerful states. These interests Brennan describes as "en-
trenched," and if given a broader range of global managerial influence, there is no
guarantee that such interests would champion the rights and aspirations of Indigenous
nations.

Second, and closely related to the first point, is the problem posed by Archibugi's extra-statist focus. Brennan's evocation of the distinction between cosmopolitanism and internationalism provides a useful illustration of the role of the state with contemporary cosmopolitanism. While cosmopolitanism, historically speaking, "designates an enthusiasm for customary differences," "projects a theory of world government and corresponding citizenship," and "envisages . . . an all-encompassing representative structure in which delegates can deliberate on a global scale," internationalism "seeks to establish global relations of respect and cooperation, based on acceptance of differences in polity as well as culture," and "does not aim to erase such differences juridically, before material conditions exist for doing so equitably." The bottom line distinction for Brennan is that internationalism "does not quarrel with the principle of national sovereignty, for there is no other way under modern conditions to secure respect for weaker societies or people."[14] By evoking this distinction, Brennan lends timely support to the nation and the state as viable structures of group survival and resistance in the face of mounting criticism against these structures for their essentialism and repression. To the extent that the political aspirations of Indigenous nations are tied for the foreseeable future to broadening self-government and self-determination efforts, theories of cosmopolitanism that deemphasize collective rights will prove less useful than theories in line with Brennan's description of internationalism.

COSMOPOLITANISM AND MULTICULTURALISM

A similar debate surrounding the nature and status of Indigenous politics is taking place on the domestic level of the nation-state where the key matter of the place of Indigenous collective rights is once again the central issue. Advocating a brand of cosmopolitanism he terms "postethnic," David Hollinger argues for a revised form of multiculturalism in American culture and politics, one with profound implications for Native nations within the present borders of the United States. In *Postethnic America: Beyond Multiculturalism*, Hollinger aims to construct an American multiculturalism that is "strong enough to process the current conflicts and convergences that make the problem of boundaries more acute than ever."[15] To achieve its purpose, this project in "postethnicity" dismantles prevailing models of American multiculturalism and then inventories positive and negative features. In this process, generally speaking, Hollinger rejects those elements within multiculturalism that preserve cultural diversity at the expense of an all-inclusive American belonging while embracing those that either enact or promise to enact a new form of American belonging more in line with the cultural diversity advanced by multiculturalism. More specifically, the postethnic perspective

> favors voluntary over involuntary affiliations, balances an appreciation for communities of descent with a determination to make room for new communities, and promotes solidarities of wide scope that incorporate people with different ethnic and racial backgrounds. A postethnic perspective resists the grounding of knowledge and moral values in blood and history, but works within the last generation's recognition that many of the ideas and values once taken to be universal are specific to certain cultures.[16]

In other words—and in the compressed terminology of contemporary theoretical discourse—the postethnic perspective "marks an effort to articulate and develop cosmopolitan instincts within this new appreciation for the ethnos."[17]

Thus, for Hollinger, cosmopolitanism, or, as he prefers, "rooted cosmopolitanism," provides the mediating function between ethnos and species and between particularism and universalism, laying the foundation for a new modality of American identification based on increased sensitivity to differences—historical, cultural, and epistemological among them. In Hollinger's reckoning, multiculturalism in its current American forms possesses two mediating functions—pluralism and cosmopolitanism—and it is in the latter, as the option with the greater responsiveness "to the potential for creating new cultural combinations," that Hollinger bases the postethnic perspective. Cosmopolitanism in Hollinger's sense is thus partially coextensive with the concept of "civic nationalism," a form of belonging based on consent rather than descent and on a shared vision of the national future. Is Hollinger's postethnic "rooted cosmopolitanism" rooted enough for tribal sovereignty?

Like Archibugi, Hollinger thinks primarily of matters of rights and justice as matters of individual rights and justice. It is true that Hollinger makes a conceptual allowance for domestic ethnic blocs and even goes so far as to grant that "exactly what place such ethno-racial solidarities should have in any particular civic nation needs to be worked out within the circumstances of that nation" (138). However, under Hollinger's formulation, these solidarities are leveled. They are seen as equal and undifferentiated components of the American ethno-racial pentagon.[18] Rather than deconstructing this reductive American system of ethno-racial categorization in the interest of highlighting either the specific historical differences between the five blocs or the specific, more precise categories of solidarity tribal peoples live, Hollinger wants primarily to loosen the pentagon's seams and reattach each segment by hyphen to the American state. As a result, differences between groups and group histories exist only to be broken down to get at the citizen underneath, each being equal, after all, under American law.

Hollinger's cosmopolitanism, however, poses an additional problem for tribal nations. This difficulty involves the tactical political orientation of Hollinger's approach. Postethnic America is not only a work of cultural theory; it is also, though secondarily, a political program. When Hollinger states that "the ideological resources of the United States are simply too useful to democratic egalitarians to be conceded to the far Right while the rest of us devote our public energies to more narrowly particularist or more broadly universalist projects," he is clearly leaving one kind of theorizing for another.[19] This shift from description to prescription brings Hollinger's project momentarily into alignment with Archibugi's because both indulge utopian visions, but Hollinger's cosmopolitan projections rely on a strong rather than weakened American nation-state, one that is capable of meeting the complex demand of mitigating differences by redefining the national character and identity while still maintaining a strong grip on the accustomed authority structures of the state. Under Hollinger's plan, in other words, Native American people would presumably find it easier to identify as members of the American nation, but they would also be required to identify with the American state, the same state they are fighting to honor their treaties and recognize their sovereignty.

Will Kymlicka, a strong critic of Hollinger's postethnic perspective, raises similar objections. One is terminological and conceptual. In the book *Multicultural Citizenship: A Liberal Theory of Minority Rights,* Kymlicka draws an important distinction between ethnic groups—Hollinger's preferred term—and national minorities. For Kymlicka, "ethnic groups" refer to "loose associations" arising from "individual and familial immigration."[20] "National minorities" refer to "previously self-governing, territorially concentrated cultures" that have been incorporated into a larger state.[21] This distinction paves the way for a theorization of political status for Indigenous groups quite apart from Hollinger's, which allows for only two options: a position within the American ethno-racial pentagon or incorporation into a more expansive system of American belonging.

However, the primary issue separating Kymlicka and Hollinger, both proponents of liberal democracy and liberal conceptions of the nation, is the issue of group rights. Unlike Hollinger, Kymlicka does not recognize an essential contradiction between individual and group rights within liberal democracies, especially as group rights pertain to national minorities.[22] Kymlicka undertakes to prove that group rights—what he here calls "group-differentiated rights" or "group-differentiated citizenship"—are compatible with the theory and practice of liberal democracy. Rather than ignoring cultural and historical particulars, Kymlicka focuses on them, for they provide the basis of his formulation to determine what kinds of minority nationalism should be endorsed. According to this basis, Kymlicka throws his support behind the group-differentiated right of self-government insofar as the exercise of self-government would work to protect the national minority from external repression for the larger state without increasing the likelihood that the citizens of the national minority would suffer from internal restrictions. In his reading of the history of social, cultural, and political impacts of gains in sovereignty on indigenous national minority populations, such internal restrictions appear only rarely while protections from external repression from the larger state have worked—however imperfectly—to help reduce "the vulnerability of minority groups to the economic pressures and political decisions of the larger society."[23] As Hollinger admits, such protections are of little consequence to the postethnic perspective. To the extent that contemporary theories of multiculturalist cosmopolitanism ignore the many ways tribal sovereignty matters to tribal nations, such theories remain disabled as analytical frameworks for understanding Native American politics, literature, and culture.

COSMOPOLITANISM: A TRIBAL IDEA

While cosmopolitanism's noted aura of effete worldliness clashes against the stereotypical parochialism of tribes, history paints a different picture. Think, for example, of the brute fact of tribal worldliness—the world-historical tribal presence on the international stage during the last five hundred years. Think, for example, of the history of early European exploration of North America and, later, of the history of treaty making, periods when international relations of a nation-to-nation variety dictated the terms of engagement. Think more recently of the work of the International Indian Treaty Council and other Indigenous organizations pursing recognition and redress through the United Nations and other international forums. Think of 1992, the Year of Indigenous Peoples, and think especially of January 1, 1994, the day the EZLN shocked the world into realizing what "free trade" means to Indians, not just in Chiapas but everywhere. Think, too, of how international travel and tribal worldliness factor in so much recent Native writing and art—witness Silko's *Garden in the Dunes,* Welch's *The Heartsong of Charging Elk,* Ortiz's *Somewhere Out There,* Harjo's *The Map to the Next World,* and Hulleah Tsinhnahjinnie's social justice photography, only a handful of prominent examples taken from a long and growing list.

More directly on the level of Indigenous political theory, think of the cosmopolitan nature of traditional Lakota political philosophy, embodied, for instance, in Black Elk's moving narrative, "The Making of Relatives," in which is recounted the historic peace negotiations between Black Elk's ancestors and the Ree. On Black Elk's account, this monumental and lasting peace between long-warring nations rests on the religious-political principle of a universal peoplehood-in-difference that reflects and is consecrated by "that real relationship" between man and the entire universe of creation. As Black Elk puts it, "we always love Wakan-Tanka first, and before all else, so we should also love and establish closer relationships with our fellow men, even if they should be of another nation than ours."[24]

As the narrative relates, a vision leads Matohoshila to discover the corn of the Ree people, which is very sacred to them but at that time unknown to the Lakota. The taking of the corn leads in turn to the Ree sending its diplomats to retrieve what has been taken by presenting a peace offering to Matohoshila and his people. Now, understanding the true meaning of his vision, Matohoshila undertakes preparing the ceremony in which each nation ritually takes the other as its relative, doing God's will by establishing a "three-fold peace" for the other nations of the world to emulate:

> The first peace, which is the most important, is that which comes within the souls of men when they realize their relationship, their oneness, with the universe and all its Powers, and when they realize that at the center of the universe dwells Wakan-Tanka, and that this center is really everywhere, it is within each of us. This is the real Peace, and the others are but reflections of this. The second peace is that which is made between two individuals, and the third is that which is made between two nations. But above all you should understand that there can never be peace between nations until there is first known that true peace which, as I have often said, is within the souls of men.[25]

The history of this significant peace, then, is the history of the creation of a cosmopolitan political philosophy that honors the sovereignty of nations, as this is created and consecrated by the ultimate sovereignty of the creator, but that also sanctifies the relatedness of all being as its necessary precondition, for only within a framework of universal connectedness can the national be the universal and the universal be the national.

Does this philosophy bear out historically? Is there reason beyond the anecdotal to think of an Indigenous, internationalist cosmopolitanism? In a recent lecture at the Newberry Library on her years of tribal research, historian Loretta Fowler began her remarks by describing the culture of the early nineteenth-century American plains as "cosmopolitan." Fowler offered the term without giving it any specific definition, but from the surrounding description of what everyday life was like in this culture, it was clear that "cosmopolitan" made sense in three separate registers: as a generalized description of the dominant systems of exchange, as a generalized description of relatively diverse and open cultural interaction, and as a generalized description of fluid and open-ended political relationships—all of which, it was suggested, prevailed on the North American plains in those years before the military campaigns to dispossess the tribes got into full swing.[26]

From these remarks, I distill a subtext that would cast this description as normative, a vision of a vibrant, diverse, and open plains culture that would later be compromised by settlers, soldiers, and the colonialist ideologies that would impose new standards of identification, belonging, and exchange. It is common anthropological knowledge that social boundaries are highly permeable in band societies and can be so in tribal societies as well. This fact is born out in my own experiences with tribal societies. On the Rocky Boy's Reservation where I teach, marriages between people from different tribes are common, and while old tribal prejudices exist in the form of jokes and teasing, this diversity is accepted as a normal matter of course—not as a function of some nebulous pan-Indian ethic but more as an ethic of intertribal respect. In fact, most problems of prejudice come as a consequence of discrimination due to scarcity of jobs, money, and resources rather than pure tribal chauvinisms. Since many if not most tribal people I know trace their identities through multiple lines of tribal descent—in fact, many I know remain active in all of the various socio-ceremonial lives of their parents and grandparents alike—it is reasonable to conclude that the kinds of bounded loyalties so roundly critiqued today by certain strains of poststructuralism and postcolonialism are not identical to the kinds of loyalties at work among today's Indigenous peoples.

This conclusion is sound, despite the strong nationalism at the heart of the tribal sovereignty movement. While the United States and the rest of the world may not always choose to recognize the historical sovereignty of tribal nations, tribal nations clearly recognize it in themselves—as polities separate and sufficient for treating with other nations of the world. For example, in July 2006 at Rocky Boy, the Chippewa-Cree tribe welcomed a delegation of Maori as part of an international symposium on Indigenous health issues. While the "international" nature of the symposium is perhaps enough to convince some of the inherent sovereign status of the Chippewa-Cree nation of Rocky Boy, the striking moment for me arrived when the two nations—Chippewa-Cree and Maori—came face to face at Rocky Boy's Pah-Nah-To recreational grounds in traditional ceremonial observances that each nation reserves specifically for such "affairs of state," as it were.

At the same time, it is important to recall that, strictly speaking, tribal nations are not national minorities. True, Native people living in the United States do possess a certain kind of minority status. First, affirmative action and other anti-discrimination statutes apply to Native Americans in the same way they apply to members of racial and ethnic minorities. After all, Native Americans born in the United States are citizens of the United States, a fact since 1924. Second, Native

Americans who are not on a tribal roll and whose tribal status is hence not recognized by federal or state governments are, for all intents and purposes, ethnic minorities no different in status from African Americans, Asian Americans, and Hispanic Americans. Conversely, the Indigenous nations of North America do possess a unique and separate status from other American ethnic minorities by virtue of legal precedent grounded in the history of treaty making and federal executive orders. Some historians and political theorists go further still and assert that tribal sovereignty is in fact inherent, that is, preexistent to the founding of the settler states and hence not delegated by constitutional fiat. Legal standing notwithstanding, there is no question that Native peoples see themselves as inherently sovereign and hence different—politically and historically—from other American minorities—but also as peoples related to all beings, to all peoples, and to all nations. Not all aspects of this uniquely cosmopolitan identity can be spelled out here. What follows can only begin to sketch its implications across disciplines.

COSMOPOLITANISM AND NATIVE AMERICAN LITERARY STUDIES

Within Native American literary studies, no single critic has pushed more forcefully for cosmopolitan views than Arnold Krupat. For over fifteen years, Krupat's self-styled brand of radical multiculturalism, which he calls "ethnocriticism," has sounded a devout but singular call for the deparochialization of Native American literature and culture. Despite its permutations over several books of literary and cultural criticism, Krupat's critical cosmopolitanism has remained constant on at least three points. First, it insists on the inclusion of Native American literature within both American and world literary canons. Second, it looks to the social and political efficacy of literature to help create a global "polyvocal polity" of nations.[27] Third, it opposes essentialisms and other restrictions placed on the cross-cultural production of knowledge. These clear gestures beyond the nation notwithstanding, Krupat's cosmopolitanism also draws heavily from anti-imperial internationalist thought, "fully acknowledg[ing] the importance of the issue of sovereignty in the political struggle of colonized peoples all over the world and at home" and recognizing, along with Robbins and Cheah, the potential compatibility between cosmopolitanism and anti-colonial nationalism.[28]

Beyond Krupat's pioneering theoretical work, there are very few cosmopolitan-inflected research programs within Native American literary studies. One such program is Eric Gary Anderson's insightful study of southwestern American literature and culture, *American Indian Literature from the Southwest*, which is important in how it showcases certain strengths and weaknesses regarding the application of cosmopolitanism to the situation of contemporary Native American cultural and political realities. Anderson's regionalist inquiry closely follows James Clifford's work on travel and translation in both its theoretical imperatives and its approach as an exercise in comparativist cultural studies. In the introduction to the study, Anderson pins the basis for much of his thinking to Clifford's observations that "'the processes of human movement and encounter are long-established and complex. Cultural centers, discrete regions and territories, do not exist prior to contacts, but are sustained through them, approving and disciplining the restless movements of people and things.'" Again following Clifford, Anderson contends, "no one 'is permanently fixed by his or her identity'"; but neither can one shed specific structures of race and culture, class and caste, gender and sexuality, environment and history.'"[29] The clear advantage to such theory is deconstructive. The impact of yoking together contradictory elements, like the grounded and the mobile, the fixed and the fluid, and the central and the peripheral, serves to call into question the ideological, cultural, and political force of borders, flatten the hierarchy between center and margin, and reimagine migration as a more normative human relation to space—and, importantly, as a mode of resistance. Because such theory is essentially comparative, the anti-colonial, counter-hegemonic possibilities of these destabilizing strategies stand out. Within the comparative Americanist framework, *American Indian Literature and the Southwest* thus more readily detaches customary ideologies of American national belonging from customary narratives of American spatial belonging and opens up new narrative as well as new political spaces to serve silenced and under-represented populations.

The pluralizing thrust of *American Indian Literature and the Southwest*, however, does not extend beyond its critique of the spatio-ideologial discourses of U.S. nationalism. When it comes to the Native American "national question," Anderson's theoretical edifice of "roots" and "routes" is unable to address the broad issue of tribal sovereignty. First and perhaps most obviously, *American Indian Literature and the Southwest*—a literary study, primarily—is mute on the status question of Native American writing, the issue at the center of the Native American literary sovereignty movement. Which category distinction should one adopt? Native American literature? American literature? Third-World literature? Indigenous literature? Tribal literature? Anderson does not mention the latter three distinctions, while the first two are used fairly interchangeably—perhaps predictably enough in a study that seeks to complicate borders and boundaries. Still, such equivocation marks an ambivalence that speaks clearly to the incapacity of one version of cosmopolitanism to address the pressing issues of tribal sovereignty.

A second and related incapacity arises as a consequence of the concept of "migration as resistance," which poses a political challenge of its own to Indigenous nationalism. This import and impact of this concept lies in the shift, following Clifford, from one conceptual base, grounded in the notion of colonial conquest, to a second conceptual base, grounded in the notion of migration. The point is not that human movements lack progressive political efficacy. To be sure, Anderson's project makes advances by teasing out moments of resistance within Native "migratory strategies." The problem is the difficulty of seeing these moments as other than isolated victories in a forgotten war because they largely concede the ongoing, historical character of the colonial relationship to a series of unconnected, "relational" episodes of "migratory" interactions that tend to equalize, dehistoricize, and reduce all human population movements, whether individual or collective, to the level of basic human necessity or choice rather than historical contingency. In this regard, migratory cosmopolitanism denies and dismantles the history of colonialism within a theoretical framework that locates the motive for population movements in an ironic "migratory" cultural universal rather than in contextualized struggle. The upshot, for tribal sovereignty, is that cosmopolitanisms too intently focused on placing norms on travel and mobility risk deterritorializing the nation, a deleterious result by any measure.

COSMOPOLITANISM AND TRIBAL SOVEREIGNTY

In much current writing on tribal sovereignty, however, it is the concept of sovereignty itself rather than its deterritorialization that is seen as problematic. It is a curious feature of this reversal that each of its claims is made in the name of a more authentic form of tribal autonomy. A brief exposition should clarify the point. Tribal sovereignty, the critique suggests, cannot deliver on its liberatory promise. Rather than articulating a vision leading to tribal self-determination, the prevailing advocacy discourses on tribal sovereignty lead only to dead-end, neo-colonialist ideologies that rearticulate and reinscribe western notions of domination from within. Instead, it is argued, "true" tribal autonomy lays down the path to culture, not the path to politics. Traditional cultural values will lead politics in the proper direction while politics, being already too saturated with the poison of power and exclusion, will lead only to more of the same.

Two scholars advancing critiques of this sort are Anishinaabe "crossblood" writer and critic Gerald Vizenor and Kahnawake political theorist Taiaiake Alfred. Despite irreconcilable differences between their positions, their respective arguments can be broken down into four basic, shared statements. First, the discourse on sovereignty compromises tribal politics because of its infectious European pedigree. Second, and directly related to the first, sovereignty instantiates internal colonialism because it throws open the back door to incompatible European political doctrines. Third, sov-

ereignty is too territorially minded and hence incompatible with a properly spiritual-
ist connection to the land. These critiques pose special difficulties for the theory and
practice of tribal sovereignty. For instance, is the concept of tribal sovereignty robust
enough to distinguish itself clearly and convincingly from its Euro-American counterparts? Can the concept of tribal sovereignty repair the split it is perceived to have
rent between political and spiritual responses to dispossession? Is nationalism antithetical to "true" tribal sovereignty? These are tough but not irresolvable questions.
Between the prevailing advocacy discourses on tribal sovereignty and the traditional-
ist, culturalist critique lies a common idiom for talking about freedom and justice that
is coextensive with cosmopolitan political idealism. It is a curious feature of these
culturalist critiques that elements of cosmopolitan idealism, rather than forming the
counter-discourse of sovereignty as we saw above, actually lie at the heart of the defense of sovereignty—that is, in its pristine, neo-traditionalist version. Against stri-
dent nationalist-sovereigntist voices, this reversal resituates the threat of internalized
colonialism squarely within the dominant discourses on sovereignty while removing
certain cosmopolitan political principles over to the side of decolonization, freedom,
and genuine tribal autonomy.

Since the late 1960s, Gerald Vizenor has developed and sustained a critique of
Indigenous nationalisms, first as a critique of AIM and militant radicalism in general,
and then, more recently, as a critique of the tribal sovereignty movement. While not
explicitly advocating in the name of cosmopolitanism, Vizenor's anti-nationalist politics and aesthetics, his anti-essentialist posture on identity questions, and his remarkably diverse life's résumé—embodied in his writing (witness the dazzling sweep of
forms from journalism, to novel writing, to autobiography, to the haiku in *Summer in
the Spring*), in his work experiences, and in his travels—all point to significant parallels with modes of "thinking and feeling beyond the nation" currently being identified
with "cosmopolitics." In addition to these autobiographical and bibliographical details, the body of Vizenor criticism also points to cosmopolitan correspondences. According to Arnold Krupat, the strongest Native Americanist advocate of
cosmopolitanism and one of Vizenor's keenest commentators, "Gerald Vizenor has
explored the possibilities of Native cosmopolitanism in his fiction and criticism, celebrating the once pitied, or despised 'halfbreed' as the 'mixedblood' or 'crossblood,'
and transforming the lowly 'mongrel' into a hero of comic invention."[30] In addition,
according to Ojibway poet and critic Kimberly Blaeser, who has written the only
book-length study of Vizenor's life and work, Vizenor can be properly characterized
as a radical, rebellious intellectual maverick whose refusal of the "manifest manners"
of dominance and the "fugitive poses" of "victimry" works toward liberating human
consciousness from the ruses of social science and the "simulations of dominance," of

which nationalist ideology is a key component.[31] Thus, while Krupat and Blaeser draw different political conclusions from Vizenor's example, such conclusions clearly concur in assessing Vizenor's project as an epistemological exercise in clearing the ground for the creation of more liberating tribal self-imaginings beyond the clarion call of nation-language and the repressive hail of the ideological apparatuses of the colonial state.

The value of Vizenor's decades-long contribution to Native American literary and cultural studies is immeasurable. On the levels of theory, politics, and culture within Native American studies, Vizenor's ecstatic iconoclasm serves the useful purpose of dogging certainty and second-guessing common sense. On the question of tribal sovereignty, as just mentioned, Vizenor has proven especially rigorous in critique. In several essays in the recent work, *Fugitive Poses* (1998), Vizenor questions current articulations of sovereignty as a form of collective resistance. On Vizenor's reading of the issue, tribal sovereignty breaks down to a contest between "territorial sovereignty," Vizenor's name for the concept's overriding meaning, and "native transmotion," Vizenor's preferred option, which draws from

> creation stories, totemic visions, reincarnation, and sovenance; transmotion, that sense of na-
> tive motion and an active presence, is sui generis sovereignty. Native transmotion is sur-
> vivance, a reciprocal use of nature, not a monotheistic, territorial sovereignty. Native stories
> of survivance are the creases of transmotion and sovereignty.[32]

While "Native transmotion" defies a neat and easy definition, the term nevertheless conjures something like a phenomenological spatialization of survivance, an abstraction of real territory into a metaphor for the omnipresence of Native space and a sense of unbounded, unrestricted movement—"Native transmotion," in other words, as a metaphor for an ontologically pure sovereignty unsullied by simulations. As a relatively new component of Vizenor's long-standing program to liberate the individual Native consciousness from the prison-house of colonialist ideologies, "Native transmotion" clearly carries a revisionary sense of sovereignty as a state of mind and heart, an inherent characteristic of being Native and spiritually tied to land and story.

Thus, the implications of "Native transmotion" for understanding the overlap between contemporary forms of cosmopolitanism and tribal sovereignty are significant. In an important way, Native transmotion bears a strong family resemblance to other forms of contemporary cosmopolitanism, for instance, Anthony Appiah's celebrated notion of "cosmopolitan patriotism" and the more general idea of "rooted cosmopolitanism," notions which recognize that attachments to place are not exhausted by the limits of country and citizenship. This transcendent territoriality is a hallmark of "Native transmotion," a notion that relocates sovereignty in motion and in the mobility that defies treaty, reservation, and other colonialist impositions on open land. As Vizenor explains, "Native transmotion is an original natural union in the stories of emergence and migration that relate humans to an environment and the spiritual and political significance of animals and other creations."[33] Within the parlance of mainstream sovereignty discourse, this means that

> sovereignty as transmotion is not the same as the notions of indigenous treaty sovereignty; transmotion can be scorned and denied, but motion is never granted by a government. Motion is a natural human right that is not bound by borders. Sovereignty as transmotion is tacit, inherent, and not the common provisions of treaties with other governments.[34]

As an Indigenous discourse on natural rights linking human freedom to the development of a consciousness beyond boundary lines and governments, Native transmotion shows a clear kinship with those brands of cosmopolitan thinking that also envision a world without borders. Within this neo-traditionalist framework of Native transmotion, tribal sovereignty thus becomes a particularly deterritorialized kind of Indigenous cosmopolitanism.

In other words, unlike the related concepts of "cosmopolitan patriotism" and "rooted cosmopolitanism" just mentioned, and especially in contrast to the progressive cosmopolitanisms mentioned earlier by Cheah, Native transmotion makes no positive allowance for the kinds of loyalties to people and place that we commonly know as nationalism. Quite to the contrary, nationalism for Vizenor holds no redeeming qualities whatsoever and functions solely as a sly variation "on narratives of dominance."[35] Moreover, the deterritorialized Indigenous cosmopolitanism of Native transmotion sees the nationalism within dominant discourses on tribal sovereignty as reductive, diminishing "discussions on natural reason and power . . . in a constitutional democracy . . . to the metes of territoriality, and mere victimry," and thus ultimately compromising the inherent sovereignty of tribal peoples since time immemorial to the freedom of "personal, reciprocal" motion across the land.[36] Nationalism, in other words, is no elixir for liberation but rather the deceptively sweet poison of internalized colonialism. To counter its effects, Vizenor looks beyond territory, domination, and power to recover Indigenous political traditions that might "actuate the observance of natural reason and transmotion in this constitutional democracy."[37]

This formulation finds a close cousin in the recent work of Kahnawake Mohawk political theorist Taiaiake Alfred. Like Vizenor, Alfred also recovers for the notion of tribal sovereignty its time-honored but submerged base in traditional cultural values.

As Alfred remarks in his most recent book *Peace, Power, Righteousness: An Indigenous Manifesto:* "Without a value system that takes traditional teachings as the basis for government and politics, the recovery will never be complete."[38] And again, as with Vizenor, this commitment to traditional values—Alfred mentions ethical principles like "respect, harmony, autonomy, and peaceful coexistence"—helps articulate an Indigenous politics that overlaps certain general cosmopolitan political values. Alfred's Indigenous cosmopolitanism, however, breaks with Vizenor's on the national question, a key distinction that points up the diversity of cosmopolitical viewpoints within contemporary indigenous politics.

With two books on tribal sovereignty and indigenous nationalism, *Heeding the Voices of Our Ancestors* and *Peace, Power, Righteousness,* and an essay, "Sovereignty," that presents perhaps the most thorough and concise statement on the issue, Alfred adds an important new critical voice to the growing conversation on contemporary Indigenous politics. Stressing the need for Indigenous theoretical frameworks that look to traditional forms of governance and seek to reinvigorate tribal political traditions, Alfred's position on sovereignty, like Vizenor's, maintains that "'sovereignty' is inappropriate as a political objective for indigenous peoples"[39] (464). Alfred bases this claim on a perceived dichotomy between sovereignty, as a European doctrine of state power, and time-honored but submerged indigenous political concepts. Alfred defines the problem thus: "The inter/counterplay of state sovereignty doctrines—rooted in notions of dominion—with and against indigenous concepts of political relations—rooted in notions of freedom, respect, and autonomy—frames the discourse on indigenous 'sovereignty' as its broadest level."[40] Having established this basic contrast, Alfred argues that the political solution to colonialism in North America lies down the path to traditional cultural values, for these will be found coextensive with traditional political values. This "Native philosophical alternative" Alfred puts forth echoes the wishes of many traditionalists:

> they [the Native traditionalists Alfred references] wish to preserve a regime that honours the autonomy of individual conscience, non-coercive forms of authority, and a deep respect and interconnection between human beings and the other elements of creation. The contrast between indigenous conceptions and dominant Western constructions in this regard could not be more severe. In most traditional indigenous conceptions, nature and the natural order are the basic referents for thinking of power, justice, and social relations. Western conceptions, with their own particular philosophical distance from the natural world, have more often reflected different kinds of structures of coercion and social power.[41]

Clearly, then, there is an undeniable and deep incompatibility between Alfred's vision of indigenous political culture and European and American forms. However, is this incompatibility necessarily reflective of the incompatibility that Alfred argues resides within "the discourse on indigenous 'sovereignty' as its broadest level"? Alfred states that "the actual history of our [Native nations and North American settler states] plural existence has been erased by the narrow fictions of a single sovereignty."[42] On the one hand, this claim is less than convincing considering that not all tribal sovereignties are the same. Some tribes enjoy self-governance compacts tailored to their historical and political circumstances; some have none; some distrust self-governance compacts as termination in sheep's clothing. Some tribes do not possess federal recognition and decide not to seek it while others have sought it for decades. In addition, some tribes hold treaties with settler nations while others have none, and yet others have arrangements determined by executive order. Each of these situations implies a unique approach to sovereignty. On the other hand, even if Alfred's claim were true, there is no logical reason to see sovereignty and Indigenous political traditions as mutually exclusive. To his credit, Alfred admits that "the positive effect of the sovereignty movement in terms of mental, physical, and emotional health cannot be denied or understated."[43] He is right when he asserts that these gains alone are not enough and that "the social ills which do continue [suggest] that an externally focused assertion of sovereign power vis-à-vis the state is neither complete nor in and of itself a solution."[44] Still, there is no good argument against a myriad approaches that would incorporate both political and cultural solutions to the challenges facing tribal nations.

At its core, the either-or approach is theoretically untenable. A commitment to traditional Indigenous cosmopolitan ideals would be well served by reconciliation with the advocacy discourses on tribal sovereignty. In Alfred's case, this commitment involves the reinvigoration of Indigenous perspectives like the "regime of respect" and "the vast potential for peace represented in Indigenous political philosophies."[45] This kind of scholarship is vital to the development of indigenous cosmopolitanism as political philosophy and political program, not to mention literary and cultural theory, but at the same time, it is unclear why theories of indigenous cosmopolitanisms are taking the hard line against tribal sovereignty. Given the prevailing negative attitude in intellectual circles toward nationalism in all its forms, such formulations are not only theoretically suspect but also potentially damaging. Energy would be well spent finding points of commensurability between theories of nationalism and cosmopolitanism. Energy would also be well spent mining from disciplines and perspectives currently outside the customary purview of Native American literary and cultural studies to examine in a different light the unique demands for sovereignty coming from North American tribal nations, i.e., from political entities, one would do well to recall, that are not states, that will not become states in the short run, that are not currently pursuing statehood, but that do seek certain powers and levels of autonomy that only states enjoy.

NOTES

1 Bruce Robbins, "Comparative Cosmopolitanisms," in *Cosmopolitics: Thinking and Feeling beyond the Nation,* edited by Pheng Cheah and Bruce Robbins (Minneapolis: University of Minnesota Press, 1998), 250. It has become conventional for essays on cosmopolitanism to open with something of a paean to the concept's amazingly diverse career across so many national, cultural, epochal, and disciplinary divides.

2 John O'Loughlin et al., "Globalization and Its Outcomes," in *Globalization and Its Outcomes,* edited by John O'Loughlin, Lynn Staeheli, and Edward Greenberg (New York: Guilford Press, 2004), 3.

3 Ibid., 3.

4 Ibid., 3.

5 Bruce Robbins, "Actually Existing Cosmopolitanisms," in *Cosmopolitics: Thinking and Feeling beyond the Nation,* edited by Pheng Cheah and Bruce Robbins (Minneapolis: University of Minnesota Press, 1998), 2.

6 Pheng Cheah, "Introduction Part II: The Cosmopolitical—Today," in *Cosmopolitics: Thinking and Feeling beyond the Nation,* edited by Pheng Cheah and Bruce Robbins (Minneapolis: University of Minnesota Press, 1998), 30.

7 Ibid., 30.

8 Oren R. Lyons, "The American Indian in the Past," in *Exiled in the Land of the Free: Democracy, Indian Nations, and the U.S. Constitution,* edited by Chief Oren Lyons and John Mohawk (Sante Fe: Clear Light Publishers, 1992), 42.

9 Ibid., 34.

10 Daniele Archibugi, "Principles of Cosmopolitan Democracy," in *Re-Imagining Political Community: Studies in Cosmopolitan Democracy,* edited by Daniele Archibugi, David Held, and Martin Kohler (Cambridge: Polity Press, 1998), 198.

11 Ibid., 199.

12 Ibid., 216.

13 Ibid., 216.

14 Timothy Brennan, "Cosmopolitanism and Internationalism," in *Debating Cosmopolitics*, edited by Daniele Archibugi (London: Verso, 2003), 41–42.

15 David Hollinger, *Postethnic America: Beyond Multiculturalism* (New York: Basic Books, 2000), 1.

16 Ibid., 3.

17 Ibid., 4.

18 According to Hollinger, the ethno-racial pentagon routinely asks U.S. citizens "to identify themselves and their contemporaries within one or another of five presumably involuntary communities of descent. This ethno-racial pentagon divides the population into African American, Asian American, Euro-American, Indigenous, and Latino segments . . . . The ethno-racial pentagon won acceptance in the context of government efforts to prevent discrimination against minorities during the 1970s," 8.

19 Ibid., 143.

20 Will Kymlicka, *Multicultural Citizenship: A Liberal Theory of Minority Rights* (New York: Oxford University Press, 1995), 10.

21 Ibid., 10.

22 See note 23, page 249 from *Postethnic America*. A sample from this note, however, should convey the general drift. According to Hollinger, "he [Kymlicka] is right, further, to fear that a failure of Americans to recognize that anomalous cases [tribes] within the United States might lead to a failure to appreciate that other civic nations, such as Canada, confront challenges more akin to dealing with the limited sovereignty of Indian tribes than to dealing with immigrant groups." Apparently, Hollinger is able to make this concession not because Kymlicka has exposed errors but because the claims to sovereignty of Indigenous nations within the United States really do not matter in "postethnic" America.

23 Kymlicka, 38.

24 Black Elk, *The Sacred Pipe: Black Elk's Account of the Seven Rites of the Oglala Sioux,* by Black Elk, Vera Louise Drysdale, and Joseph Epes Brown (Norman: University of Oklahoma Press, 1982), 101.

25 Ibid., 115.

26 Loretta Fowler, "Lecture on the Ethnohistory of the Northern Arapaho", D'Arcy McNickle Center for American Indian History, Newberry Library, Chicago, June 8, 2004.

27 Arnold Krupat, *The Voice in the Margin: Native American Literature and the Canon* (Berkeley: University of California Press, 1989), 216.

28 Arnold Krupat, *Red Matters: Native American Studies* (Philadelphia: University of Pennsylvania Press, 2002), 22.

29 Eric Gary Anderson, *American Indian Literature and the Southwest* (Austin: University of Texas Press, 1999), 3.

30 Krupat, *Red Matters*, 20.

31 Kimberly M. Blaeser, *Gerald Vizenor: Writing in the Oral Tradition* (Norman: University of Oklahoma Press, 1996).

32 Gerald Vizenor, *Fugitive Poses: Native American Indian Scenes of Absence and Presence* (Lincoln: University of Nebraska Press, 1998), 15.

33 Ibid., 183.

34 Ibid., 189.

35 Ibid., 181.

36 Ibid., 182.

37 Ibid., 199.

38 Taiaiake Alfred, *Peace, Power, Righteousness: An Indigenous Manifesto* (Don Mills, Ontario: Oxford University Press, 1999), 2.

39 Taiaiake Alfred, "Sovereignty," in *A Companion to American Indian History,* edited by Philip J. Deloria and Neal Salisbury (London: Blackwell, 2002), 464.

40 Ibid., 460.

41 Ibid., 470.

42 Ibid., 460.

43 Ibid., 465.

44 Ibid., 465.

45 Ibid., 471.

BIBLIOGRAPHY

Alfred, Taiaiake. *Peace, Power, Righteousness: An Indigenous Manifesto*. Don Mills, Ontario: Oxford University Press, 1999.

———. "Sovereignty." In *A Companion to American Indian History*, edited by Philip J. Deloria and Neal Salisbury. London: Blackwell, 2002.

Anderson, Eric Gary. *American Indian Literature and the Southwest*. Austin: University of Texas Press, 1999.

Archibugi, Daniele. "Principles of Cosmopolitan Democracy." In *Re-Imagining Political Community: Studies in Cosmopolitan Democracy*, edited by Daniele Archibugi, David Held, and Martin Kohler. Cambridge: Polity Press, 1998.

Black Elk. *The Sacred Pipe: Black Elk's Account of the Seven Rites of the Oglala Sioux*, by Vera Louise Drysdale, and Joseph Epes Brown. Norman: University of Oklahoma Press.

Blaeser, Kimberly M. *Gerald Vizenor: Writing in the Oral Tradition*. Norman: University of Oklahoma Press, 1996.

Brennan, Timothy. "Cosmopolitanism and Internationalism." In *Debating Cosmopolitics*, edited by Daniele Archibugi. London: Verso, 2003.

Cheah, Pheng. "Introduction Part II: The Cosmpolitical—Today." In *Cosmopolitics: Thinking and Feeling beyond the Nation*, edited by Pheng Cheah and Bruce Robbins. Minneapolis: University of Minnesota Press, 1998.

Fowler, Loretta. "Lecture on the Ethnohistory of the Northern Arapaho." Lecture, D'Arcy McNickle Center for American Indian History Newberry Library, Chicago, IL, June 8, 2004.

Hollinger, David. *Postethnic America: Beyond Multiculturalism*. New York: Basic Books, 2000.

Krupat, Arnold. *Red Matters: Native American Studies*. Philadelphia: University of Pennsylvania Press, 2002.

———. *The Voice in the Margin: Native American Literature and the Canon*. Berkeley: University of California Press, 1989.

Kymlicka, Will. *Multicultural Citizenship: A Liberal Theory of Minority Rights*. New York: Oxford University Press, 1995.

Lyons, Oren R. "The American Indian in the Past." In *Exiled in the Land of the Free: Democracy, Indian Nations, and the U.S. Constitution*, edited by Chief Oren Lyons and John Mohawk. Santa Fe: Clear Light Publishers, 1992.

O'Loughlin, John, et al. "Globalization and Its Outcomes." In *Globalization and Its Outcomes*, edited by John O'Loughlin, Lynn Staeheli, and Edward Greenberg. New York: Guilford Press, 2004.

Robbins, Bruce. "Actually Existing Cosmopolitanisms." In *Cosmopolitics: Thinking and Feeling beyond the Nation*, edited by Pheng Cheah and Bruce Robbins. Minneapolis: University of Minnesota Press, 1998.

————. "Comparative Cosmopolitanisms." In *Cosmopolitics: Thinking and Feeling beyond the Nation*, edited by Pheng Cheah and Bruce Robbins. Minneapolis: University of Minnesota Press, 1998.

Vizenor, Gerald. *Fugitive Poses: Native American Indian Scenes of Absence and Presence*. Lincoln: University of Nebraska Press, 1998.

3 PONDERING SOVEREIGNTY FOR NATIV HAWAIIANS

Kauila Clark

INTRODUCTION: A BRIEF SEGMENT OF HAWAI'I'S HISTORY

On January 17, 1893, 167 United States Marines from the USS Boston marched on the Iolani Palace, the royal residence of the Queen of Hawai'i.[1] In a bloodless revolution, they overthrew the Monarch and thus captured the Kingdom of Hawai'i. Queen Lili'uokalani (1838–1917) became a prisoner in her own palace, while American businessmen restructured the government and tried to persuade the United States of America to annex Hawai'i as United States territory. American business interests aimed for the control of the Hawaiian lands to continue their immensely profitable sugar operations with sales to the United States.

Despite President Grover Cleveland's refusal to annex Hawai'i and his unequivocal acknowledgment that Hawai'i was a sovereign nation illegally overtaken, the small group of American businessmen who instigated the overthrow proceeded to form and operate a "Republic of Hawai'i" for five consecutive years. The next United States President, William McKinley, supported American business interests and manipulated the United States Congress, through an illegal joint resolution, to take Hawai'i as a territory. The annexation became ceremonially formalized on August 12, 1898. Through the Treaty of Paris (1898), which concluded the Spanish American War, the United States received Guam, Puerto Rico, and the Philippines. Ironically, Hawai'i was added to the list, even though Hawai'i had nothing to do with the war.

Queen Lili'uokalani relinquished her throne under threat in the overthrow, but she never surrendered Hawaiian land or her title as Monarch of Hawai'i.[2] The United States government acknowledged the legitimacy of her royal acts by putting Royal Hawaiian Government lands in a trust to be held until Native Hawaiians could again rule themselves. The trust lands comprise about two million acres and subterranean ocean lands.[3]

These briefly sketched historical events have shaped the premise for Native Hawaiian sovereignty today. In light of the United Nations' definition of a sovereign nation, the Hawaiian case for sovereignty differs from that of many Native American Nations on the American Continent.[4] To begin with, the sovereign Nation of Hawai'i was under numerous international treaties of commerce and peace with many international countries. At the time of the overthrow, for example, the Nation of Hawai'i was under two treaties of commerce with the United States of America. Furthermore, the Nation of Hawai'i comprised a distinct population, possessed clearly defined geographical boundaries, enjoyed a succession of rulers for at least a thousand years, and was governed by a legitimate political system recognized as such by the

Hawaiian people. All of these characteristics identified the Nation of Hawai'i as an internationally viable and legitimate entity when President Cleveland rejected the annexation of Hawai'i as United States possession. The United Nations was formed in 1947, but its definitions of sovereignty draw from a long and internationally recognized history.[5] At the end of the nineteenth century, President Cleveland applied criteria of sovereignty internationally valid today by affirming Hawai'i as an innocent victim of ruthless business ventures and as a nation enjoying inherent sovereign rights.

The last decade of the twentieth century has witnessed the resurgence of addressing the illegitimacy of Hawai'i's annexation. In 1993, President Bill Clinton signed an Apology Bill to Native Hawaiians for the illegal overthrow of the monarchy.[6] The Apology Bill is the basis for Native Hawaiians to pursue renewed recognition as a sovereign nation and to establish a nation-to-nation relationship with the United States. The United States Congress is presently considering the Akaka Bill. The Akaka Bill, if passed, will provide Native Hawaiians with a platform to begin the legal process of re-developing full sovereignty.[7] Once Hawaiian sovereignty will again be recognized by the United States of America, the Nation of Hawai'i will be in a position to renegotiate terms and conditions of its relationship with the United States, including economic issues.

This summary of historical events brings us to the present situation of the Hawaiian sovereignty movement and the controversies it must resolve. The following sections will present reflections on external and internal barriers to Native Hawaiian sovereignty, and some thoughts on the objectives and characteristics that are unique to the situation of Hawaiian nation building today.

EIGHT EXTERNAL ISSUES AND BARRIERS TO NATIVE HAWAIIAN SOVEREIGNTY

I. To begin with, several United States constitutional issues frame Hawaiian sovereignty as a *race-based initiative*. In this framework, the United States government may define contemporary sovereignty as pertaining to the Native Hawaiian population exclusively. However, at the time of the overthrow, at least three percent of the population of the Nation of Hawai'i was multiethnic, including Japanese, Portuguese, Chinese, American, and European ethnicities. Many voices against Hawaiian Sovereignty thus can argue that a race-based Nation of Hawai'i ought to be considered illegal by the United States Constitution.

However, a convincing case can be made for a race-based definition of Hawaiian sovereignty beyond the Nation of Hawai'i's multiethnic reality. It is easy to identify the majority of the Nation of Hawai'i as Native Hawaiians are defined as the contemporary remnant of the original people inhabiting the Islands.[8] It would be more difficult identifying other ethnic groups as indigenous to Hawai'i, even though they are recognized as Hawai'i Nationals today.

II. *Four Royal Hawaiian estates*, created for Native Hawaiians as sole beneficiaries, are still in existence today. Contemporary sovereignty issues include the protection and restoration of these estates and wills, and they necessitate a definition of Hawaiian sovereignty as race-based. The royal estates and royal family and monarchs who set up these wills and estates include Bernice Pauahi Bishop (Kamehameha Schools), King Kamehameha the IV and his Queen Emma (The Queen's Hospital and Medical Center), King Lunalilo (The Lunalilo Home for the Elderly), and Queen Lili'uokalani's Children's Center for Orphaned and Indigent Children. These organizations are currently under scrutiny by the Internal Revenue Service for 501 (c) 3 status precisely because of their race-based beneficiaries. Many Native Hawai'ians fail to see that the mandate of protecting the wills and estates necessitates a race-based definition of sovereignty in negotiation with the Constitution of the United States and the IRS tax exempt code.[9]

III. Some Non-Hawaiians resist Native Hawaiian Sovereignty because of the belief that the Hawaiian Nation would continue to pose *an economic burden* to the Non-Hawaiian community. There is a fear that Non-Hawaiians will be excluded from the benefits and governance of the developing nation yet still would have to *support welfare programs*. In this scenario, the only obvious aid given to Non-Hawaiians would consist of reparations and repayment for past land use. Ceded lands now controlled by the Federal Government and the State would be removed from the authority of Non-Hawaiian entities, yet Non-Hawaiians would have to fund Native Hawaiian assistance and support programs indeterminably. Opponents to Hawaiian sovereignty consider the U.S. government's provision of funds for the new Nation of Hawai'i as the creation of a dependency cycle without end. The current high percentage of Native Hawaiians in the Federal Welfare System and housing assistance programs seems to offer evidence for the truth of this opinion.[10] Many Non-Hawaiians can only see present poverty and welfare programs as a prediction of the future relationship between the United States and the Nation of Hawai'i. Even deeper lies the condescending assumption that Native Hawaiians are incapable of generating national self-sufficiency. What proponents of this argument overlook is that the current dependency model was put into place not by Native Hawaiians, but by the U.S. government in order to control the "Native Hawaiian Problem" in the post-overthrow era.

IV. The *United States of America and its Constitution* form a barrier to Native Hawaiian Sovereignty. Whereas the United States has a Trust relationship with the Native

Hawaiian People to compensate for the illegal overthrow, it seems an act of treason to suggest that the Hawaiian Nation could once more form an independent country. In the view of the United States Congress, the most favorable position for granting nationhood to Native Hawaiians is to support a form of semi-autonomous government known as "a nation within a nation." This is precisely the legal status that has been granted to American Indian Nations.[11] At this point in history, the U.S. Congress does not conceive of or recommend a nation status fully independent of the United States of America. The Constitution allows "nation within a nation" status, but not secession from the United States of America. Even though the Constitution of the United States was violated in the illegal acquisition of Hawai'i, it still seems a strongly held view that it is right to deprive Native Hawaiians of due justice in the international arena and to deny the re-development of an independent Nation of Hawai'i. This position is perpetuated because of the existence of United States military bases in Hawai'i, especially Pearl Harbor, with their mandate to protect the West Coast of the United States.[12]

V. *Hawaiian lands are held in trust* by the United States of America as a result of the overthrow and Queen Lili'uokalani's refusal to surrender to the United States. These areas are known as the "ceded lands."[13] The government declared that they were to be held in trust until Native Hawaiians could govern themselves. The ceded lands of the Hawaiian Nation are located across the State of Hawai'i and are not contiguous. This reality presents a problem. If sovereignty were achieved, the nation's discontinuous geography could create a political nightmare in terms of police enforcement, regulation, commerce, water, ocean access, and tradition-based access to land resources.

VI. *Gaming* posits a distinct problem in the formation of nationhood. The easy way to provide economic benefits is to allow and promote gaming in the Nation of Hawai'i. The financial gain could turn into a boon to Native Hawaiians. However, this is a decision that has to be seriously considered by the leadership of the Nation because it may very well become the downfall of the people in the Nation. The direct distribution of funds to Native Hawaiians based on equal and unearned opportunities may increase alcohol and drug addiction, provide disincentives for individual career development and promote dysfunction in the community. Any funds earned for the Nation of Hawaii should provide an incentive and support for national efforts in basic education, higher education, career development, and housing incentives. All of the funding should be spent on the people by a governing entity that will promote education, career, investments, and community building by providing housing and opportunity for all rather than individual monetary distribution.[14]

VII. The current *prison population* in the State of Hawai'i includes a high number of incarcerated Native Hawaiians. There are many questions in need of answers by the leadership of the new Nation, and the legal system is a crucial part of this process. What rights and privileges should be granted to prison populations if nationhood were to be achieved once again? If the Nation is established, will incarcerated Native Hawaiians enjoy full access to its benefits and governance structures? Will the Hawaiian Nation exclude Hawaiians who are currently a ward of the State of Hawai'i? Will Native Hawaiians have to build prisons and accept the laws and structures of the U.S. judicial system in order to carry out sentences? What credentials will be acceptable to practice law in the Nation of Hawai'i? How will the court system be set up? Will it be a mere reflection of the Western system? Will there be a community, regional, and a supreme court? What will the status of prisoners be in the Hawaiian Nation? Will they be rehabilitated in the traditional Native Hawaiian system of Nā Pu'uhonua (Cities of Refuge)?[15]

VIII. The biggest question of perceived barriers to Hawaiian sovereignty concerns funding, taxes, and other national sources of income. The Hawaiian Nation may utilize numerous funding opportunities on the basis of governmental agreements with the United States. Other possibilities include leases designed for the use of trust lands to various entities such as already established telescope companies on ceded lands, the ocean, and all of its resources. Other economic pursuits such as gas sales may prove beneficial as well. In the State of Hawai'i, commodities of high cost and heavily taxed items that are sold to the general public such as gasoline, pharmaceutical drugs, tobacco, and alcohol could be sold for much less on National land.

SIX INTERNAL ISSUES AND BARRIERS TO THE FORMULATION OF THE NATION

I. A barrier to the collaborative development of a blueprint for Native Hawaiian sovereignty can be found in the lack of a *commonly shared agreement on process and procedures*. The general population seems intent on defining everything before formulating and establishing a process by which to reach definitions and consensus. The debate for individual Native Hawaiians frequently focuses on personal issues and needs which then become the basis for more general and far-reaching nation building decisions. Personal agendas thus can dominate the debate, even though they are tangential in terms of a sovereign entity and whether they support the pursuit of sovereignty or not.[16]

II. Many Native Hawaiians demand a *completely and perfectly defined model of sovereignty* before they will commit to the process of nation building. This is indeed the greatest barrier to Native Hawaiian unity: the current inability to pursue a common goal with a common understanding. We could engage in the process of becoming a sovereign nation more successfully; but a process for the development of a sovereignty model needs to be designed with the shared agreement that such a process would be exploratory, and with the shared acceptance that mistakes and faults will always be an integral part of the process. As a people, many Native Hawaiians do not yet share a common grasp of the vocabulary, systems, and history necessary to achieve consensus and harmony in collaboration. They appear to want a process that is perfect and flawless before the process is even set in motion. At this point in our history, there seems to be a general failure to understand that it is the process itself that will develop character, commitment, and experience for building and running a Nation.

III. Health issues are a barrier to Hawai'i as a sovereign nation. Sick people will build a sick nation. The data for contemporary Native Hawaiian health is appalling. Native Hawaiians have the highest rate of hypertension, heart disease, kidney failure, obesity, respiratory disease, diabetes, and other chronic diseases of any peoples on the globe.[17] The failing health of the nation would bar its people from making healthy choices for the life of the nation. The national budget would be plagued with monumental health costs and issues. A major emphasis in the process of nation building must be placed on preventative medicine and traditional healing.[18]

IV. Traditional Native Hawaiian culture is a barrier to nationhood. Traditional Native Hawaiian culture and values are a barrier in at least one way: they may not allow new ideas and processes to be included in the process of cultural development because their inclusion must breach cultural context. For example, many questions would have to be asked about the use of electronics as a tool. From a traditional perspective, such use constitutes a breach of the Hawaiian spirit. It does not allow for many important cultural practices, including *Aloha*, *pono* (correctness), healing, Native Hawaiian ceremonies, energy work, and the personal touch that is an integral part of Native Hawaiian culture and energy.[19]

V. Another difficult barrier is the *divide between generations* in regard to views on sovereignty. Those who are under the age of forty seem to be much more inclined to think in terms of complete independence from the United States. One reason for this position lies in young people's low investment in the United States retirement system. Those over the age of forty are, however, invested in Social Security, Medicare, and Medicaid. Aging Native Hawaiians are thus more concerned about the possible losses that may occur if an independent nation were formed. Their concerns reach beyond personal worries in asking how the Hawaiian nation can survive economically if independence were achieved.

VI. Contemporary Western lifestyles and attitudes among Native Hawaiians block the pursuit of nation building. Native Hawaiians may be so steeped in the contemporary lifestyle of the West that it becomes difficult to forge the civic-minded attitudes and behaviors that define the independence of a sovereign nation.[20] It is attitudes and behaviors that shape a Nation, its policies, laws, constitution, and form of government. Because many Native Hawaiians are only familiar with a Western lifestyle and form of government, these values would very likely shape the constitution and form of government that would prevail. In this future scenario, it would be difficult to be true to the beliefs, values, and understanding of the traditions taken from the people in the overthrow, when the Hawaiian government mirrored the times, needs, and benevolence of the nation back to its people.

CHOOSING A FORM OF GOVERNMENT AND CONSTITUTION

Based on the United Nations guidelines, Native Hawaiians must decide on one of three possible forms of government in forming a new nation. The choices are to become a "nation within a nation," a "compact nation," or a fully independent Nation. The Akaka bill, now before the United States Congress and aiming to grant Native Hawaiians recognition, strongly suggests that the form of government be the "nation within a nation" model. This choice closely resembles the governmental structures granted Native American Nations.[21]

One strategy to keep the trust benefits intact while forming a new government system is to pursue the guidelines of nationhood as provided by the United States Congress to protect entitlement programs, wills, and estates for Native Hawaiians as the beneficiaries. This arrangement would agree with the form of government suggested by the Congress of the United States in the Akaka Bill.

There are deeper issues and concerns, however, in defining a government system, and present stumbling blocks in the advancement of nationhood. Nationhood involves much more than simple concepts and outward appearance or physical, material problems. The issues are multilayered, yet the core issue of coming together as a nation is spiritual. If the spiritual dimension is put into place first, it will place the more superficial issues such as physical and material in a manageable and sensible context. The political debate about forms of government and a constitution has no base unless government and constitution are discussed as the physically manifest features of the deep core and meaningful values of Hawaiian spirituality and identity.

In my view, the major problem is thus to identify who we are as Native Hawaiians. Even though we fought against attitudes, behaviors, and the vision of the colonizers, after many years of colonization, Hawaiians may use the attitudes and behaviors of the colonizers in the development of the Nation of Hawai'i. Will we be like our colonizers and fail to understand and practice who we are as Hawaiians and what we do to our own people? Native Hawaiians believe that we were created spiritually before we were created physically. This concept then should be our guiding principle: to establish spiritual values before the physical formation of the government.[22]

UNDERSTANDING SOVEREIGNTY DEMANDS A REDEFINITION OF KEY TERMS

There needs to be redefinition of several terms and concepts if Native Hawaiians embrace sovereignty in a traditional understanding.

I. The first definition concerns *sovereignty*. Sovereignty seems to have a different meaning for different people. It ranges from a sovereign being to sovereign royalty to a nation. Every Native Hawaiian needs a common understanding of what the word means and how it can be applied to nation building. In my view, sovereignty means that each and every person has to be a sovereign and independent entity that comes together with others in harmony as a sovereign nation. Individualism forms the basis of sovereignty, but it is established in oneness as a nation.

II. The second concept in need of clarification is *economy*. The most popular definition refers narrowly to a cash economy. The Native Hawaiian concept of economy has been much more comprehensive. It considers the resources, places, and needs of the people. The *ahupua'a*, the Native Hawaiian economic understanding of land use, illustrates a more comprehensive economic system. Within this grid of land division, people could trade for their needs and produced what was best for the land they lived on. The *ahupua'a* was usually a piece of pie-shaped geographic area that reached from the top of the mountain to the ocean, with the larger dimension located at the ocean shore. The subsistence economic system of the *ahupua'a* fit the Native Hawaiian lifestyle and a Pacific Island existence. I believe that Native Hawaiians today would be best served by a combination of cash and subsistence economies in order to maximize natural resources and human potential.

III. The third area in need of definition is *Native Hawaiian values*. The whole of Native values today must include both traditional and contemporary interpretations of these values as well as the application of their core principles. A comprehensive educational and practice-oriented effort must be made to bring alive the meaning and application of these values.[23] I believe that the people would be served best if Native Hawaiian spiritual values would set the national standard for all understanding and practice in a contemporary setting.

IV. The last challenge is to define the term *Native Hawaiian*. There are currently three definitions of *Hawaiian* in use. The first is Hawaiian as it refers to anyone born in Hawai'i. The second definition is narrower and refers to ancestral Hawaiians, which refers to Hawaiians with less than a fifty percent blood quantum. The third and most prominent definition is the designation Native Hawaiian by the United States Congress in the Hawaiian Homes Act. This definition refers to Hawaiians with more than a 50% blood quantum. It has divided families, friends, and large groups of Hawaiian people into "haves" and "have-nots" with the intent that individuals can qualify for federal government benefits.[24]

Hawaiians must progress beyond these fractured definitions and agree to one inclusive understanding, so the people can heal and move toward becoming one nation once again. The definition I believe to serve the Native Hawaiian people best is to be a citizen of the Nation of Hawai'i. This would be the one and only classification of Hawaiian.

THE CORE UNDERSTANDING IN BEING A SOVEREIGN NATION IS FOUND IN IDENTITY AND VALUES

The core issue facing sovereignty is our unity. Our unity as a nation should be one in diversity. Furthermore, the traditional understanding of *Aloha* must be incorporated in the identity and values of our people, into the core of our being. Native Hawaiians must come together on a spiritual level before they can achieve harmony on a physical level: Native Hawaiian traditional belief is that everything was created spiritually before it was created physically.[25] This belief will show itself in the behaviors and protocols used in leading, organizing, and establishing the Nation. Those who lead the pursuit of sovereignty need to identify with Native Hawaiian understanding and values and identify with them in the depth of their being. If this approach can become the protocol and the process used to achieve sovereignty, then there is hope for the nation to come together and to achieve sovereignty once more. That hope is present in the everyday expression and behavior of *Aloha*. *Kupuna* (Elder) Pilahi Paki explained *Aloha* by using ALOHA as an acronym[26]:

A-Akahai: Kindness to be expressed with Tenderness
L-Lokahi: Unity to be expressed with Harmony
O-OluOLu: Agreement to be expressed with Pleasantness
H-HaaHaa: Humility as expressed with Modesty
A-Ahonui: Patience to be expressed with Perseverance.

Aloha will bring Native Hawaiians together to form a nation for the people by the people and with unity under the creator.

RESOLVE FOR THE ESTABLISHMENT OF NATIVE HAWAIIAN SOVEREIGNTY

The most effective and efficient way Native Hawaiians can establish a sovereign entity for the people is through an extensive and continuous education program. This education program should cover the elements of discussion in this text as well as broader concepts of cultural socialization and nationhood. It may well be the next generation that will establish what has been lost for one hundred and fifteen years. It is up to the present generation to teach the younger generations all facets of sovereignty and to work toward that dream to make it a reality. We, as Native Hawaiians, must learn, understand, and strive toward the hopes and visions of the last five generations.

NOTES

1 See Thomas J. Osborne, *Annexation Hawai'i: Fighting American Imperialism* (Waimanalo, HI: Island Style Press, 1998).

2 See Helena G. Allen, *The Betrayal of Queen Lili'uokalani, Last Queen of Hawaii 1838–1917* (Honolulu: Mutual Publishing, 1982), and Queen Lili'uokalani, *Hawai'i's Story by Hawai'i's Queen* (reprint; Honolulu, HI: Mutual Publishing, 1991).

3 For a review of the dynamics of the trust, see Thomas A. Loudat, *A Historical Performance Review of the Hawaiian Home Lands Trust, State of Hawai'i (August 21, 1959, to June 30, 1988)* (Honolulu: Hawaiian Claims Office, Dept. of Commerce and Consumer Affairs, 1994).

4 Ken E. Iyall Smith, *The State and Indigenous Movements: Indigenous Peoples and Politics* (New York: Routledge, 2006).

5 For a contemporary context, see Ward Churchill and Sharon H. Venne with Lilikala Kame'eleihiwa, *Islands in Captivity: The International Tribunal on the Rights of Indigenous Hawaiians* (Boston: South End Press, 2004).

6 President Bill Clinton signed United States Public Law 103–150 on November 23, 1993 (107 Stat. 1510). The "Apology Resolution" acknowledged the illegal overthrow of the sovereign Hawaiian government.

7 The "Akaka Bill," now titled the *Native Hawaiian Government Reorganization Act of 2007* (S. 310, H.R. 505), aims to re-establish a government to government relationship with sovereign Native Hawaiian citizens. However, there are significant differences to U.S. federal recognition of American Indian tribal nations.

8 On the issue of race based versus cultural definitions of identity, see Kan Terry Young, *Rethinking the Native Hawaiian Past* (New York: Garland, 1998) and Noenoe K. Silva, *Aloha betrayed: Native Hawaiian Resistance to American Colonialism* (Durham, NC: Duke University Press, 2004).

9 See Hawaiian Homes Commission Act, 1920 (42 Stat. 108, chapter 42).

10 For the historical trauma that has determined many current social woes, see Martha H. Noyes, *Then There Were None* (Honolulu: Bess Press, 2003).

11 See David E. Wilkins and K. Tsianina Lomawaima, *Uneven Ground: American Indian Sovereignty and Federal Law* (Norman: University of Oklahoma Press, 2001).

12 For details see, among others, Tom Coffman, *Nation Within: The Story of America's Annexation of the Nation of Hawai'i* (Kane'ohe, HI: Epicenter, n. d.).

13 See Tom Coffman, *The Island Edge of America: A Political History of Hawai'i* (Honolulu: University of Hawaii Press, 2003).

14 The current Akaka Bill does not permit Native Hawaiians to establish casinos (Section 9a).

15 On Native Hawaiians and imprisonment statistics, see the Office of Hawaiian Affairs, *2006 Data Health Book* (Honolulu: Unknown Author), <*http://www.oha.org/*>, last updated December 11, 2006.

16 On the challenge of shared protocol, see Lilikala Kame'Eleihiwa, *Native Land and Foreign Desires: Pehea LA E Pono Ai? How Shall We Live in Harmony?* (Honolulu: Bishop Museum Press, 1992) and Rona Tamiko Halualani, *In the Name of Hawaiians: Native Identities and Cultural Politics* (Minneapolis: University of Minnesota Press, 2002).

17 On health statistics, see the Office of Hawaiian Affairs, *2006 Data Health Book* (Honolulu: Unknown Author) (<http://www.oha.org/>, last updated December 11, 2006).

18 On traditional healing, see David Malo, *Hawaiian Antiquities* (Honolulu: Bishop Museum, 1951) and more recently, Makana Risser Chai, *Na Mo'olelo Lomilomi: Traditions of Hawaiian Massage & Healing* (Honolulu: Bishop Museum, 2005).

19 For an introduction to the principle and use of *pono* (righteousness, respect), especially in Native Hawaiian sovereignty movements, see Lawrence H. Fuchs, *Hawai'i Pono: An Ethnic and Political History*, 3d ed. (Honolulu: Bess Press, 1997).

20 See Ronald H. Heck and Maenette K. P. Benham, *Culture and Educational Policy in Hawai'i: The Silencing of Native Voices,* Sociocultural, Political and Historical Studies in Education Series (Mahwah, NJ: Lawrence Erlbaum, 1998).

21 For the origin of the concept, see Vine Deloria, Jr. and Clifford M. Lytle, *The Nations Within: The Past and Future of American Indian Sovereignty* (Austin: University of Texas Press, 1984).

22 See Kilipaka Kawaihonu Nahili Pae Ontai, "A Spiritual Definition of Sovereignty from a Kanaka Maoli Perspective," in *Sovereignty Matter: Locations of Contestation and Possibility in Indigenous Struggles for Self-Determination,* edited by Joanne Barker (Lincoln: University of Nebraska Press, 2005), 153–69.

23 See essay by David Kekaulike Sing in this volume.

24 On the destructive impact of blood quantum on Native American identity, see Eva Marie Garroutte, *Real Indians: Identity and the Survival of Native America* (Berkeley: University of California Press, 2003); on the issue for Native Hawaiians, see J. Kehaulani Kauanui, "The Politics of Hawaiian Blood and Sovereignty in *Rice vs. Cayetano,*" in *Sovereignty Matter: Locations of Contestation and Possibility in Indigenous Struggles for Self-Determination,* edited by Joanne Barker (Lincoln: University of Nebraska Press, 2005), 87–109.

25 See Martha Beckwith, *Hawaiian Mythology* (New Haven, CT: Yale University Press, 1940).

26 *Kapuna* Pilahi Paki, private and public teachings, no date.

BIBLIOGRAPHY

Office of Hawaiian Affairs. *2006 Data Health Book.* Honolulu: Unknown Author, 2006. <*http://www.oha.org/*>.

Allen, Helena G. *The Betrayal of Queen Lili'uokalani, Last Queen of Hawai'i 1838–1917*. Honolulu: Mutual Publishing, 1982.

Beckwith, Martha. *Hawaiian Mythology*. New Haven, CT: Yale University Press, 1940.

Chai, Makana Risser. *Na Mo'olelo Lomilomi: Traditions of Hawaiian Massage & Healing*. Honolulu: Bishop Museum Press, 2005.

Churchill, Ward, and Sharon H. Venne with Lilikala Kame'eleihiwa. *Islands in Captivity: The International Tribunal on the Rights of Indigenous Hawaiians*. Boston: South End Press, 2004.

Coffman, Tom. *The Island Edge of America: A Political History of Hawai'i*. Honolulu: University of Hawaii Press, 2003.

———. *Nation Within: The Story of America's Annexation of the Nation of Hawai'i*. Kane'ohe, HI: Epicenter, 2003.

Deloria, Vine, Jr., and Clifford M. Lytle. *The Nations Within: The Past and Future of American Indian Sovereignty*. Austin: University of Texas Press, 1984.

Fuchs, Lawrence H. *Hawai'i Pono: An Ethnic and Political History*. Honolulu: Bess Press, 1997.

Garroutte, Eva Marie. *Real Indians: Identity and the Survival of Native America*. Berkeley: University of California Press, 2003.

Halualani, Rona Tamiko. *In the Name of Hawaiians: Native Identities and Cultural Politics*. Minneapolis: University of Minnesota Press, 2002.

Heck, Ronald H., and Maenette K. P. Benham. *Culture and Educational Policy in Hawai'i: The Silencing of Native Voices*. Sociocultural, Political and Historical Studies in Education. Mahwah, NJ: Lawrence Erlbaum, 1998.

Kame'Eleihiwa, Lilikala. *Native Land and Foreign Desires: Pehea LA E Pono Ai? How Shall We Live in Harmony?* Honolulu: Bishop Museum Press, 1992.

Kauanui, J. Kehaulani. "The Politics of Hawaiian Blood and Sovereignty in *Rice vs. Cayetano.*" In *Sovereignty Matters: Locations of Contestation and Possibility In Indigenous Struggles for Self-Determination*, edited by Joanne Barker. Lincoln: University of Nebraska Press, 2005.

Lili'uokalani, Queen. *Hawai'i's Story by Hawai'i's Queen*. Honolulu, HI: Mutual Publishing, 1991.

Loudat, Thomas A. *A Historical Performance Review of the Hawaiian Home Lands Trust, State of Hawaii (August 21, 1959, to June 30, 1988)*. Honolulu: Hawaiian Claims Office, Dept. of Commerce and Consumer Affairs, 1994.

Malo, David. *Hawaiian Antiquities*. Honolulu: Bishop Museum Press, 1951.

Noyes, Martha H. *Then There Were None*. Honolulu: Bess Press, 2003.

Office of Hawaiian Affairs. *2006 Data Health Book.* Honolulu: Unknown Author, 2006. <*http://www.oha.org/*>.

Ontai, Kilipaka Kawaihonu Nahili Pae. "A Spiritual Definition of Sovereignty from a Kanaka Maoli Perspective." In *Sovereignty Matters: Locations of Contestation and Possibility in Indigenous Struggles for Self-Determination,* edited by Joanne Barker. Lincoln: University of Nebraska Press, 2005.

Osborne, Thomas J. *Annexation Hawai'i: Fighting American Imperialism.* Waimanalo, HI: Island Style Press, 1998.

Silva, Noenoe K. *Aloha Betrayed: Native Hawaiian Resistance to American Colonialism.* Durham, NC: Duke University Press, 2004.

Smith, Ken E. Iyall. *The State and Indigenous Movements: Indigenous Peoples and Politics.* New York: Routledge, 2006.

Wilkins, David E., and K. Tsianina Lomawaima. *Uneven Ground: American Indian Sovereignty and Federal Law.* Norman: University of Oklahoma Press, 2001.

Young, Kan Terry. *Rethinking the Native Hawaiian Past.* Garland, NY: Routledge, 1998.

4 PRACTICING SOVEREIGNTY: LUMBEE IDENTITY, TRIBAL FACTIONALISM, AND FEDERAL RECOGNITION, 1932–1934

Malinda M. Maynor

Many Indigenous people in the United States know the Lumbee tribe for its 120-year-old quest for federal recognition. The Bureau of Indian Affairs (BIA) has not granted the tribe recognition, it is thought, because the tribe cannot rely on the usual criteria for acknowledgment. Over time, the U.S. government has developed a variety of ways to make decisions about a tribe's Indian identity. Before the Indian New Deal in the 1930s, the BIA based recognition on the petitioning tribe's prior treaty relationship to the United States, or on whether the United States had ever held land in trust for the tribe. Under the leadership of Commissioner of Indian Affairs John Collier, the Indian New Deal incorporated anthropological definitions of "Indianness," including a certain percentage of "Indian blood" and corresponding evidence of "Indian culture." In 1978, the BIA added more measures of identity to the acknowledgment process, including documented evidence of a continuous social and political organization among the tribe that outsiders have recognized as such. A bevy of scholars have pointed out the inherent flaws in these criteria, most prominent among them the fact that the government's ideas about Indian identity have little to do with Indians' own markers.[1] These well-founded criticisms, however, have not affected Lumbees and the many other eastern tribes who are hard-pressed to find an extant treaty their ancestors signed, or who never lived on a reservation, or whose languages and religious rituals have been hidden by colonization. Their appeals to the federal government have fallen on deaf ears.

But wait—the Lumbees are federally recognized, just not by the BIA. In 1956, Congress passed the Lumbee Act, which gave the tribe its current name and a limited form of federal acknowledgment. Congress declared that the Lumbees were indeed an Indian tribe but also stated that the tribe should receive no benefits or services normally due to Indians. The Lumbees are therefore unique among federally recognized tribes—they are not eligible for the funding that other tribes receive, yet the government has repeatedly acknowledged their Indian identity. 1956, in fact, was not the first time Congress proposed a limited acknowledgment for Lumbees; the tribe's recognition efforts in 1932 and 1933 resulted in a similar proposal, but those bills failed to pass. These two bills proposed recognition for the group under the names "Cherokee Indians of Robeson County" in 1932 and "Siouan Indians of Lumber River" in 1933. The bills fell short of even limited recognition because of an intractable conflict between Congress and the BIA over the nature of Indian identity and the assumptions behind federal acknowledgment. North Carolina's congressional delegation saw recognition as a political matter. They aimed to please their white and Indian constituents and satisfy the concerns of other Congressmen about questions such as racial purity and legitimate Indian leadership. The BIA, on the other hand, approached recognition from an academic perspective, measuring Robeson County Indians' identity against intellectual and legal categories of "Indianness" that included evidence of particular tribal ancestors and whether their descendants qualified for federal services. These criteria mattered (and still matter) far more to non-Indian policymakers than to Indian people's everyday ways of reckoning their identity.

The "Cherokee" and "Siouan" names proposed in the 1932 and 1933 bills stemmed from this conflict between Congress and the BIA. The quandary of a tribal name has persistently shadowed the Lumbees on this path to federal recognition, although nowhere in the government's tortuous history of Indian identity discussions has it required a historic tribal name to authenticate the petitioning group's Indian identity. Rather, tribal names constitute powerful symbols of a historic ancestry, a visible culture, and a distinct identity. Names represent identity; they do not constitute identity themselves, but their power has made trouble for southern and eastern Indian groups.[2] Similar to other Indians in the post-Removal South, Lumbees lived within a system of legal segregation that only countenanced two races—"white" and "colored." Their appeals for recognition went to elected officials who supported white supremacy and hoped to use Indian identity as a way to uphold segregation. For southern politicians, a tribal name meant greater success in their quest to separate the races—Indians from blacks and blacks from whites. For policy makers at the BIA, however, a name signaled anthropological authenticity, a criterion that had little relevance to southern racism. This conflict, brought by segregation and aggravated by political agendas, doomed recognition for Lumbees in the 1930s.

Even so, the government's failure to recognize the tribe did not mean that the Lumbees failed to exercise their sovereignty and affirm their Indian identity. The federal government does not grant sovereignty. Rather, Lumbees' strategies to advocate for these bills demonstrated how tribal leaders put sovereignty into practice. Confronted with a disagreement within the federal government, Lumbee leaders deployed their traditional social and political organization by dividing into political factions. Each faction negotiated with the government branch that most closely identified with its own beliefs about how the tribe should achieve federal recognition. While both groups sought federal recognition to shield them from the uncertainties inherent in the "Jim Crow" system, the factions disagreed on how to achieve such acknowledgment. Those who supported the "Cherokee" designation, "Cherokees" in this chapter, believed that Indians should reinforce their support of white supremacy to gain congressional favor. Those Indians who favored the "Siouan" name, however, looked to prove their identity to the BIA directly and avoided ingratiating themselves with white politicians. To articulate their identity in terms the federal government understood, "Siouans" built a tribal government modeled on the United States' notions of sovereignty. The factions also reflected pre-existing social divisions between kin and settlement groups, divisions that had characterized the community for hundreds of years and served to clearly distinguish Indians from non-Indians. Lumbees' efforts to obtain federal recognition from Congress in the 1930s demonstrate an astute political strategy that practiced sovereignty in all of its forms as a way to affirm their identity in the segregated South.

A NATION OF NATIONS: NEGOTIATING A DIVERSE PAST

Lumbees forged their identity in a crucible of cultural and political diversity. In the late seventeenth and eighteenth centuries, Indian families from different Iroquoian, Siouan, and Algonkian language groups migrated from distant places to the swampy lands in what is now Robeson County, North Carolina. They sought refuge from European diseases, warfare, and slavery. Oral tradition consistently points to their origins in three regions: the Roanoke River in northeastern North Carolina and southern Virginia, the Outer Banks of North Carolina, and the piedmont region south and west of present-day Robeson County. Indian groups in these areas included the Cheraw, Waccamaw, and Peedee (Siouan speakers) in upper South Carolina; the Tuscarora (Iroquoian speakers) and Saponi (Siouan speakers) in piedmont and eastern North Carolina; the Hatteras (Algonkian speakers) at the North Carolina coast; and small Indigenous communities such as the Yeopim, Potoskite, Nansemond, and Weanoke in the Roanoke River region.[3] Cheraw and Seneca groups traveled through the remote area around the Lumber River in Robeson County, but a Waccamaw community resided there as well, and Cheraw settlers joined them later.[4] By the late eighteenth century, an Indian community had coalesced in Robeson County. Some had lived there for many years, while others had arrived relatively recently. In the nineteenth century, this Indian community shaped its core identity around kin ties and the specific settlements that extended families constructed. An ethic of reciprocity knit these social and geographic communities together. In this context of migration and settlement, they must have minimized the value of a single name for their emerging communities. Like the Catawbas, Creeks, Choctaws, Seminoles, and other Indian groups in the East, Robeson County's Indians are a "nation of nations," for whom a formal name became necessary primarily for negotiating with colonial, state, and federal authorities.[5] Tribal names, constitutions, bounded territories and the other aspects of tribal life we take for granted today had no place in the eighteenth- and nineteenth-century world of the Lumbees. The area's cultural and linguistic diversity and the nature of Indians' coalescence thus make it difficult to define one particular group from which the present-day Lumbee descend.[6]

However, the lack of a single name, a bounded territory, or a centralized government did not mean that Lumbees were not a sovereign community. "A sovereign nation defines itself and its citizens," according to scholars David E. Wilkins and K. Tsianina Lomawaima, and Lumbees had plenty of ways to define themselves apart from their political structure.[7] Kinship ties governed Indigenous people and influenced Indians' identification with their group. Both before and after European contact, an individual was an "Indian" because he or she was born into or adopted by a clan that had specific roles within the larger society. During the seventeenth and eighteenth centuries, few people—even Europeans—would have assumed that identity was exclusively linked to racial ancestry. Race had little to do with Indian identity until the Removal era, when European Americans began to declare Indians racially inferior in order to justify the United States' expansion.[8] Throughout the colonial period, Indian communities commonly incorporated members of other races and ethnic groups through marriage or captivity rituals.[9]

Lumbees' adoption of Christianity and their widespread landholding in the nineteenth century transformed the matrilineal relations that characterized eastern Native societies in the eighteenth century. Indian children thus came to trace their kin relations not only through their mother's line, but through their father's as well. The influence of the Protestant church and the inability of married women to own land reduced women's visible roles in community governance. Although the system of reckoning kinship changed, gender roles continued to uphold kinship networks in Robeson County. Men and women tended to identify positively with their respective roles, each accepting responsibility for distinct areas of family and community life. A father claimed his role as the head of the household, the family's primary provider, and the person most responsible for negotiating with outside institutions. These duties corresponded with whites' recognition of an Indian man's status as a landowner, but they also co-existed with an Indian mother's position as mistress within the home. In addition to providing for the family through her work in the fields and in the garden, mothers made the decisions regarding children's discipline and socialization; women also transmitted the oral tradition and kept kinship connections intact by caring for in-laws and by keeping the family in church.[10]

By 1930, Lumbees had been shaping their kin network in their place for over 150 years, and one's family and home settlement were the fundamental way to identify oneself as an Indian. To be a Hammonds from Saddletree, a Lowry from Pembroke, a Brooks from White Hill, or an Oxendine from Union Chapel meant something to other Indians. It was their way of identifying another Indian's family and thus his likely reputation, economic background, political influence, and overall social "place" in the larger community. Locale thus reinforced family relations and cultural values and shaped the social cooperation and conflict that occurred within the Indian community.[11] These Indians have claimed different political affiliations since their coalescence, yet all acknowledge that they are part of the same extended kinship group and share a deep attachment to their family's settlement and to their larger homeland in Robeson County. Their ability to disagree politically yet preserve their underlying unity, their kinship and place connections, suggests that their sense of themselves as Indians is the product of a kind of layering process.[12] This layering allows for disagreement within the tribe on some levels while they preserve their common identity and their distinctiveness from their black and white neighbors.

GRASSROOTS DEMOCRACY: LUMBEE POLITICAL LEADERSHIP

Just as an Indian's ties to family and place were intensely localized, so was the group's political leadership. Men's responsibility as negotiators placed them in leadership roles, especially as the language of white supremacy became increasingly gendered in the late nineteenth and early twentieth centuries.[13] Scattered communities formed the larger Indian community, which kinship linked and common concerns occasionally brought together. An Indian's sense of "Indianness" stemmed first from his family and locality and then from the "tribe" as a whole. Like their pre-Columbian ancestors, tribal identity—as opposed to family or clan identity—did not reside in a governmental body that exercised influence over all tribal members. Rather, particular issues and particular leaders stimulated an Indian's sense of identification with his tribe.

Attached as they were to kin and to settlement, Indian leaders pulled apart more often than they pulled together on many issues. Leadership was individualistic and entrepreneurial, heavily influenced by family or personal charisma. Having no single spokesperson, Indians tolerated a wide diversity of opinion within the community, and tribal members placed great emphasis on respect for the opinions of family patriarchs and matriarchs, as well as pastors and teachers. Each community had its own set of acknowledged leaders who influenced individual conduct, religious doctrine, voting, school admission, employment, and a host of other issues. Leaders routinely challenged one another's authority. Though not strictly hereditary, some families held status as "leading families" for several generations.[14] Overall, the words "fragmented" and "contested" best described Indian leadership, but this political structure was not detrimental to the community's survival, however different it seemed from Western models of democracy. Rather, a decentralized leadership worked well for a community focused primarily on local attachments to family and home that wanted to avoid political entanglements with whites.

However, as southern whites struggled to recapture their supremacy after the Civil War, Indians needed new ways to affirm their identity. No longer would knowledge of one's ancestors and allegiance to one's home place suffice to mark an individual as an Indian. White southerners based their new society on the existence of two social categories: white and "colored." Indians rejected whites' attempts to classify them as "colored" and sought ways to remind others of their "Indianness." Indian families from different settlements disagreed, however, on how to approach these issues. For example, members of the Brooks family, who lived in what was called the Brooks Settlement, chose to articulate their Indian identity by reaching out to Native Americans from other places. They invited a group of Mohawks from upstate New York to Robeson County to help them establish a Haudenosaunee Longhouse and remind surrounding Indians and non-Indians of their distinctiveness.[15] Indians in other settlements took a different approach to reinforcing their separate place in the southern racial hierarchy. These Indians chose to embrace racial segregation and press for Indian-only schools. The community's segregated social institutions brought Lumbees together across kin and settlement boundaries and gave some Indians greater political influence, both within and outside the community.

In the creation of Indian-only schools, Indians' ideas about identity began to engage with white segregationists' ideas about the racial hierarchy. North Carolina's 1868 constitution provided only for schools for white and black children. Under this system, Indians had no choice but to attend school with blacks, which they refused to do. Attending black schools would have undermined their distinctiveness as Indians and encouraged whites to classify them, legally and socially, as "colored." In 1885, the North Carolina state legislature passed a law that recognized Robeson County Indians as "Croatan Indians" and provided for separate Indian schools. In 1887, the legislature passed another law establishing a normal school, or teacher-training institution, for Indian teachers. With schools of their own, Indians proceeded to express their separate identity through education. Native Americans also retained the ballot, in contrast to their black neighbors whom Conservative Democrats disfranchised in 1900. With white politicians recognizing their tribal identity and their votes, Indians capitalized on their schools to gain political influence. This creation of a legally recognized "tribe" generated a political layer of Indian identity. Identification as a "tribe" formed the basis for negotiations with white supremacists and for disagreements within the group about the strategies that Indians should use to preserve their separate identity.

BATTLING "JIM CROW" IN INDIAN COUNTRY

The development of Indian-only schools and the coincident formal tribal organization also created an internal class differentiation among Lumbees. Before the early twentieth century, Indians had largely avoided such competition and internal differentiation by focusing their economic resources on opportunities that sustained their kinship networks: subsistence farming, seasonal wage work in the turpentine and lumber industries, and land ownership.[16] Landownership, in particular, was an important vehicle for Indian identity; owning land reinforced the markers of kinship and reciprocity. The adult children and grandchildren of Indian landowners worked their parents' farm cooperatively, and sometimes they purchased land from the head of the household or from aunts and uncles. Tradition also assured children that when their parents died, the land would not be sold but instead passed on to them.[17]

Landowning had even deeper meanings in the Indian world. Robeson County was their homeland, and to paraphrase anthropologist Karen Blu, landowning, more than a means of livelihood, was an end in itself. Owning land took precedence over the money that could be made from the land. For example, James E. Chavis bought a twenty-acre farm in 1933 and admitted to a government agent that his land "was not so good as other, more expensive places" in other parts of the county.[18] This land was not the best, not even enough to feed his family, but the farm sold at a price Chavis could afford and gave him a material stake in the community. Typically, landowners in the 1930s owned small parcels—five to ten acres. Some Indians dedicated a large portion of their income to buying land, even small amounts, in order to preserve their connection with past and future generations. Owning land in Robeson County was an important part of how Indians identified one another and how Indians maintained their identity over time. With land, one could always provide a place for one's children to grow up, for one's grandchildren and great-grandchildren to identify as "the home place," where Indians nurtured and preserved their values.[19]

A decline in Indian-owned land in the decades after 1900, due to bank foreclosures, drove Indians into sharecropping and reduced their economic opportunity as farmers. As a result, some of the Indians who lived in rural areas moved to Pembroke, a growing railroad town that since 1909 had been the home of the Indian Normal School. These migrants increased the Indian population of the town and launched the development of the small but influential Lumbee middle class.[20] Many Indians who moved to Pembroke took advantage of the availability of education at the Normal School for their children and themselves. A new group of Indian teachers emerged and the community schools quickly became overcrowded with teachers. Segregation prevented Indians from teaching in non-Indian schools, and educated Indians typically could not go into factories. Companies only made manufacturing jobs available to white workers.[21]

Some Indians responded to this discrimination by adopting a middle-class identity in values and in lifestyle and presenting an image to whites that they thought whites would approve. Those Indians believed that appealing to white values helped them escape white prejudice. Depicting Indian people as "progressive" had become, by the 1930s, a powerful way to articulate Indian identity to non-Indians. "Progressive" Indians, like their white and black counterparts, valued education, temperance, and civic engagement. "Progressive" values, coincidentally, also reinforced the ethic of self-reliance on which most Indian families depended to earn a living on the farm. In this way, the Indian middle class did not lose its sense of itself as connected to other Indians. Rather, the Indian middle class saw itself as leading the Indian people in a direction towards greater autonomy and freedom from white control.[22] The future of the Indian people as a whole mattered more as Indians became increasingly characterized as a "tribe." A tribe needed leaders, and from the perspective of the goals of the Pembroke middle class, this tribe needed leaders who had friendly, rather than antagonistic, relationships with the whites in power. While Indian leaders enhanced Indian autonomy and strengthened identity through these values and the Indian-only institutions they supported, their success in having their Indian identity recognized ultimately depended on whether their appeal to "progressive" values worked.

In the meantime, land loss turned most Indian landholders into tenant farmers in the rural areas around Pembroke. Compared to the two hundred estimated Indian landowners in Robeson County in 1935, eighteen hundred were tenant farmers. Under the tenant farming system, landlords controlled the farmer's labor and severely constrained a farmer's ability to produce a crop that could feed and clothe his family.[23] A landlord typically restricted the amount of food he permitted a sharecropper to raise, so that the farmer could grow a maximum amount of cotton on the land. In some cases, the landlord exercised total authority over the family's labor—if he wanted the farmer to keep his children out of school to work, the farmer had to obey the landlord. Similarly, if a wife had tasks to do like canning or making clothes, and a landlord or overseer sent her to the field, she had to go. Consequently, families bought clothes and canned food on credit, which usually trapped them in debt.[24] Tenant houses were in poor repair, some did not have windows, and perhaps ten or more people lived in a two- or three-room house. Diseases such as pellagra, pneumonia, and malaria were common, and some tenant families had only rags to wear. Lumbee sharecropper Ellen Jacobs, for example, produced an excellent cotton crop in 1935 for the Fletcher Plantation, but she had no shoes or stockings for herself or her children.[25]

Indians felt particularly victimized by the sharecropping system in Robeson County. Starting in the late 1920s, white-owned merchant-landholding companies, such as the McNair Corporation, began traveling to other tobacco-farming counties in North Carolina and inviting white tenant farmers to come to Robeson County. A superintendent at McNair's claimed that they brought in white farmers because they could "drive a better bargain" with them than with Indians. Certain landowners simply dispossessed some Indians entirely.[26] Segregation disempowered these rural Indians; they did not benefit from the system in the ways that some of their "middle-class" kin in Pembroke did. Consequently, these rural Indians sought assistance from the federal government to escape the economic ills under "Jim Crow."

Social and economic divisions between "town" and "country" Indians acquired a political significance as the tribe's leadership began to pursue federal recognition in the 1930s. Those who came to support a "Cherokee" designation identified most closely with Pembroke's "progressive" leaders, who had developed a symbiotic relationship with local whites. Other Pembroke leaders, however, equally identified with the values of the middle class but rejected the idea that cooperating with local whites would gain federal recognition and protection of Indian land, Indian schools, and Indian families. They did not hold such politically sensitive occupations as the "progressive" leaders did, but they nevertheless placed value on education and on civic duty and aspired to earning comfortable livings for their families. These men, who would come to lead the "Siouan" movement, viewed local whites as political adversaries, and whites therefore excluded these Indians from their patronage. Their power derived from the settlements lying outside of Pembroke, from "country" Indians who believed primarily in kinship as a basis for identity and desperately needed economic relief. Regardless of how it affected their relations with whites, these men believed that an improvement in Indians' economic situation could only be achieved under Indian leadership and with full Indian autonomy. However, their vision for Indian autonomy still depended on whites, just not the local ones who promoted segregation. These Indian leaders needed the favor of white policymakers and legislators in Washington, DC.

FROM "CROATAN" TO "CHEROKEE INDIANS OF ROBESON COUNTY"

By 1932, the state of North Carolina had recognized three tribal designations for Robeson County Indians—"Croatan," "Indians of Robeson County," and "Cherokee Indians of Robeson County." By all accounts, Indians themselves requested these name changes in response to the social conditions of segregation. Soon after 1900, whites in Robeson County began using "Croatan" as a racial slur towards Indians, shortening it to "Cro" (as in black crows, or "Jim Crow"). What started as a way to gain some measure of tribal autonomy through a state-sanctioned identity became whites' favorite way to humiliate Indians. "Croatan" became a reminder of Indians' racial ambiguity under segregation; regardless of their actual identity, or their efforts to promote "progressive" values, local whites still refused to acknowledge their autonomy.[27]

Indians responded by appealing for protection to a higher authority, the U.S. Congress. In 1910, Congressman Hannibal Godwin, a Democratic lawyer from Harnett County, North Carolina, introduced legislation to recognize Robeson County's Indians as "Cherokee Indians," presumably an attempt to claim a historic identity that whites could not associate with blackness but instead with an authentic Indianness. An influential white Democrat, Angus McLean, obtained and publicized evidence of the tribe's Cherokee ancestry. He had been long acquainted with the Indian population and was a friend of some of Pembroke's "progressive" leaders, particularly Rev. Doctor Fuller Lowry. Over the previous years, McLean listened to elders relay the tribe's oral tradition, and he became convinced that their true ancestry was Cherokee.[28] The 1910 bill did not pass in the House, and Congress left no record of the objections to it—perhaps the Eastern Band of Cherokees, who did have federal recognition, protested.[29]

In 1911, Indians petitioned the state legislature to change their name simply to "Indians of Robeson County," a name that seemed neutral. Within two years, however, Indians realized that this name still left them vulnerable to losing their already fragile social autonomy, since the name itself provided little insight into the issue the federal government cared most about: the tribe's connection to historically documented people with recognizable "tribal" names and affiliation.[30] Consequently a group of Indians representing various families and settlements, with McLean's friend D. F. Lowry as chairman, lobbied for Congressional legislation to recognize them as "Cherokees" and grant funds for a federal Indian school in Robeson County. The bill requested $50,000 for construction of the school and $10,000 for maintenance but nothing for salaries and other costs. A bill passed the Senate in 1912, but encountered more challenges in the House.[31] Angus McLean testified on the Indians' behalf before the House Committee on Indian Affairs in 1913.

One exchange between a Congressman and McLean in 1913 illustrates Congress's assumptions about federal recognition. Segregationists' racial agenda played a major role in how Congress viewed Robeson County Indians' request. White southerners and their sympathizers in the federal government marked Indian identity according to how Indians distinguished themselves from blacks. Representative Charles H. Burke of South Dakota, a Republican real estate developer who became Commissioner of Indian Affairs in 1921, explicitly linked Robeson County Indians' status with that of blacks when he stated that, "It is my belief that these Indians have no right to enter any Indian school because they are not full-blooded Indians. I will also say that I have great sympathy with people in the South in dealing with the Negro. You refuse to recognize them. I presume that it is due to the prejudice that exists in the mind of the people on account of color." McLean replied, "The Indians themselves recognize this feeling and respect it." Burke's assertion that "these Indians" were not "full-blooded," followed by his comment on Southern racism, implied his suspicion that "these Indians" were actually "Negroes," or in any case did not have enough "Indian blood" to justify federal interference with the South's race problem by recognizing them as a separate group with separate rights. McLean, a Southerner and conservative Democrat, dodged any question about the tribe's Indian ancestry and appealed to Burke's prejudice, telling him that these Indians felt the same way as whites did about blacks. McLean told Burke that he should recognize Robeson County's Indians as Indians, not because of their pure Indian ancestry, but because they were as prejudiced as he was.[32] Racial prejudice lay at the core of Southern whites' view of Indian identity. A month following the 1913 House committee hearings, the state legislature changed Indians' name to "Cherokee Indians of Robeson County." The Eastern Band objected, disavowing any historic or contemporary connection with Robeson County's Indians, but the legislature applied the name anyway.

McLean's reasoning reveals a basis for Indian identity that appeared logical under Jim Crow but remained far outside the mainstream of federal definitions of Indianness and indicates why Lumbees have had so much difficulty gaining federal acknowledgment. Southern whites did not care what kind of Indians the Robeson County Indians were—for the purposes of taking their land, exploiting their labor, and controlling their social behavior, it was sufficient simply that they were Indians, or rather that they were not white. Their status as Indians needed no special historical or biological reinforcement for whites at the top of the racial hierarchy; designating them as Indians simply required that Indians prove that they were not black. In this way, a separate Indian identity reinforced the legitimacy of the racial hierarchy in the minds of powerful whites, because Indians themselves acquiesced to it. Indians adopted this method of reckoning identity in the presence of their white neighbors, partly because it achieved concrete gains in social autonomy and partly because it did not threaten their own markers of family and place, which had little to do with a tribal name and everything to do with social organization and behavior. Rather than reject the state's authority, Indians resigned themselves to a relationship that the social needs of whites governed.

Historically, however, the federal government and Indian nations had a political, rather than social, relationship, that is, a relationship between two governments. From the perspective of federal officials, an Indian's identity was intrinsically linked to his tribal ancestry and whether that historic tribe had a relationship to the United States government. Congress, which preferred to deal in political favors, assigned the

Bureau of Indian Affairs the task of legitimizing the petitioning tribe's claim. Accordingly, the BIA concerned itself with the historical origins of the Indian group that applied for assistance, so that they could determine the authenticity of these appeals. They based their findings on historical and anthropological research that established links between the contemporary Indian group and a past people whom the government considered a "tribe." The BIA's judgment included assumptions about racial ancestry and a proper "Indian" phenotype, but such assumptions did not form the exclusive criteria for Indian identity. Prior to the 1930s, BIA officials found the key identity test in whether the "tribe" had a historic relationship with the United States and the right to treaty-based assistance. Not surprisingly, given these assumptions, the BIA did not approve of the 1913 "Cherokee" bill.[33]

"PASSING THE BUCK": RECOGNIZING THE "CHEROKEES" IN CONGRESS

Hoping to find a way to circumvent the conflict between Congress and the BIA, Indians in Robeson County took yet another approach to federal recognition in 1932. Rather than work through Congressional Democrats, whose efforts on behalf of recognition seemed ineffective relative to the BIA, Indians first went directly to Washington and discussed their situation with the foremost Indian policy activist of the day, John Collier. In March of 1932, a delegation of Indians met with Collier, who at that time served as Executive Secretary of the American Indian Defense Association (AIDA). The AIDA had a reputation as the most controversial organization lobbying for changes in Indian policy. The group advocated reversing the devastation induced by the government's goal of allotting Indian lands and assimilating Indians to white norms. Robeson County Indians reviewed a new draft bill with Collier for recognition as "Cherokees," and he agreed to help them introduce it. Collier then wrote to Senator Josiah W. Bailey, North Carolina's senior Senator. "Being myself from Georgia," he wrote, "I am able to appreciate the desire of these Indians for some status by which they would be, at least in their own thinking, clearly distinguished from Negroes. And as a matter of fact, my impression of the group who came here was that they had strong Indian characteristics."[34] Collier recognized that segregation drove Indians' new attempt to gain federal assistance, and he sympathized with their position.

Three days later, Senator Bailey and North Carolina's Senator Cameron Morrison received a petition signed by more than six hundred Indians requesting introduction of a "Cherokee" bill. The petition listed B. G. (or "Buddy") Graham, A. B. Locklear, and two other men as officers of the group's "Business Committee"; they apparently constituted the tribe's formal political leadership at that time. Graham owned land in the Saint Annah community, outside Pembroke. A. B. Locklear had led a community group known as "the lodge" in the rural Union Chapel community during the 1920s.[35] "Country" Indians may have recognized that the strategies of their leadership in 1913 did not work and gave other men a chance to try. The Indian "town" leaders who derived their influence from the community's segregated social institutions did not appear to play a significant role in the effort to become federally recognized as "Cherokees" in 1932.

This "Cherokee" bill proposed three types of assistance: to recognize the Indians formerly known as "Croatans" as "Cherokees," to permit these Indians to attend federal Indian schools, and to examine Robeson County "Cherokees'" circumstances, probably to provide a basis for further federal assistance. The bill also forbade any change in the Indians' current property rights or "present status" and denied them any tribal rights or monies due to the Eastern Band of Cherokees or the Western Cherokee in Oklahoma.[36] Philosophically, this legislation fit squarely in the tradition of the tribe's previous attempts to gain federal recognition: the bill declared a historic tribal affiliation and asked for educational assistance. The measure intended to secure an Indian identity through enhancing educational opportunities for Indians, a strategy that had worked well at state and local levels in the past and reinforced the social institutions that Indians already used to monitor their community's boundaries. However, the approach involved an important strategic difference; rather than soliciting the help of white Democrats, Indians asked for assistance from a white activist, John Collier, perhaps believing that his experience with federal Indian policy would prove more effective in Congress than segregationist logic. Bailey introduced the "Cherokee" bill in May 1932, including all the provisions set forth in the original draft except the request for an additional investigation.[37] The investigation would have paved the way for future assistance from the federal government and empowered Indians to see their interests as separate from those of North Carolina's white citizens.

The Senate Committee on Indian Affairs asked Commissioner of Indian Affairs C. J. Rhoads to report on the bill. But Rhoads's concerns echoed those of earlier BIA officials, and, in fact, Rhoads's report clouded the issue of tribal ancestry and unintentionally deepened the confusion between BIA and congressional criteria for federal designation. Rhoads left the ultimate decision about tribal ancestry up to Congress, but his articulation of Indian identity alarmed white southerners.

In his memorandum, Rhoads quoted ethnologist James Mooney's 1907 writings about the "Croatans." Mooney wrote, "The theory of descent from Raleigh's lost colony of Croatan may be regarded as baseless, but the name itself serves as a convenient label for a people who combine in themselves the blood of the wasted native tribes, the early forest rovers, the run-away slaves or other Negroes, and probably also of stray seamen of the Latin races from coasting vessels in the West Indian or Brazilian trade."[38] This portrayal of Robeson County Indians' ancestors provided no definitive evidence of their tribal affiliation and simultaneously introduced the notion of miscegenation about which Charles Burke questioned Angus McLean in 1913. Segregationists saw Mooney's assessment of Robeson County Indians' ancestry as an attack on their social order. To acknowledge that racial mixing existed undermined the righteousness of segregation. White southerners justified segregation with arguments that separation promoted social advancement for all races, while miscegenation led to degeneracy and violence.[39] However, we must read Mooney's statements in light of his own assumptions as an ethnographer and the assumptions of the federal officials for whom he wrote. Mooney knew that Robeson County's Indians were not exceptional among other Indian tribes in their multiracial ancestry; in another, later memorandum, he stated that "Indian blood" predominated in the tribe and compared the Croatans' ancestry with that of other acknowledged tribes in the Southeast—he cited the Nanticoke, Pamunkey, Chickahominy, Creek, Catawba, Shawnee, and Cherokee.[40] To Mooney, mixed ancestry did not mean that the Robeson County Indians were not actually Indians. Accordingly, Rhoads did not explicitly deny their Indian identity. Rather, Rhoads discussed identity in terms relevant to the BIA in order to answer the question about eligibility for federal services. He used Mooney's assessment to establish that they had never entered into a treaty relationship with the United States and were therefore ineligible for assistance.

Rhoads added another warning to his report: "We believe that the enactment of this legislation would be the initial step in bringing these Indians under the jurisdiction of the Federal Government." The text of the bill asked for nothing more than for "Cherokees" to be admitted into federal Indian schools and did not ask for an additional report to be made. Rhoads's warning was unnecessary, but he added it because he wanted to make certain that his office assumed no responsibility for these people. To substantiate his reasoning, Rhoads might have denied that Robeson County's Indians were Indians at all, but he chose not to. Instead, Rhoads acknowledged their identity repeatedly in the report, but he left the question of their specific tribal affiliation to Congress. He avoided a definitive statement because he knew that if he affirmed the historic identity they claimed, Congress could recognize the Robeson County Indians and make Rhoads responsible for the education and welfare of another eight to twelve thousand people. Alternately, if he expressly denied any Indian identity on the part of Robeson County Indians based on their mixed ancestry, he would be going against an eminent scholar's assessment and setting a double-standard for federal relationships to Indian tribes, none of whom had "pure" Indian pedigrees. Furthermore, he would be critiquing the racial order that North Carolina's Congressmen supported. Like his predecessors, Rhoads did not commit to the subject of Robeson County Indians' historic tribal affiliation and "passed the buck" back to the Senate Committee on Indian Affairs. Not surprisingly, Congress adjourned and the committee did not act on the bill.[41]

"I HAVE TRIED TO SHOW MY COLOR…": FORGING NEW STRATEGIES

In March of 1933, when Robeson County leaders received news that their campaign had failed, Indians demanded new leadership. Rather than withdraw their support from Bailey, however, Indians turned their hostility on A. B. Locklear. "People got mad with him [Locklear]," remembered one ninety-nine-year-old resident of the Saint Annah community. "[They] claimed that he was just after money, taking their money and spending it on something else."[42] True to the Indian community's tendency to challenge their leadership, Indians transferred their support to Buddy Graham and Joseph Brooks. Brooks apparently took Locklear's place as "spokesman" for Graham, and the two men launched a direct appeal to Senator Bailey to gain support for the bill.[43] They organized a letter-writing campaign, and over one hundred Indians from various settlements urged Bailey to reintroduce the bill in exchange for their votes in the next election. They structured their campaign according to families and settlements, a method consistent with their community's social organization.

These letters reminded Bailey of his vulnerability as an elected official and let him know that Indians expected benefits in return for their support of his career specifically and white supremacy more generally. The letters outlined Indians' reciprocal relationship with white supremacy and segregation and showed how they used their distinct identity as a tribe of Indians to enforce this reciprocity. Shaw Deese, a tenant farmer in the Brooks Settlement and brother-in-law of Joseph Brooks, wrote Bailey: "I am an Indian of Robeson County and has [sic] never been recognized by the US Government, even though I am a voter and has [sic] been for a number of years…. [Y]ou has [sic] never represented me as a Cherokee Indian of Robeson County, I have tried to show my color for you and thought was empressing me that you would do something for me…. [U]nless [you do] something in the behalf of us as a tribe of Cherokee Indians, your Hope for votes will be in vain."[44] Deese's attempt to "show his color" to Bailey reveals how deeply congressional politicians entwined segregation, Indian identity, and federal recognition. In exchange for Bailey's support for recognition, Deese implied that he accepted segregation by "showing his color" and assuring Bailey and other white politicians that he knew his place in the racial hierarchy. Deese's letter disclosed disappointment that Bailey did not honor his part of the bargain and help mitigate Deese's tenuous place in Southern society by granting Indians greater economic security. Colon Brooks, a landowner and member of the Brooks Settlement Longhouse, also wrote to Bailey, emphasizing his identity as an Indian and his respect for the color line. He admonished Bailey for not representing their interests as "Cherokee" Indians: "I am a real Indian of Robeson County and always have been a citizen of our country and voted as our white friends[.]... [O]ur [congressman] has never represented us as a tribe of Cherokee Indians and I think we should be recognized and cared for as much so as any Indians in the USA[.] Unless this is done no Indian in Robeson County and adjoining ones will never throw another vote for a [congressman]."[45] Bailey received over one hundred letters like these, with most authors representing themselves not just as voters but as Indians who had a right to recognition. The principle of reciprocity, so important for gauging Indian identity within the group, also extended to their congressmen. Rather than protest the system that oppressed them, Indians demanded that the system keep its part of the bargain.[46]

Armed with community support, Graham and others traveled to Washington to meet with government officials in March. A. B. Locklear stayed in Robeson County and tried to undermine their efforts from afar. Locklear told Bailey that "the President of our committee, Mr. B. G. Graham ... have [sic] joined in with a bunch of folks who are enimies [sic] to white people and are habitual fighters who will not agree to have any white man to represent us at a hearing before the commitie [sic] on Indian Affairs." Locklear thus urged Bailey to "defer any action on the matter[,] as we understand that Graham and his crowd is on the way up there now[,] until you hear from [Angus] McLean.... Just a line from you to the effect that you will see that Mr. McLean will have a say in the matter will be appreciated." Despite the community's apparent selection of new leaders to represent their interests, Locklear persisted in soliciting a white Southern Democrat's help in gaining federal recognition. Locklear believed that McLean's guidance would achieve the best results in Congress. To accomplish his goal, Locklear planted mistrust in Bailey's mind about the intentions of Graham "and his crowd" and called them "enemies to white people" and "habitual fighters"; Locklear intended to characterize the faction led by Graham and Brooks as against the "progress" that his own faction promoted, and therefore as unreliable representatives of the Robeson County Indians. Bailey replied to Locklear that "it would be to the distinct advantage of the Indians in Robeson County to have Governor McLean present their case to the Secretary of the Interior." Bailey perhaps agreed with Locklear philosophically, but Locklear's voice did not dominate the negotiations in Washington. While we do not know the exact outcome of Graham's meeting, Graham did give Bailey a strong message: A. B. Locklear no longer spoke for the tribe; Graham did.[47]

Negotiating the 1932 legislation for "Cherokee" recognition divided the Indian community along ideological lines. The issues involved in passing the bill—maintaining the racial hierarchy and determining a tribal affiliation—mandated cooperation from white segregationists such as Angus McLean. However, the strategy did not work when confronted with the concerns of the Bureau of Indian Affairs, and Indians suffered another delay in their long-sought goal of federal recognition. In response to that disappointment, some Indians looked for new leadership and a new strategy, while others remained confident that McLean would serve their interests. Congress's and the BIA's different attitudes about federal recognition undoubtedly strengthened the tribe's internal factionalism. In the next attempt to gain federal recognition, this division, rather than the racial hierarchy, dominated the negotiations. Kin differences and residency patterns, not just ideological disagreements, characterized these internal tribal divisions.

FROM "CHEROKEE" TO "SIOUAN"

Graham and Brooks began lobbying for another recognition bill less than a month after their March, 1933, trip to Washington. In April, they asked Bailey for another meeting, where they wanted to present "information which we have obtained from public records and History" regarding "our original and ancient Name," which "we believe will be of great help in behalf of having favorable action taken" on the bill. They thanked Bailey for "past favors" and assured him that they were "your supporters" and reminded him, as so many other Indian constituents had, of his duty to them as voters. Their evident efforts to research their documentary history demonstrated their acquiescence to the BIA's criteria for Indian identity, and their confidence in their own case for federal acknowledgment grew.[48]

After their meeting with Bailey, the delegation met with John Collier, whom Harold Ickes, the new Secretary of the Interior, had recently appointed Commissioner of Indian Affairs.[49] Collier knew the group, since he had met with some of them in 1932, when he seemed convinced of their Indian ancestry and their eligibility for federal recognition. He may have pointed out to the delegation that "Cherokee" would not satisfy the BIA as a tribal affiliation, however, since ethnologist James Mooney had debunked the name, and the Senate Committee on Indian Affairs had rejected it as well. Nevertheless, he seemed convinced of their Indian ancestry; the only question was their proper tribal name.

To arrive at a suitable tribal affiliation to recommend to Congress, Collier sent the delegation to see John R. Swanton, an anthropologist who specialized in southeastern Indians in the Bureau of American Ethnology (BAE) at the Smithsonian Institution. Swanton, too, was familiar with Indians from Robeson County, having met one in James Mooney's office some years before. Swanton gladly accepted the challenge and spent "a few days" looking into the Robeson County "Cherokees'" true tribal heritage. Apparently he never visited Robeson County, but instead interviewed the delegation and conducted documentary research in government and anthropological records in Washington, DC. He investigated the tribe's genealogy, their oral tradition, the colonial records of North Carolina, the census records, and old correspondence in the BAE files. His extant notes reveal little about his thought process or methodology, but they do indicate that Swanton looked into the surviving records of every major Indian community in colonial North and South Carolina for evidence related to the contemporary Indian group in Robeson County. He then made some logical deductions based on indirect evidence, which placed particular Indian groups at certain places during the colonial period. He concluded that the core ancestors of the Robeson County group came from the Keyauwee and Cheraw tribes, two Siouan-speaking groups that had good reasons for migrating to the swampy area around Drowning Creek. He disavowed the "Cherokee" and "Croatan" theories, arguing that the former represented a confusion with the name "Cheraw," and that there was simply no evidence for the latter. He did acknowledge, however, that other Iroquoian or Algonquian groups probably made "contributions" to the Robeson County Indians. Swanton declared that "Cheraw" would be the most appropriate name for the tribe since it was well-known to whites.[50]

Senator Bailey and House Representative J. Bayard Clark introduced companion bills on behalf of the Robeson County Indians on May 1, 1933. Rather than recognize the tribe as "Cherokees," the bills proposed recognition as "Cheraw Indians," a change that reflected Swanton's conclusions. The bill was nearly identical to the previous "Cherokee" bill, including the stipulation that the legislation not "affect the present status or property rights of any such Indians or prohibit the attendance of children of such Indians at Government Indian schools." Furthermore, it prevented the "Cheraws" from having any rights to "the tribal lands or moneys of other bands of Indians in the United States." According to James Chavis, Joseph Brooks drafted the bill naming them "Cheraws" and returned home to confirm the legislation with his followers in Robeson County. Both congressional and Indian leaders had reason to think that the name satisfied at least some of the BIA's concerns since the BIA's anthropological consultant suggested the tribal designation. The Committee on Indian Affairs requested that the Department of the Interior report on the bill.[51]

In the summer of 1933, the tribe divided into two opposing groups on the question of which tribal name best served their interests in the South's racial hierarchy. The groups differed over how best to sustain an Indian identity in the context of white supremacy. Those who favored keeping the name "Cherokee" believed that that name would protect their hard-fought victories for education in the state, victories secured by white supremacists' notions of Indian identity. Those who favored the name "Cheraw," however, looked to the federal government's standards of Indian identity to support their social autonomy in the "Jim Crow" South.

That summer, Joseph Brooks and others began organizing a representative council of the Indians in Robeson County. Referred to as the "Cheraw Indians of Robeson and Adjoining Counties," self-government demonstrated to the BIA their serious desire to gain protection for their schools by asserting tribal self-rule and their accommodation to Western concepts of sovereignty. They elected a "Business Committee" consisting of B. G. Graham as President, Joseph Brooks as Vice-President, and James E. Chavis as Secretary. The Senate Committee on Indian Affairs accepted their government and Joseph Brooks as the duly elected representative of the tribe to the federal government. The Senate committee expected the council to govern democratically in order to be legitimate. They warned, for example, that Brooks should honestly represent the Council and that the Council should stand by the majority of tribal members.[52] In December, "Cheraws" met to elect their representatives to the Council and passed a resolution declaring their affiliation with the Cheraw Indians, based on their belief in the research of "the very learned gentleman of the Ethnology Dept.," John R. Swanton. They also appointed B. G. Graham and Joseph Brooks to proceed to Washington "to foster the passage of certain bills to recognize [sic] and enroll us as Indians by the U.S.A." They then gave Graham and Brooks sole authority to transact business in the council's stead, perhaps anticipating challenges from other members of the tribe. They sent a copy of the resolution to Senator Bailey.[53]

The Senate Committee on Indian Affairs held hearings on the bill in late January of 1934, a positive step when compared with the previous "Cherokee" bill, which did not even receive a hearing. Brooks and Graham along with Senator Bailey testified in support of the bill.[54] Harold Ickes, Secretary of the Interior, wrote to the committee that he did not favor the bill in its present form, but that "legislation to clarify the status of these Indians is desirable." Without explanation, Ickes asked that the name "Cheraw" be changed to "Siouan Indians of Lumber River." James Chavis remembered that this change was a result of the Indian Affairs Committee chairman's knowledge of the multiple tribal ancestors of the Robeson County Indians; he felt that "Siouan" would "cover all the small tribes and groups represented in and among the Siouan people."[55]

Furthermore, Ickes recommended that the Senate strike any provisions regarding education from the bill. Ickes suggested that they replace those provisions with the following: "Provided, that nothing contained herein shall be construed as conferring

Federal wardship or any other governmental rights or benefits upon such Indians."
Such language accommodated both Congress's and the BIA's agendas: it acknowledged Robeson County's Indians as Indians and upheld the racial hierarchy, but it also
preserved the BIA's historic policy of refusing responsibility for their education and
welfare. In his opinion, Secretary Ickes quoted the reports issued by previous com-
missioners and reached a similar conclusion: "As the Federal Government is not under
any treaty obligation to these Indians, it is not believed that the United States should
assume the burden of the education of their children, which has heretofore been
looked after by the State of North Carolina." The Committee recommended the bill's
passage, with Secretary Ickes's amendments. In contrast to previous reports from the
Department of the Interior, this one affirmed a tribal ancestry for Robeson County
Indians and satisfied at least part of the concerns of Bailey's constituents. The bill did
not, however, provide for federal assistance in education, a key provision to protect
Indians' control over their schools in Robeson County. While previous bills did not
reconcile congressional and Indian Bureau definitions of Indian identity, the approved
bill represented the BIA's and Senate Committee on Indian Affairs' compromise with
white supremacy. They gave Robeson County Indians a nominal recognition but left
control of Indian schools in the hands of the state so as to not empower Indians further.[56]

Although the bill as recommended by the Committee on Indian Affairs did not
accomplish everything that Joseph Brooks and B. G. Graham wanted, it legitimated
their tribal government and provided an avenue to federal aid that circumvented the
state. Other Indians in Robeson County, however, disputed the "Siouan" government's authority and challenged the bill and the new name. Their motivations centered on preserving the state's authority and Indian control of admission to Indian-
only schools. Although their overriding concern was the conflict between the state-
sanctioned identity as "Cherokee" and the federal identity as "Siouan," they attacked
the authority of Graham and Brooks to speak for the tribe. Graham's and Brooks's
opponents became known as the "Cherokees," because of their insistence on that designation for the tribe. "Cherokee" leaders not only disagreed with the "Siouans" ideo-
logically, but their leadership came from different kinship and settlement
communities. The Lowry and Oxendine families in Pembroke dominated the
"Cherokee" leadership. These families' home settlements were in Hopewell and
Prospect, and the leaders descended from some of the community's most active nineteenth-century religious and educational leaders.[57]

PRACTICING SOVEREIGNTY

Clifton Oxendine, principal of Pembroke's Indian elementary school, wrote Senator Bailey the first of several letters and telegrams opposing the "Siouan" bill. "The majority of the Indians in Robeson County are absolutely opposed to the passing of such a bill by congress," he wrote. "The persons . . . who are in Washington trying to get this bill passed are not the leaders of our race. They are of that class that believes that the government owes us something. . . I realize that our privilege[s] are very meager and limited as it is, but with the passage of the proposed bill we will be in much worse shape than we are at present. It's true that we as a people need help from the Federal Government but I feel that the bill which is before congress concerning us would be very detrimental to us if passed." While Oxendine saw the obvious need for and benefits of federal assistance, he opposed the bill in its present form because, as recommended by the Committee, the legislation did nothing to alter the situation of Robeson County Indians, other than changing the name. Oxendine also objected to the persons who proposed the name change and the unforeseen effects the change might have on Indian schools.[58]

In response to Oxendine's letter, a group representing the "Siouan" faction wrote to Bailey assuring him that the name had the support of the majority of Indians. The men told Bailey that over two thousand Indians had attended a meeting and affirmed the legislation as proposed, with one dissenting vote.[59] This assurance did not satisfy Bailey, who wanted unanimous approval and asked for signed petitions assenting to the name change. "If there is any serious opposition to [the bill]," he wrote, "I see no reason why I should take a course calculated to offend good people."[60] Bailey left considerable room to hear individuals' objections to the bill, in spite of the two thousand who approved of it. Two days later he received a telegram from ten Indians representing themselves as "leaders of the Indian people of Robeson County" who "request you to use every effort to defeat the bill."[61] D. F. Lowry also wrote to Bailey, questioning the legitimacy of the "Siouan" leadership. The bill, according to Lowry, "is not what the people want. It has a big following thinking it will bring lands and money." Lowry implied that the "Siouans" manipulated the two-thousand person vote, saying that they called the meeting because "it was announced that our Representative Clark was to speak. Had he been present and explain[ed] the meaning of the provision on the bill he would not have gotten very many votes for its passage." Driving a nail into the coffin, Lowry wrote, "Senator, we are depending on you for the non-passage of this bill."[62]

Bailey threw his definitive support to the "Cherokees" late in February of 1934, when a committee that included D. F. Lowry and his nephew James R. Lowry pro-

posed another bill to designate them as "Cherokees." They wrote the letter on sta-
tionery from the Indian Normal School, where James R. Lowry was Dean of Students. "We are unanimous for National recognition in accordance with our present
State recognition i.e. Cherokee, with the same rights and privileges of other citizens."
They wanted federal recognition as much as the "Siouan" group did, but they felt
more comfortable with a bill and a history that pleased southern whites. They asked
that James Mooney's report, which had raised the specter of miscegenation in their
history, be "discarded, for the reason that it is . . . misleading." The bill they proposed was identical to the one that failed in 1932, and they promised Angus McLean's
presence "before any committees that may be necessary."[63] In spite of the same bill's
previous failure, Bailey replied, "This is entirely agreeable to me. I shall have the
Siouan Bill killed and withdrawn from the Senate."[64]

Bailey's role in killing the bill did not alleviate the internal controversy of the
tribe, so the Senate Committee on Indian Affairs called a meeting of the two factions
in Washington in late March, 1934. Representative J. Bayard Clark from the House
and Angus McLean were also present at the conference. Graham and Brooks claimed
that ninety percent of the Indian population approved of the name "Siouan," and they
believed that duty called them to stand by the majority, as the Committee had directed them to do a year earlier. Representatives of the minority "Cherokee" faction
did not dispute the claim of the "Siouans" in the meeting, but according to committee
staff member A. A. Grorud, "the attitude of the delegates who represent the minority
. . . would not yield." Grorud thought that John R. Swanton's "Siouan" designation
was the most appropriate for the tribe, but because the "Cherokee" faction would not
compromise, nothing came of the conference.[65]

The delegates from both sides returned to Robeson County and held meetings
with their supporters; the Cherokees met in Pembroke, while the Siouans met at
Saint Annah Church, just north of Pembroke. Gertrude Bonnin, also known as Zit-
kala-Sa, a Sioux Indian and president of the National Council of American Indians
(NCAI), spoke to the Siouan group and urged them to continue to fight for federal
recognition. The group voted to join the NCAI at the meeting, sending a message to
the Cherokees and non-Indians that they would use outside resources in their cause.[66]
"We'll run our own affairs," Joseph Brooks said to a Robeson County sheriff's deputy
whom the sheriff had sent to police the two thousand-person meeting.[67]

The locations of these meetings sent a powerful message to other Indians. In
some ways the locations reflect typical distinctions based on kin and settlement that
had existed for decades in the Indian community. However, the negotiations with the
federal government in the early 1930s gave these distinctions a new political importance for how the tribe maintained its identity and its autonomy. Leaders of each fac-

tion believed they held the key to vast resources and to a moderation of the crippling social, political, and economic effects of segregation. Cherokees saw themselves as closely affiliated with the town of Pembroke and the Normal School, places that were Indian-controlled but heavily dependent upon white patronage. Siouans, however, met in the church, another symbol of Indian autonomy and power over which whites had less control. Furthermore, their seat of power was a rural community that was close to Pembroke but dominated by Indian landowners.[68] Each faction defined itself in opposition to the other. For an Indian who was not a member of the leadership class, then, choosing to attend a meeting at the Normal School or at the church signified which faction he preferred and with which of the tribe's growing social classes he most identified. The identity markers embedded in these political events hardened the distinction between "town" and "country" Indians that had developed in the 1920s.

CONCLUSIONS

These differences implied that there were wide, irreconcilable gulfs between supporters of the Cherokee and Siouan names. However, the two groups had a great deal in common. Leaders of both sides were landowners and relatively well-educated. Both sides embraced education for their people, as indicated by the text of the bills that they proposed, and both sides clearly saw the limitations that poverty and segregation placed on their people. Both sides recognized the value of federal acknowledgment; validation from the federal government as a tribal people with a distinct history could empower them to assert greater control over their own affairs and perhaps gain positions of influence in the segregated South. Furthermore, both sets of leaders saw value in making contacts with whites outside their community to improve their circumstances and enhance their own influence within their kin networks and settlements.

Despite these broad areas of agreement, two main factors separated the groups. Kin and settlement patterns, and an ideological disagreement concerning the role that white supremacy should play in their affairs, divided the factions. As indicated by the names of those involved in the negotiations, "town" leaders promoted the "Cherokee" name. These men almost without exception resided in the town of Pembroke and belonged to that town's middle class. Several of them were also close kin to one another. The Cherokees appeared to have no formal political organization and did not keep membership or registration lists. The Siouan group's leaders came from both Pembroke and rural Indian communities. The Siouan faction also included many members of the Brooks Settlement, who were also distantly related to Joseph Brooks's family but constituted their own kin network. As indicated by the letter-writing campaign that Brooks and Graham organized to support the "Cherokee" bill, their network reached beyond Pembroke. By the spring of 1934, what was formerly the "Cheraw" Council had become the "General Council of Siouan Indians of Lumber River," with 2,181 members who elected councilmen representing seventeen Indian settlements. Graham, Brooks, and James E. Chavis continued to serve as the group's executives.[69] These divisions reflected the political diversity that had been an ongoing feature of community life.

These kin and settlement differences did not by themselves mean disagreement on the question of which tribal name they would accept. After all, many of those who supported the 1932 "Cherokee" bill, including Joseph Brooks and B. G. Graham, became Siouan supporters in 1933 and 1934. To the majority of those who desired federal recognition, the question of which name to choose mattered little. Indians certainly recognized that whites and their notions of identity controlled the discussion. They persistently pushed for support in the face of the injustices of segregation under whatever tribal name whites wanted, whether they were local southerners or federal officials. Kin and settlement differences became significant when Indians factored attitudes about segregation into the discussion. Pursuing a name with which whites felt comfortable resulted in disappointment, due to the federal government's ambivalent attitude about Southern segregation and its consistent refusal, until 1933, to recognize a tribal affiliation for these Indians. No single name pleased everyone at any one time and neither the Indian Office nor Congress acted on the question because of uncertainty about how it would affect Southern white power. Indians had their own reactions to the names, and when the government finally applied a definitive label in 1933, Indians themselves divided on the question, due to their various opinions about how best to deal with segregation.

The primary disagreement between the Cherokee and Siouan supporters was not over whether the federal government should recognize the tribe, but what strategy should be used to accomplish this goal. Cherokees put their faith in their political contacts in Congress, the local white community, and state government, while Siouans followed the lead of the Bureau of Indian Affairs in Washington. These political actions affected how each group articulated and chose to maintain their identity as Indians. The Cherokee leadership called on their forty-plus years of experience working within the Jim Crow system, in which proving they were Indians depended on proving they were "not black" and, at least in some ways, aspired to "be white." Maintaining Indian-only schools, where it was evident to non-Indians that Indians were a distinct and socially autonomous people, was critical to maintaining an Indian identity in this context. They saw the Siouan name as a potential threat to their schools because the state government had not recognized that name and they feared future lawsuits between the real Indians of Robeson County and people of "doubtful" ancestry who might claim affiliation with the Siouan tribe.

Siouan supporters, on the other hand, called on their experience with Jim Crow and decided that they could maintain their schools with the federal government's help, rather than the state's. They sought to distinguish themselves from blacks and whites, not just on the basis of values that local whites thought were important, but on markers that whites in Washington thought were important, namely, a tribal designation. Believing that an inconclusive tribal affiliation was the main obstacle to federal recognition, they pursued a name that federal government representatives suggested. They also created a representative tribal government to signal to the Congress and the BIA that the Robeson County Indians functioned politically and socially as a distinct Indian tribe, similar to other tribes that the federal government assisted. "Siouans" organized politically as a tribe in order to prepare themselves for what they believed was near-certain government assistance to alleviate their precarious position under "Jim Crow." Unlike the Cherokees, who believed that persons of doubtful ancestry assaulted their Indian identity, the absence of equal opportunity most threatened Siouans' sense of themselves as Indians. Thus, they allied themselves with another set of powerful policymakers in Washington.[70]

These conflicting views had profound ramifications for how Indians expressed their identity in the 1930s, 1940s, and 1950s, up to the passage of the 1956 Lumbee Act. The two factions agreed on many things, and the tribe's social organization, which revolved around kinship and place, encompassed all sides. However, the differences between how Cherokees and Siouans expressed their identity became the source of much conflict within the community. Cherokees demonstrated a progressive attitude that appealed to white middle-class values and also helped convince whites that Indians were a unique people, deserving of separate status from blacks. This expression of their progressive qualities—the fact that they represented the "best class" and the "best educated" of the Indian population—reveals a certain resignation to the Jim Crow system. In the face of segregation and a pervasive racial hierarchy, these men saw the power of white standards as inescapable. However, the Cherokee leaders also kept their Indian community and Indian identity in mind. There is no evidence that they tried to escape being Indian, but they articulated their Indian identity in terms of the Indian community's progressiveness.[71] Ultimately, Cherokee supporters after 1933 believed that self-help was the key to maintaining Indian identity, a view that prompted Clifton Oxendine to deride "a class that believes the government owes them something." Cherokees wanted to be self-contained and self-supporting, and they believed that receiving direct benefits from the federal government would constrain their own power and their community's opportunities to become equal to the whites among whom they lived.

Siouans also wanted to be self-supporting, but they envisioned using the federal government to help them attain that status. In contrast to the Cherokee leadership, they did not appear resigned to segregation or anxious to assert their progressive values. Instead, their communications to federal officials reveal an insistence on their tribe's sovereignty and right to self-rule, objectives that were antithetical to segregation, a system in which whites ruled everyone, although they permitted some Indian autonomy. To a certain extent, the emergence of an identity expressed by membership in a tribal organization was a reaction to the progressive identity put forward by the tribe's Cherokee leaders and by earlier generations. However, Siouan leaders' rejection of racial politics did not make them necessarily less self-interested than Cherokee leaders. The Siouan leadership surely recognized that connections to the BIA benefits in Washington augmented their own standing within the Indian community. Furthermore, federal assistance put them on the same playing field with other Indians across the nation, such as those who founded the NCAI. With this in mind, they continued to cultivate outside contacts and resources to make their existence and their cause known.[72]

The 1932 and 1933 Cherokee and Siouan bills failed to accomplish recognition for the Lumbee tribe, but they did not fail to affirm the tribe's identity and sovereignty. They asserted their sovereignty by practicing a political strategy to negotiate with both branches of government's ideas about Indian identity and federal recognition. That strategy entailed tribal division, but that division only mirrored the policy differences at the federal level. Furthermore, tribal factionalism was also consistent with the community's pre-existing markers of identity. Local community action developed a concept of sovereignty that asserted the tribe's independence from federal ideas about identity and affirmed their own markers of identity in a unique way.

NOTES

1 I use the term "Indian" throughout much of this essay for practical reasons—it is the word most of Robeson County's Indigenous people use when defining themselves to one another and to outsiders. It also happens to be the term most often used in the historical documents on which this essay is based, and so that label provides for an easier narrative. Of course, preferences within the community vary, as they do in every community; I have no particular personal attachments to any one label. Like many tribal names, "Indian," "American Indian," "Native American," and so on are inventions of convenience for English speakers and are products of colonization. For critiques of the federal government's identity criteria, see Eva Marie Garroutte, *Real Indians: Identity and the Survival of Native America* (Berkeley: University of California Press, 2003); Circe Sturm, *Blood Politics: Race, Culture, and Identity in the Cherokee Nation of Oklahoma* (Berkeley: University of California Press, 2002); Melissa L. Meyer,

"American Indian Blood Quantum: Blood Is Thicker Than Family," in *Over the Edge: Remapping the American West*, edited by Valerie J. Matsumoto and Blake Allmendinger (Berkeley: University of California Press, 1999), 231–49; M. Annette Jaimes, "Federal Indian Identification Policy: A Usurpation of Indigenous Sovereignty in North America," in *The State of Native America: Genocide, Colonization, and Resistance*, edited by M. Annette Jaimes (Boston: South End Press, 1992), 123–38; Margo S. Brownwell, "Note: Who Is an Indian? Searching for an Answer to the Question at the Core of Federal Indian Law," *University of Michigan Journal of Law Reform* 34 (Fall-Winter 2000–2001): 275–320; David E. Wilkins, "Breaking into the Intergovernmental Matrix: The Lumbee Tribe's Efforts to Secure Federal Acknowledgement," *Publius* 23 (Fall 1993): 123–42; Angela A. Gonzales, "American Indian Identity Matters: The Political Economy of Identity and Ethnic Group Boundaries" (Ph.D. diss., Harvard University, 2001); Bruce Granville Miller, *Invisible Indigenes: The Politics of Nonrecognition* (Lincoln: University of Nebraska Press, 2003).

2 See N. Brent Kennedy and Robyn Vaughan Kennedy, *The Melungeons: The Resurrection of a Proud People* (Macon, GA: Mercer University Press, 1994); William H. Gilbert, Jr., "The Wesorts of Maryland: An Outcasted Group," *Journal of the Washington Academy of Sciences* 35 (August 15, 1945): 237–46; Dave D. Davis, "A Case of Identity: Ethnogenesis of the New Houma Indians," *Ethnohistory* 48 (Summer 2001): 473–94.

3 The Lumbee and Tuscarora oral tradition about their origins can be best understood by carefully reading the various texts compiled by government officials such as Hamilton McMillan, Angus W. McLean, Charles F. Pierce, O. M. McPherson, Carl C. Seltzer, and John R. Swanton. See Hamilton McMillan, *Sir Walter Raleigh's Lost Colony: An Historical Sketch of the Attempts of Sir Walter Raleigh to Establish a Colony in Virginia, with the Traditions of an Indian Tribe in North Carolina. Indicating the Fate of the Colony of Englishmen Left on Roanoke Island in 1587* (Wilson, NC: Advance Press, 1888); O. M. McPherson, *Report on Condition and Tribal Rights of the Indians of Robeson and Adjoining Counties of North Carolina*, 63d Cong., 3d sess., January 5, 1915, S. Doc. 677, hereafter cited as McPherson Report; Angus W. McLean, "Historical Sketch of Indians of Robeson County," cited in McPherson Report; Charles F. Pierce, *[Visit Among the Croatan Indians, Living in the Vicinity of Pembroke, North Carolina]*, Report, in the Field at Pipestone, Minn., to the Commissioner of Indian Affairs, U.S. Indian Service, Department of the Interior, March 2, 1912 [National Archives and Records Administration, Record Group 75, Entry 161, File no. 23202–1912–123 General Services], hereafter cited as Charles Pierce Report; Seltzer Report; John R. Swanton, "Probable Identity of the 'Croatan' Indians," 1933 [National Anthropological Archives, Smithsonian Insitution, MS 4126], 3, hereafter cited as Swanton Report. Robert K. Thomas undertook this kind of close reading for an unpublished report he completed around 1976 for the Lumbee Regional Development Association. He discusses his methodology in Robert K. Thomas, *A Report on Research of Lumbee Origins*, unpublished typescript, no date [1976?] [North Carolina Collection, UNC-Chapel Hill], 22–24, hereafter cited as Thomas Report. The relative contributions of these groups are a point of much debate within the modern-day Lumbee and Tuscarora communities, but most acknowledge that their ancestry stems from some combination of all of these peoples.

4 Rebecca S. Seib, *Settlement Pattern Study of the Indians of Robeson County, NC, 1735–1787* (Pembroke, NC: Lumbee Regional Development Association, 1983), 3, 8–13, 54, 62, 79 [copy in personal possession of the author]; Thomas Report, 31; Julian T. Pierce and Cynthia Hunt-Locklear, et al., *The Lumbee Petition*, 3 vols. (Pembroke, NC: Lumbee River Legal Services, 1987), 12, 16.

5 Scholars call this process of recombining "ethnogenesis," and a great deal of work has been done to demonstrate that ethnogenesis is the process which led to many of the Indian groups we now consider to be "tribes." See James H. Merrell to Charlie Rose, October 18, 1989, in U.S. Congress, House, Committee on Natural Resources, *Report Together with Dissenting Views to Accompany H.R. 334*, 103rd Cong., 1st sess., October 14, 1993, H.Rpt. 290; Pierce et al., 1–2; Gerald Sider, *Living Indian Histories: Lumbee and Tuscarora People in North Carolina* (Chapel Hill: University of North Carolina Press, 2003), 239–41. See also Patricia Galloway, *Choctaw Genesis: 1500–1700* (Lincoln: University of Nebraska Press, 1995); James H. Merrell, *The Indians' New World: Catawbas and Their Neighbors from European Contact Through the Era of Removal* (Chapel Hill: University of North Carolina Press, 1989). Gerald Sider takes this point further by arguing that the notion of a "tribe" and the European definition of an "Indian," were subject to the demands of the European market economy, which depended heavily on deerskins and Indian slaves (see Sider, 190). As the State of North Carolina eroded the status of Indians and other free persons of color in the 1835 State Constitution, Indians may have believed that a particular tribal name may have been secondary to "the legal and social battles over who was to be classified as 'White' or 'Indian' or 'Negro.'" See Peter H. Wood, Deborah Montgomerie, and Susan Yarnell, *Tuscarora Roots: An Historical Report Regarding the Relation of the Hatteras Tuscarora Tribe of Robeson County, North Carolina, to the Original Tuscarora Indian Tribe* (Durham, NC: Hatteras Tuscarora Tribal Foundation, 1992), 46 [copy in personal possession of the author].

6 Pierce et al., 3–22, 159–65.

7 David E. Wilkins and K. Tsianina Lomawaima, *Uneven Ground: American Indian Sovereignty and Federal Law* (Norman: University of Oklahoma Press, 2001), 4.

8 Charles M. Hudson, *The Southeastern Indians* (Knoxville: University of Tennessee Press, 1976), 185; Theda Perdue, *"Mixed Blood" Indians: Racial Construction in the Early South* (Athens: University of Georgia Press, 2003), 4, 71, 80–81, 95. For the development of the racial hierarchy, also see Edmund S. Morgan, *American Slavery, American Freedom: The Ordeal of Colonial Virginia* (New York: W. W. Norton, 1975), 316–19.

9 See Perdue, 4–5, 28–29; Claudio Saunt, *A New Order of Things: Property, Power, and the Transformation of the Creek Indians, 1733–1816* (Cambridge: Cambridge University Press, 1999), chapter on the Seminoles.

10 Christopher Arris Oakley, "The Reshaping of Indian Identity in Twentieth Century North Carolina" (Ph.D. diss., University of Tennessee, Knoxville, 2002), 54; John G. Peck, "Urban Station— Migration of the Lumbee Indians," (Ph.D. diss., University of North Carolina-Chapel Hill, 1972), 67–68, quoted in Vernon Ray Thompson, "A History of the Education of the Lumbee Indians of Robeson County, North Carolina From 1885 to 1970" (Ed.D. diss., University of Miami, 1973), 24–25.

11 These settlements, with the exception of Pembroke, are not towns, but instead are social and cultural centers usually with an Indian school and church and one or more "stations" (or country grocer, gas station, and small restaurant). When a Lumbee refers to his home "community," he typically means the rural area around these social centers, where his family's home is. Karen I. Blu, "'Where Do You Stay At?' Home Place and Community Among the Lumbee," in *Senses of Place*, ed. Steven Feld and Keith Basso (Santa Fe: School of American Research Press, 1996), 201, 205–6. For the development of the modern-day Lumbee in Robeson County, see Thomas Report, 55.

12 Much of the historical literature on Indian ethnicity has defined an "Indian" as individuals who are racially different from American immigrant groups, who have a historical, continuous attachment to a

particular place, and who belong to a community that share a common political organization and set of rituals different from their neighbors. As historian Alexandra Harmon summarized, "Too often Indians' history is written as if protagonists, authors, and readers have no reason to wonder who is Indian," yet Indian people are burdened with defending their identity more often and more extensively than any other ethnic group in America. Historians' criteria seem to stem from organic characteristics of Indian tribes, but sociologists and legal historians have identified how such criteria depend more on non-Indian concerns than on anything true or "natural" about Indian communities. Many Indian communities are more accurately characterized by geographic movement (rather than attachment to one specific place) and expansive attitudes about adoption and cultural exchange (resulting in racial mixing and cultural adaptation). However, their identities as Indians do not dissipate as a result of these changes. In response to these trends, ethnic identity has been described more accurately as a process resulting from one group's attempt to differentiate itself from another group, or, as sociologist Fredrik Barth called it, "boundary maintenance." In this work, I define identity as a group's process of inclusion and exclusion, a constant renegotiation that can include racial ancestry but is not exclusively linked to it. See Harmon, *Indians in the Making: Ethnic Relations and Indian Identities Around Puget Sound* (Berkeley: University of California Press, 1998), 3; Barth, "Introduction," in *Ethnic Groups and Boundaries: The Social Organization of Culture Difference*, edited by Fredrik Barth (London: George Allen & Unwin, 1969). For a summary of the "natural" categories on which Indian identity are based, see Raymond D. Fogelson, "Perspectives on Native American Identity," in *Studying Native America: Problems and Prospects*, edited by Russell Thornton (Madison: University of Wisconsin Press, 1998) and Joane Nagel, "American Indian Ethnic Renewal: Politics and the Resurgence of Identity," *American Sociological Review* 60 (December 1995): 947–65. Sociologists and legal historians who have questioned these categories are Angela Gonzales, "The (Re)Articulation of American Indian Identity: Maintaining Boundaries and Regulating Access to Ethnically Tied Resources," *American Indian Culture and Research Journal* 22 (1998): 199–225; Anne Merline McCulloch and David E. Wilkins, "'Constructing' Nations Within States: the Quest for Federal Recognition by the Catawba and Lumbee Tribes," *American Indian Quarterly* 19 (Summer 1995): 361–87; Jaimes; C. Matthew Snipp, *American Indians: First of this Land* (New York: Russell Sage, 1989), chapter 2; James A. Clifton, "Alternate Identities and Cultural Frontiers," in *Being and Becoming Indian: Biographical Studies of North American Frontiers*, edited by James Clifton (Chicago: Dorsey Press, 1989), 11, 21–22. For treatments of American Indian history that encompass this view, see Harmon; Karen I. Blu, *The Lumbee Problem: The Making of an American Indian People* (New York: Cambridge University Press, 1980); Morris W. Foster, *Being Comanche: A Social History of an American Indian Community* (Tucson: University of Arizona Press, 1991); Loretta Fowler, *Shared Symbols, Contested Meanings: Gros Ventre Culture and History, 1778–1984* (Ithaca, NY: Cornell University Press, 1987).

13 See Glenda Elizabeth Gilmore, *Gender and Jim Crow: Women and the Politics of White Supremacy in North Carolina, 1896–1920* (Chapel Hill: University of North Carolina Press, 1996).

14 Pierce et al., 48–61, 227–30; Sider, 31–32.

15 Elisha Locklear and Cecil Hunt, Interview by Author and Willie Lowery, tape recording, Pembroke, NC, 23 February 2004 [Lumbee River Fund Collection, Sampson-Livermore Library, UNC-Pembroke]; Ella Deloria to Franz Boas, August 7, 1940 [Franz Boas Papers, American Philosophical Society]; Wood et al., 109; Colan Brooks and Rosetta Brooks, Interview by Adolph Dial, tape recording, Pembroke, NC, September 2, 1969 [The Adolph Dial Tapes, 1969–1971, Native American Resource Center, UNC-Pembroke], hereafter cited as Adolph Dial Tapes.

16 Angelina Okuda-Jacobs, "Planting Health, Culture, and Sovereignty: Traditional Horticulture of the Lumbee Nation of North Carolina" (master's thesis, University of Wisconsin-Madison, 2000), 31; Karen I. Blu, "'Reading Back' to Find Community: Lumbee Ethnohistory," in *North American Indian Anthropology: Essays on Society and Culture*, edited by Raymond DeMallie and Alfonso Ortiz (Norman: University of Oklahoma Press, 1993), 287–88; Malinda Maynor, "People and Place: Croatan Indians in Jim Crow Georgia, 1890–1920" (master's thesis, University of North Carolina, 2002).

17 Ruth Dial Woods, "Growing Up Red: The Lumbee Experience" (Ph.D. diss., University of North Carolina-Chapel Hill, 2001), 26; Pierce et al., 133–35; Fred A. Baker to Commissioner of Indian Affairs, 9 July 1935, in Fred A. Baker, *Report on Siouan Tribe of Indians in Robeson County, North Carolina* [NARA, RG 75, Entry 121, File no. 36208–1935–310 General Services], hereafter cited as Baker Report; R. T. Melvin and A. M. Johnson, "Final Plans for the Pembroke Indian Resettlement Project" [NARA, RG 96, Entry 85, Region IV, Project Plans File of C. B. Faris, Box 1], 3, hereafter cited as Melvin and Johnson, "Final Resettlement Plan."

18 John Pearmain, "Report . . . . On the Conditions of the Indians in Robeson County, North Carolina," November 11, 1935 [NARA, RG 75, Entry 121, File no. 64190–1935–066 Part 1-A], 29, hereafter cited as Pearmain Report.

19 Fred A. Baker to Commissioner of Indian Affairs, July 9, 1935, in Baker Report; also see Blu, *The Lumbee Problem*, 163–67; A. M. Johnson and R. T. Melvin, "Report of Reconnaissance Survey of Pembroke Indian Community Resettlement Project Area" [NARA, RG 96, Entry 85, Region IV, Project Plans File of C. B. Faris, Box 1], 2.

20 Okuda-Jacobs, 32–33; Sider, 151–53; Wood et al., 78; Melvin and Johnson, "Final Resettlement Plan," 3.

21 Ella Deloria to Franz Boas, August 7, 1940 [Franz Boas Papers, American Philosophical Society]; J. O. Walker to George S. Mitchell, March 24, 1937 [NARA-Atlanta, RG 96, Entry 79, Region IV, Box 39 Folder Wolf Pit/Pembroke-913]; Pearmain, "Reservation," 44; Fred A. Baker to Commissioner of Indian Affairs, July 9, 1935, in Baker Report; Pearmain Report, 29; Waltz Maynor, conversation with author, Pembroke, NC, July 31, 2003.

22 cf. Blu, *The Lumbee Problem*, 140–42, 187–89.

23 Pearmain, "Reservation," 44; Fred A. Baker to Commissioner of Indian Affairs, July 9, 1935, in Baker Report.

24 Pearmain Report, 30, 47; Fred A. Baker to Commissioner of Indian Affairs, July 9, 1935, in Baker Report.

25 Pearmain Report, B, 4, 6, 7, 19, 27, 43, 48; Fred A. Baker to Commissioner of Indian Affairs, July 9, 1935, in Baker Report.

26 A. M. Johnson to Bruce Poundstone, December 20, 1935 [NARA, RG 96, Entry 85, Region IV, Project Plans File of C. B. Faris, Box 1]; Pearmain Report, 13, 14, 29, 41, 51, 53.

27 James E. Henderson, "The Croatan Indians of North Carolina," December 11, 1923 [NARA, RG 75, Entry 121, File no. 93807–1923-CHEROKEE SCHOOL-150], 1; Blu, *The Lumbee Problem*, 78.

28 See A. W. McLean, "Historical Sketch of the Indians of Robeson County" and accompanying letters, in McPherson Report, 120–32.

29 Pierce et al., 51–52.

30 Garroutte, chapter 1; Harmon, 138–39; Blu, *The Lumbee Problem*, 36, 79.

31 Pierce et al., 52–53.

32 Blu, *The Lumbee Problem*, 79.

33 Cindy D. Padget, "The Lost Indians of the Lost Colony: A Critical Legal Study of the Lumbee Indians of North Carolina," *American Indian Law Review* 21 (1997): 404–6; see also Garroutte, chapter 1 and Harmon, 138–39.

34 John Collier to Josiah W. Bailey, March 26, 1932, in Josiah W. Bailey Collection, Box 310, Folder: Interior, 1932, January-March [Duke University Rare Book, Manuscript, and Special Collections Library], hereafter cited as Bailey papers.

35 For the backgrounds of the members of the Business Committee, see Tamer Graham, Interview by Author and Maureen Dial, tape recording, Pembroke, NC, May 19, 2004 [copy in personal possession of the author]; Business Committee of the Cherokee Indians of Robeson and Adjoining Counties, North Carolina to Cameron Morrison and Josiah W. Bailey, March 29, 1932, in Bailey Papers, Box 310, Folder: Interior, 1932, January-March.

36 John Collier to Josiah W. Bailey, March 26, 1932, in Bailey Papers, Box 310, Folder: Interior, 1932, January-March; Business Committee of the Cherokee Indians of Robeson and Adjoining Counties, North Carolina to Cameron Morrison and Josiah W. Bailey, March 29, 1932, in Bailey Papers, Box 310, Folder: Interior, 1932, January-March.

37 Thaddeus Page to Elwood P. Morey, May 13, 1932, in Bailey Papers, Box 310, Folder: Interior, 1932, April-June.

38 C. J. Rhoads to Secretary of the Interior, May 24, 1932, in Bailey Papers, Box 310, Folder: Interior, 1933, January-March 15.

39 Miscegenation was of particular concern to Southern whites because the presence of mixed-race individuals "militated against the white man's sense of identity," according to historian Joel Williamson. He wrote, "Indeed, the white sense of self depended in part upon maintaining that separateness, and white 'being' somehow lay close to the tensions involved in maintaining and refining the distinction" between blacks and whites. It was thus crucial for those distinctions to be rigidly maintained if whites were to occupy a superior place in society. See Joel Williamson, *New People: Miscegenation and Mulattoes in the United States* (New York: The Free Press, 1980), 95. The logic behind separation of the races is found in Williamson, *The Crucible of Race: Black-White Relations in the American South Since Emancipation* (New York: Oxford University Press, 1984), 414–58 and C. Vann Woodward, *The Strange Career of Jim Crow* (New York: Oxford University Press, 1955), 44–65.

40 James Mooney, "Croatan Indians," no date [National Anthropological Archives, Washington, D.C., MS 1921]. I believe the document is later than 1907 because it contains the express statement, "They are not Cherokee Indians," followed by a paragraph demonstrating why. This statement leads me to believe that the document was written sometime after 1910, when it was first proposed that Robeson County Indians be designated as "Cherokees."

41 C. J. Rhoads to Secretary of the Interior, May 24, 1932, in Bailey Papers, Box 310, Folder: Interior, 1933, January-March 15.

42 Tamer Graham, Interview by Author and Maureen Dial, tape recording, Pembroke, NC, May 19, 2004 [copy in personal possession of the author].

43 Locklear's replacement by Joseph Brooks is indicated in three letters: one from Brooks and Graham to Bailey, one from Bailey to Locklear, saying that Bailey "had been recently advised that [Locklear] had severed [his] connection with the Association of Indians in Robeson County," and one from Boss Locklear to Bailey, telling him that "We as Indians is sending our Chief and Spokesman B. G. Graham, Chief, Joe Brook[s] Spokesman[.]" See Joseph Brooks and B. G. Graham to Josiah W. Bailey, March 13, 1933, in Bailey Papers, Box 310, Folder: Interior, 1933, January-March 15, and Josiah W. Bailey

to A. B. Locklear, March 29, 1933, in Bailey Papers, Box 311, Folder: Interior, 1933, March 16-May; Boss Locklear to Josiah W. Bailey, April 18, 1933, in Bailey Papers, Box 311, Folder: Interior, 1933, March 16-May.

44 Shaw Deese to Josiah W. Bailey, March 7, 1933, in Bailey Papers, Box 310, Folder: Interior, 1933, January-March 15.

45 Colon Brooks to Josiah W. Bailey, March 15, 1933, in Bailey Papers, Box 310, Folder: Interior, 1933, January-March 15.

46 Several scholars have demonstrated a similar reaction among other Indian tribes, including the Cherokee and Lakota. See Biolsi, chp. 7 and Sturm, 48.

47 A. B. Locklear to Josiah W. Bailey, March 20, 1933, in Bailey Papers, Box 311, Folder: Interior, 1933, March 16-May; Josiah W. Bailey to A. B. Locklear, March 29, 1933, in Bailey Papers, Box 311, Folder: Interior, 1933, March 16-May.

48 B. G. Graham and Joseph Brooks to Josiah W. Bailey, April 4, 1933, in Bailey Papers, Box 311, Folder: Interior, 1933, March 16-May.

49 Thaddeus Page to John Collier, April 22, 1933, in Bailey Papers, Box 311, Folder: Interior, 1933, March 16-May.

50 Swanton Report, 1–2, 3–5; see notes and correspondence accompanying Swanton Report [National Anthropological Archives, Smithsonian Institution, Washington, D.C., MS 4126].

51 Pierce et al., 67; Copy of S. 1632 [NARA, RG 75, Entry 121, File no. 45499–1937–066 General Services]; James E. Chavis, Interview by Adolph Dial, tape recording, Pembroke, NC, August 19–20, 1971, in Adolph Dial Tapes; *Robesonian,* April 23, 1934.

52 A. A. Grorud to James Chavis, July 28, 1933, quoted in Pierce et al., 71.

53 Resolution of Cheraw Indians of Robeson and Adjoining Counties, December 2, 1933, in Bailey Papers, Box 311, Folder: Interior, 1933, November 25–1934 February 5.

54 Pierce et al., 71.

55 James E. Chavis, Interview by Adolph Dial, tape recording, Pembroke, NC, August 19–20, 1971, in Adolph Dial Tapes; U.S. Congress, Senate, *Recognition as Siouan Indians of Lumber River of certain Indians in North Carolina* (73rd Cong., 2d sess., 23 January 1934, S. Rpt. 204), 2, hereafter cited as S. Rpt. 204.

56 S. Rpt. 204, 2–3.

57 See Malinda Maynor, "Native American Identity in the Segregated South: The Indians of Robeson County, North Carolina, 1872–1956" (Ph.D. diss., University of North Carolina-Chapel Hill, 2005), introduction and chapter 1.

58 Clifton Oxendine to Josiah W. Bailey, February 1, 1934, in Bailey Papers, Box 311, Folder: Interior, 1934, Feb. 6-March 13; Clifton Oxendine, Interview by Carol Hunt and Jennings Bullard, tape recording, Pembroke, NC, July 17, 1982 [PSU Oral History Project, Public Schools of Robeson County Indian Education Resource Center, Pembroke, NC].

59 L. W. Jacobs, James Cummings, and W. J. Jacobs to Josiah W. Bailey, February 6, 1934, in Bailey Papers, Box 311, Folder: Interior, 1934, Feb. 6–March 13.

60 Josiah W. Bailey to W. J. Jacobs, February 8, 1934, in Bailey Papers, Box 311, Folder: Interior, 1934, Feb. 6–March 13.

61 J. H. Sampson, W. G. Revels, C. L. Maynor, E. B. Martin, William R. Locklear, W. H. Godwin, J. C. Oxendine, Jas. W. Smith, Eddie Lowrey, N. P. Cummings to Josiah W. Bailey, February 10, 1934, in Bailey Papers, Box 311, Folder: Interior, 1934, Feb. 6–March 13.

62 D. F. Lowry to Josiah W. Bailey February 2, 1934, in Bailey Papers, Box 311, Folder: Interior, 1934, Feb. 6–March 13.

63 E. B. Sampson, D. F. Lowry, J. R. Lowry, W. H. Godwin, to J. Bayard Clark, February 22, 1934, in Bailey Papers, Box 311, Folder: Interior, 1934, Feb. 6–March 13.

64 Josiah W. Bailey to W. H. Godwin, February 24, 1934, in Bailey Papers, Box 311, Folder: Interior, 1934, Feb. 6–March 13.

65 A. A. Grorud to James E. Chavis, March 28, 1934, quoted in Pierce et al., 75–76.

66 *Robesonian,* April 12, 1934; April 16, 1934; April 23, 1934.

67 *Robesonian,* April 23, 1934.

68 Rebecca S. Seib, *Indians of Robeson County Land Ownership Study, 1900–1910* (Pembroke, NC: Lumbee Regional Development Association, no date), Map II, [copy in personal possession of the author], hereafter cited as Seib, *Land Ownership Study.*

69 *Robesonian*, April 23, 1934.

70 The previous two paragraphs follow closely on an argument presented in Pierce, et al., 203.

71 Blu, *The Lumbee Problem*, 137–42.

72 cf. Pierce et al., 203.

BIBLIOGRAPHY

Bailey, Josiah W. to A. B. Locklear, March 29, 1933. In Bailey Papers, Box 311, Folder: Interior, 1933, March 16-May.

Bailey, Josiah W. to W. H. Godwin, February 24, 1934. In Bailey Papers, Box 311, Folder: Interior, 1934, Feb. 6-March 13.

Bailey, Josiah W. to W. J. Jacobs, February 8, 1934. In Bailey Papers, Box 311, Folder: Interior, 1934, Feb. 6-March 13.

Baker, Fred A. to Commissioner of Indian Affairs, July 9, 1935. In Fred A. Baker, *Report on Siouan Tribe of Indians in Robeson County, North Carolina* [NARA, RG 75, Entry 121, File no. 36208–1935–310 General Services].

Barth, Fredrik. "Introduction." In *Ethnic Groups and Boundaries: The Social Organization of Culture Difference*, edited by Fredrik Barth. London: George Allen and Unwin, 1969.

Blu, Karen I. *The Lumbee Problem: The Making of an American Indian People.* New York: Cambridge University Press, 1980.

———. "'Reading Back' to Find Community: Lumbee Ethnohistory." In *North American Indian Anthropology: Essays on Society and Culture*, edited by Raymond DeMallie and Alfonso Ortiz. Norman: University of Oklahoma Press, 1993.

———. "'Where Do You Stay At?' Home Place and Community Among the Lumbee." In *Senses of Place*, edited by Steven Feld and Keith Basso. Santa Fe: School of American Research Press, 1996.

Boss Locklear to Josiah W. Bailey, April 18, 1933, in Bailey Papers, Box 311, Folder: Interior, 1933, March 16-May.

Brooks, Colan to Josiah W. Bailey, March 15, 1933 in Bailey Papers, Box 311, Folder: Interior, 1933, March 16-May.

Brooks, Colan, and Rosetta Brooks. Interview by Adolph Dial, tape recording, Pembroke, NC, September 2, 1969. [The Adolph Dial Tapes, 1969–1971, Native American Resource Center, UNC-Pembroke].

Brooks, Joseph, and B. G. Graham to Josiah W. Bailey, March 13, 1933, in Bailey Papers, Box 310, Folder: Interior, 1933. January-March 15 and Josiah W. Bailey to A.B. Locklear, March 29, 1933. In Bailey Papers, Box 311, Folder: Interior, 1933, March 16–May.

Brownwell, Margo S. "Note: Who Is An Indian? Searching for an Answer to the Question at the Core of Federal Indian Law." *University of Michigan Journal of Law Reform* 34 (Fall-Winter 2000–2001): 275–320.

Business Committee of the Cherokee Indians of Robeson and Adjoining Counties, North Carolina to Cameron Morrison and Josiah W. Bailey, March 29, 1932. In Bailey Papers, Box 310, Folder: Interior, 1933, April-June.

Chavis, James E. Interview by Adolph Dial, tape recording, Pembroke, NC, August 19–20, 1971, in Adolph Dial Tapes.

Clifton, James A. "Alternate Identities and Cultural Frontiers." In *Being and Becoming Indian: Biographical Studies of North American Frontiers*, edited by James A. Clifton. Chicago: Dorsey Press, 1989.

Collier, John to Josiah W. Bailey, 26 March 1932. In Josiah W. Bailey Collection, Box 310, Folder: Interior, 1932, January-March [Duke University Rare Book, Manuscript, and Special Collections Library].

Davis, Dave D. "A Case of Identity: Ethnogenesis of the New Houma Indians." *Ethnohistory* 48 (Summer 2001): 473–94.

Deese, Shaw to Josiah W. Bailey, March 7, 1933, in Bailey Papers, Box 310, Folder: Interior, 1933, January-March 15.

Deloria, Ella to Franz Boas, August 7, 1940. [Franz Boas Papers, American Philosophical Society].

Fogelson, Raymond D. "Perspectives on Native American Identity." In *Studying Native America: Problems and Prospects*, edited by Russell Thornton. Madison: University of Wisconsin Press, 1998.

Foster, Morris W. *Being Comanche: A Social History of an American Indian Community*. Tucson: University of Arizona Press, 1991.

Fowler, Loretta. *Shared Symbols, Contested Meanings: Gros Ventre Culture and History, 1778–1984*. Ithaca, NY: Cornell University Press, 1987.

Galloway, Patricia. *Choctaw Genesis: 1500–1700*. Lincoln: University of Nebraska Press, 1995.

Garroutte, Eva Marie. *Real Indians: Identity and the Survival of Native America*. Berkeley: University of California Press, 2003.

Gilbert, William H., Jr. "The Wesorts of Maryland: An Outcasted Group." *Journal of the Washington Academy of Sciences* 35 (August 15, 1945): 237–46.

Gilmore, Glenda Elizabeth. *Gender and Jim Crow: Women and the Politics of White Supremacy in North Carolina, 1896–1920*. Chapel Hill: University of North Carolina Press, 1996.

Gonzales, Angela A. "American Indian Identity Matters: The Political Economy of Identity and Ethnic Group Boundaries." PhD diss., Harvard University, 2001.

———. "The (Re)Articulation of American Indian Identity: Maintaining Boundaries and Regulating Access to Ethnically Tied Resources." *American Indian Culture and Research Journal* 22 (1998): 199–225.

Graham, B. G., and Joseph Brooks to Josiah W. Bailey, April 4, 1933, in Bailey Papers, Box 311, Folder: Interior, 1933, March 16–May.

Graham, Tamer, Interview by Author and Maureen Dial, tape recording, Pembroke, NC, May 19, 2004.

Grorud, A. A. to James E. Chavis, March 28, 1934.

Harmon, Alexandra. *Indians in the Making: Ethnic Relations and Indian Identities Around Puget Sound*. Berkeley: University of California Press, 1998.

Henderson, James E. "The Croatan Indians of North Carolina." December 11, 1935. [NARA, RG 75, Entry 121, File no. 93807–1923–CHEROKEE SCHOOL-150], 1.

Hudson, Charles M. *The Southeastern Indians*. Knoxville: University of Tennessee Press, 1976.

Jacobs, L.W., James Cummings, and W. J. Jacobs to Josiah W. Bailey, February 6, 1934. In Bailey Papers, Box 311, Folder: Interior, 1934, Feb. 6–March 13.

Jaimes, M. Annette. "Federal Identification Policy: A Usurpation of Indigenous Sovereignty in North America." In *The State of Native America: Genocide, Colonization, and Resistance*, edited by M. Annette Jaimes. Boston: South End Press, 1992.

Johnson, A. M., and R. T. Melvin. "Report of Reconnaissance Survey of Pembroke Indian Community Resettlement Project Area" [NARA, RG 96, Entry 85, Region IV, Project Plans File of C.B. Faris, Box 1], 2.

Johnson, A. M. to Bruce Poundstone, December 20, 1935 [NARA, RG 96, Entry 85, Region IV, Project Plans File of C.B. Faris, Box 1].

Kennedy, N. Brent, and Robyn Vaughan Kennedy. *The Melungeons: The Resurrection of a Proud People.* Macon, GA: Mercer University Press, 1994.

Locklear, Elisha, and Cecil Hunt, Interview by Author and Willie Lowery, tape recording, Pembroke, NC, February 23, 2004 [Lumbee River Fund Collection, Sampson-Livermore Library, UNC-Pembroke].

Lowry, D. F. to Josiah W. Bailey February 2, 1934, in Bailey Papers, Box 311, Folder: Interior 1934, Feb. 6–March 13.

Maynor, Malinda. "Native American Identity in the Segregated South: The Indians of Robeson County, North Carolina, 1872–1956." PhD diss., University of North Carolina-Chapel Hill.

———. "People and Place: Croatan Indians in Jim Crow Georgia, 1890–1920." Master's thesis, University of North Carolina, 2002.

Maynor, Waltz, conversation with author. Pembroke, NC, July 31, 2003.

McCulloch, Anne Merline, and David E. Wilkins. "'Constructing' Nations Within States: The Quest for Federal Recognition by the Catawba and Lumbee Tribes." In *American Indian Quarterly* 19 (Summer 1995): 361–87.

McMillan, Hamilton. *Sir Walter Raleigh's Lost Colony: An Historical Sketch of the Attempts of Sir Walter Raleigh to Establish a Colony in Virginia, with the Traditions of an Indian Tribe in North Carolina. Indicating the Fate of the Colony of Englishmen Left on Roanoke Island in 1587.* Wilson, NC: Advance Press, 1888.

McPherson, O. M. *Report on Condition and Tribal Rights of the Indians of Robeson and Adjoining Counties of North Carolina.* 63rd Cong., 3d sess., January 5, 1915, S. Doc. 677.

Melvin, R. T., and A. M. Johnson. "Final Plans for the Pembroke Indian Resettlement Project." [NARA, RG 96, Entry 85, Region IV, Project Plans File of C.B. Faris, Box 1], 3.

Merrell, James H. *The Indians' New World: Catawbas and Their Neighbors From European Contact Through the Era of Removal.* Chapel Hill: University of North Carolina Press, 1989.

Merrell, James H. to Charlie Rose, October 18, 1989 in U.S. Congress, House, Committee on Natural Resources, *Report together with Dissenting Views to Accompany H.R. 334,* 103rd Cong., 1st sess., October 14, 1993, H. Rpt. 290.

Meyer, Melissa L. "American Indian Blood Quantum: Blood Is Thicker Than Family." In *Over the Edge: Remapping the American West,* edited by Valerie J. Matsumoto and Blake Allmendinger. Berkeley: University of California Press, 1999.

Miller, Bruce Granville. *Invisible Indigenes: The Politics of Nonrecognition.* Lincoln: University of Nebraska Press, 2003.

Mooney, James. "Croatan Indians." No date. [National Anthropological Archives, Washington, D.C., MS 1921].

Morgan, Edmund S. *American Slavery, American Freedom: The Ordeal of Colonial Virginia.* New York: W. W. Norton, 1975.

Nagel, Joane. "American Indian Ethnic Renewal: Politics and the Resurgence of Identity." *American Sociological Review* 60 (December 1995): 947–65.

Oakley, Christopher Arris. "The Reshaping of Indian Identity in Twentieth Century North Carolina." PhD diss., University of Tennessee, 2002.

Okuda-Jacobs, Angelina. "Planting Health, Culture, and Sovereignty: Traditional Horticulture of the Lumbee Nation of North Carolina." Master's thesis, University of Wisconsin-Madison, 2000.

Oxendine, Clifton. Interview by Carol Hunt and Jennings Bullard, tape recording, Pembroke, NC, July 17, 1982 [PSU Oral History Project, Public Schools of Robeson County Indian Education Resource Center, Pembroke, NC].

Oxendine, Clifton to Josiah W. Bailey, February 1, 1934. In Bailey Papers, Box 311, Folder: Interior, 1934, Feb. 6–March13.

Padget, Cindy D. "The Lost Indians of the Lost Colony: A Critical legal Study of the Lumbee Indians of North Carolina." *American Indian Law Review* 21 (1997): 404–6.

Page, Thaddeus to John Collier, April 22, 1933 in Bailey Papers, Box 311, Folder: Interior, 1933, March 16–May.

Pearmain, John. "Report . . . On the Conditions of the Indians in Robeson County, North Carolina." November 11, 1935 [NARA, RG 75, Entry 121, File no. 64190–1935–066 Part 1-A], 29.

Peck, John G. "Urban Station—Migration of the Lumbee Indians." PhD diss., University of North Carolina, 1972.

Perdue, Theda. *"Mixed Blood" Indians: Racial Construction in the Early South.* Athens: University of Georgia Press, 2003.

Pierce, Charles F. *[Visit Among the Croatan Indians, Living in the Vicinity of Pembroke, North Carolina]*, Report, in the Field at Pipestone, Minn., to the Commissioner of Indian Affairs, U.S. Indian Service, Department of the Interior, 2 March 1912 [National Archives and Records Administration, Record Group 75, Entry 161, File no. 23202–1912–123 General Services].

Pierce, Julian T., and Cynthia Hunt-Locklear, et al. *The Lumbee Petition.* 3 vols. Pembroke, NC: Lumbee River Legal Services, 1987.

Recognition as Siouan Indians of Lumber River of certain Indians in North Carolina. U.S. Congress, Senate. 73rd Cong., 2d sess., January 23, 1934, S. Rpt. 204, 2.

Resolution of Cheraw Indians of Robeson and Adjoining Counties, December 2, 1933. In Bailey Papers, Box 311, Folder: Interior, 1933, November 25, 1934–February 5.

Rhoads, C. J. to Secretary of the Interior, May 24, 1932, in Bailey Papers, Box 310, Folder: Interior, 1933, January-March 15.

Sampson, E. B., D. F. Lowry, J. R. Lowry, W. H. Godwin, to J. Bayard Clark, February 22, 1934. In Bailey Papers, Box 311, Folder: Interior, 1934, Feb. 6-March 13.

Sampson, J. H., W. G. Revels, C. L. Maynor, E. B. Martin, William R. Locklear, W.H. Godwin, J. C. Oxendine, Jas. W. Smith, Eddie Lowrey, N. P. Cummings to Josiah W. Bailey, February 10, 1934. In Bailey Papers, Box 311, Folder: Interior, 1934, Feb. 6–March 13.

Saunt, Claudio. *A New Order of Things: Property, Power, and the Transformation of the Creek Indians, 1733–1816.* Cambridge: Cambridge University Press, 1999.

Seib, Rebecca S. *Indians of Robeson County Land Ownership Study, 1900–1910.* Pembroke, NC: Lumbee Regional Development Association, no date.

————. *Settlement Pattern Study of the Indians of Robeson County, NC, 1735–1787.* Pembroke, NC: Lumbee Regional Development Association, 1983.

Sider, Gerald. *Living Indian Histories: Lumbee and Tuscarora People in North Carolina.* Chapel Hill: University of North Carolina Press, 2003.

Snipp, C. Matthew. *American Indians: First of This Land.* New York: Russell Sage, 1989.

Sturm, Circe. *Blood Politics: Race, Culture, and Identity in the Cherokee Nation of Oklahoma.* Berkeley: University of California Press, 2002.

Swanton, John R. "Probable Identity of the 'Croatan' Indians." 1933. [National Anthropological Archives, Smithsonian Institution, MS 4126].

Thomas, Robert K. *A Report on Research of Lumbee Origins.* Unpublished, undated manuscript. [North Carolina Collection, UNC-Chapel Hill].

Thompson, Ray. "A History of the Education of the Lumbee Indians of Robeson County, North Carolina from 1885 to 1970." EdD diss., University of Miami, 1973.

Walker, J. O. to George S. Mitchell, March 24, 1937. [NARA-Atlanta, RG 96, Entry 79, Region IV, Box 39 Folder Wolf Pit/Pembroke-913].

Wilkins, David E. "Breaking into the Intergovernmental Matrix: The Lumbee Tribe's Efforts to Secure Federal Acknowledgement." *Publius* 23 (Fall 1993): 123–42.

Wilkins, David E., and K. Tsianina Lomawaima. *Uneven Ground: American Indian Sovereignty and Federal Law.* Norman: University of Oklahoma Press, 2001.

Williamson, Joel. *The Crucible of Race: Black-White Relations in the American South Since Emancipation*. New York: Oxford University Press, 1984.

————. *New People: Miscegnation and Mulattoes in the United States*. New York: The Free Press, 1980.

Wood, Peter H., Deborah Montgomerie, and Susan Yarnell. *Tuscarora Roots: An Historical Report Regarding the Relation of the Hatteras Tuscarora Tribe of Robeson County, North Carolina, to the Original Tuscarora Indian Tribe*. Durham, NC: Hatteras Tuscarora Tribal Foundation, 1992.

Woods, Ruth Dial. "Growing Up Red: The Lumbee Experience." PhD diss., University of North Carolina-Chapel Hill, 2001.

Woodward, C. Vann. *The Strange Career of Jim Crow*. New York: Oxford University Press, 1955.

5 THE CATAWBA NATION UNDER SIEGE: A TROUBLED HISTORY OF TRIBAL SOVEREIGNTY

E. Fred Sanders and Thomas J. Blumer

HISTORICAL OVERVIEW

Once there were hundreds of American Indian nations located on the lands that are now called the United States. Each had a unique culture and language. Each had its own government and provided for its own justice. Some punished bad acts by requiring the person to correct the harm he or she had done. Sometimes, for example, a troublemaker was sent away from his home and his family and was never allowed to return. Decisions were often made by mutual agreement. The elders selected community leaders. Some people took responsibility more seriously than others. Some had special gifts. Some were selected as healers, some as spiritual leaders, as warriors, or as storytellers. Many were hunters and followed the game across the land. Others were known as warriors. These included the Seneca and Catawba Nations.

Some, like the Pueblo Indians, were farmers. American Indians knew the plants and herbs and used them for medicine as well as for food. Religious beliefs and practices were important to all activities. Each living thing was seen as a part of the circle of life. Whenever herbs or an animal's life was taken from the forest, a prayer was offered to the spirit world. The land was not to be owned. It was a gift from the Creator. Land belonged to the people, animals, and plants. The earth sustained life.

In 1492, Christopher Columbus got lost as he searched for India. Instead he found himself on the homelands of the Taino people. Because he thought he had arrived in India, he called the people Indians. After he realized his mistake, he tried to claim the entire country for the Spanish Queen Isabella. Soon other Europeans came and called this continent the New World. Because many of the American Indian people were primarily hunters rather than farmers, the colonists thought they needed to be "civilized." Civilization, to the Europeans, meant dividing the land, so that it could be fenced and farmed. Europeans never understood American Indians' ideas about land ownership. American Indians never saw the need for fences. Because American Indians were not Christians, the Europeans thought they were not religious. They called American Indians "savages," even though they would not have survived in the new world without the kindness of the Indians. Thanksgiving is a reminder of Indigenous generosity.

Settlers gradually took more and more of the land for farming and for building homes. As the land was taken, Indigenous people lost their traditional hunting grounds and sacred sites for medicine, burial, and worship. Often the land was stolen by the Europeans. Disputes arose, and sometimes blood was shed.

Peace was often made, and treaties were signed between Indigenous nations and European countries. However, these treaties were always written in English. The treaties were sometimes used to remove First Peoples from their homelands to a smaller area. Sometimes the treaty came after the land had already been taken. Each treaty promised to protect the new tribal homelands. American Indians' right to live peacefully was guaranteed. However, these promises were frequently broken. More land was always needed. Many difficulties were created by settlers who simply entered Indian territory and claimed land ownership.

In 1763, the King of England established a new policy. Only Great Britain could obtain legal title to Indian land. Individuals or colonial governments could not buy land from any Indian or Indian tribe. One of these Indian tribes was the Catawba Nation. The Catawba's first treaty was with Great Britain in 1760. The Treaty of Pine Tree Hill offered the Catawba protection from the colonists who were taking Catawba lands illegally. In exchange, the Catawba Nation agreed to cede over eight million acres, a large part of both South Carolina and North Carolina. The Catawba kept only a fifteen square mile area (144,000 acres). They reserved their right to hunt in customary Catawba hunting grounds throughout South Carolina. Hunting was essential to Catawba survival. In 1763, a second treaty was signed at Augusta, Georgia. The Treaty of Augusta reaffirmed the protection of the Catawba's 144,000 acre homeland.[1]

In 1776, after gaining independence from Great Britain, the colonists began to form a new nation. They incorporated democratic principles of government, which they had learned from the Iroquois Confederacy. They also identified the unique status of Indigenous nations in the United States Constitution. The new government assumed responsibility for honoring promises made by Great Britain's treaty obligations. For the Catawba, this was the Treaty of 1763. The first Congress implemented the already existing policies of Great Britain. Only the United States could obtain legal title to Indian land.

In 1828, Andrew Jackson was elected president of the United States. He wanted to move all American Indian Nations west of the Mississippi River and seize their land. In 1830, the Indian Removal Act became law. It authorized the American Indian removal to the west.

In 1831, the Cherokee Nation sued the State of Georgia. Georgia had enacted a series of laws that were aimed at destroying the Cherokee government, removing the Cherokee Nation, and taking their lands. The Cherokees asked the Supreme Court to stop Georgia from violating treaties made with Great Britain and the United States and protect their rights. The majority of the Supreme Court justices said that they had no power to hear this case. Most were saddened by Georgia's destructive actions.

Chief Justice John Marshall believed that American Indian Nations could not be called foreign countries. He proposed that American Indian tribes should be called domestic nations because their homelands were located inside the United States. He called them "dependent" nations because they were forced to depend on the United States to honor the treaties. He proposed that the United States must protect the Indians since the Cherokees and other American Indian nations could no longer protect themselves.

Justice Thompson disagreed. He said American Indian Tribes were clearly foreign nations with unique governments and ancient cultures. American Indian nations existed on this continent long before the United States. He proposed that the treaties were not made as favors to American Indian nations but were based upon the needs of both sides and were signed as equals. He argued that the tribes, recognized as nations when the treaties were made, now were unjustly denied the right to enforce them.

Georgia officials did not answer the Cherokee complaint and did not defend their actions before the Supreme Court. President Andrew Jackson ignored the rights of the Cherokee Nation. In 1835, the United States obtained the consent of a minority faction within the Cherokee Nation to the Treaty of New Echota, which exchanged all Cherokee lands in Georgia for lands west of the Mississippi River. In 1838, the Cherokees were forcibly removed by the United States. They traveled, mostly on foot, over a thousand miles to lands in what is now called Oklahoma. Because over 4,000 Cherokees died during this forced removal, this tragic episode is called the "Trail of Tears."

Two years later, in 1840, South Carolina tried to take all of the Catawba lands through an agreement called the "Treaty of Nation Ford." South Carolina promised to find a new homeland for the Catawba people and to pay a very small amount of money for their 144,000 acres. After taking the land, South Carolina broke these promises. Since there was no federal approval of the treaty, the Catawba lands were never legally transferred. The Treaty of Nation Ford was void.

In 1842, having failed to provide a new homeland for the Catawba people, South Carolina bought back approximately one square mile of land within the original 144,000 acres. These lands, the Old Reservation, continue to be held in trust by South Carolina for the Catawba Nation. In 1848, the United States Congress appropriated funds for the removal of the Catawba people to a location west of the Mississippi River. This removal was never carried out.[2]

The Catawba kept insisting that the land issue be settled. As a result, the Catawba were federally recognized in 1941, and 3,400 acres within the treaty lands were placed in trust by the United States. A little more than ten years later, in 1953, the United States Congress established a policy called termination. One by one, Congress ended the federal relationship with over one hundred American Indian nations. The United States no longer had to keep the promises made in treaties to these tribes.

The Catawba Nation was one of the tribes targeted in 1954 for termination. In 1958 and 1959, the Bureau of Indian Affairs (BIA) sent agents from Washington, DC. They tried to convince the Catawba people to agree to end the federal relationship. The BIA agents wrote the Catawba's resolution approving the end of federal trust responsibility. The BIA gave Congress information about the Catawba that supported termination, even though some of it was not correct. Catawba leaders continued to insist that the United States honor the promises made in the treaties of Pine Tree Hill (1760) and Augusta (1763) to protect the Catawba's claim to the remaining 141,000 acres. Over and over again, the United States promised to protect the Catawba's land claim.

In 1959, Congress passed the Catawba termination law, called "The Division of Assets." This law ended federal services and United States trust responsibility over 3,400 acres of tribal land, but it did not terminate the existence of the Catawba Indian Nation. Catawba tribal members received either land or money from the sale of this land. The acreage held in trust by the State of South Carolina for the Catawba Nation remained. The rest of the Catawba treaty lands (about 141,000 acres) were not part of the Division of Assets.

The United States termination policy lasted only fifteen years. The effect was disastrous for all the tribes subjected to this policy. In 1973, the Menominee Tribe of Wisconsin became the first American Indian nation to ask Congress to restore their relationship. Almost all of the tribes who were caught in this policy have been restored.

Meanwhile, the Catawba tribal government continued to operate under its own governing documents. Tribal leaders were still seeking a final settlement with South Carolina for the remaining 141,000 acres of treaty lands. When negotiations finally broke down, the Catawba filed suit against South Carolina. The Catawba asked for the return of the lands, which were taken in the Treaty of Nation Ford, or fair payment. South Carolina tried to claim that when the Catawba's federal relationship with the United States ended, the tribe's claim to the remaining 141,000 acres also ended.

The Supreme Court said that the Catawba did not lose their claim to the 141,000 acres when the federal relationship was terminated. However, the Court also said that the laws of South Carolina would apply to these lands from the effective date of the Catawba Division of Assets (1962) until the law suit was filed in 1980.

The Catawba people were stunned. How could this land now be taken from Catawba by placing it under South Carolina law? These lands were under the treaty protection of the United States. The transfer to South Carolina in the Treaty of Nation Ford had never been approved by Congress. Federal agents, including Congressman Robert Hemphill, had promised to safeguard the Catawba's claim to these lands. Without this promise, the Catawba would not have agreed to termination.

On June 21, 1990, the Catawba Nation filed a second lawsuit. This suit was against the United States for failure to protect the land claim as promised in the treaties and during termination. Would the United States fulfill promises made over two hundred years ago, or would these promises also be broken, like so many others? Would the State of South Carolina finally accept responsibility for the illegal taking of the Catawba's homelands? Would they cooperate in a fair settlement of the Catawba claim? Would the people of the United States carry out the promise of this nation, act as a "civilized" people, and treat these First Americans with fairness and equity? The Catawba won their lawsuit in 1992 and negotiated a settlement act in 1993. The United States and Catawba government-to-government relationship was restored, but major concessions were extracted by South Carolina.[3]

THE CATAWBA NATION'S ANCIENT GENERAL COUNCIL: A DIFFICULT SURVIVAL

The Catawba Indian Nation is one of the few Southeastern Indian tribes to retain its democratic form of government even when external and internal circumstances seem to conspire against its survival. The Catawba, from the most ancient of times, have exercised political rule through a General Tribal Council, the legislative branch of the Catawba government, hereafter referred to as the General Council. The council has elected rulers (unknown date to 1775), generals (1775–1840), and chiefs (1840 to the present) to represent it. The General Council is most akin to ancient Greek democracy. Today the *Landesgemeinde* (legislature) of the Swiss Forest Cantons may be looked at as a close parallel; however, the Catawba General Council from ancient times has been so democratic to include women in its ranks, while the *Landesgemeinde* has only recently included women. Today, the General Council consists of all enrolled Catawba men and women over the age of eighteen. When in session, the General Council governs the Nation by passing resolutions, approving tribal actions, and tending to all tribal business. This governmental device is crucial to perform a set of checks and balances built into Catawba social structures over the centuries. It is formally encoded in writing in Catawba constitutions from 1944 to the present (see Appendix B for the 1944 Constitution and Appendix C for the 1975 Constitution). The Catawba General Council is currently drafting a new constitution to address the changes brought by the Settlement Act of 1993.

Between the American Revolution and the present, the Catawba have retained two key cultural practices. First is the Catawba pottery tradition. Catawba pottery constitutes the oldest clay-based art form east of the Mississippi. Its origin in the Woodland Period makes the Catawba tradition possibly older than that craft practiced by the famed Pueblo tribe of the Southwest.[4] The other continuously existing cultural practice is not quite so easily perceptible to non-Native observers. This cultural treasure is the Catawba Nation General Council and the tribalism which supports its functions. Its obscurity is partially due to the fact that only Catawba Indians may attend General Council meetings. Outsiders are only occasionally invited. These two cultural practices, pottery and the General Council, have breathed life into the Catawba Nation for many centuries.

By the time John Lawson made his exhausting journey through the Carolina Back Country in 1700 and his subsequent publication of his *New Voyage to Carolina* almost ten years later, this Renaissance man was recognized as an authority of Indigenous nations in the Carolinas. In his *New Voyage*, Lawson provides a description of the General Council, which is worth repeating despite its problematic mix of European and Indigenous concepts:

> The King is the Ruler of the Nation, and has others under him, to assist him, as his War Captains, and Counsellors, who are pick'd out and chosen from among the ancientest Men of the Nation he is King of. These meet him in all general Councils and Debates, concerning, War, Peace, Trade, Hunting, and all the Adventures and Accidents of Humane Affairs, which appear within their Verge; where all Affairs are discoursed of and argued pro and con, very deliberately (without making any manner of Parties or Divisions) for the good of the Publick; as they meet there to treat, they discharge their Duty with all the Integrity imaginable, never looking towards their Own Interest, before the Publick Good. After every Man has given his Opinion, that which has most Voice, or, in Summing up, is found the most reasonable, that they make use of without any Jars and Wrangling, and put it in Execution, the first Opportunity that offers.[5]

Once other Europeans began to study the governmental structures of the Catawba Nation, the General Council was noticed as of primary importance. Council Houses or State Houses were recorded immediately and described as large thatched buildings central to every community in the Carolinas. Lawson, for example, stated that "on our way, we met with several Towns of Indians each town having its Theater or State House, such Houses being found all along the road...."[6] This observation was also made among the Esaw or Catawba people. In some instances, a tribe lived in their Council Houses. In other communities, the representative, "king," or "ruler" lived in this structure. In every case, however, the Council House was resorted to for all business.

One of the earliest European glimpses of the workings of the General Council occurred in October 1750. Young Warrior (Yanabe Yalangway), Haigler's predecessor, visited Charleston to attend a conference (see Appendix A). Most of his headmen, in today's parallel, members of the Executive Committee, joined Young Warrior in this effort. When they left Charleston to return to the Catawba Nation, the party was ambushed by a Haudenosaunee war party. The entire Catawba delegation was massacred.[7] Upon hearing the news of this tragedy, the Catawba Nation's General Council met and learned that only one member of the ruling family, Nop-ke-he, had escaped the Haudenosaunee. The young man did not join the delegation in Charleston, but was on a hunting trip elsewhere. Nop-ke-he was still not aware of what had happened to the Charleston party and had no idea the General Council was in an emergency session. Nop-ke-he was elected ruler. A party was sent from the General Council to find the young man in the forest and inform him of the decision. Later, this young man became known as King Haigler. He signed the 1769 Treaty of Pine Tree Hill with the British Government.[8] The vast written records left by King Haigler abound with speeches that were often made before his General Council.[9]

On August 20, 1763, after having served for thirteen years, King Haigler suffered the same death as Young Warrior. He was murdered by a Shawnee war party not far from Van Wyck, South Carolina.[10] Apparently, the Catawba General Council judged the political situation to be different from the circumstances triggered by the death of Young Warrior. One might speculate that the impending Treaty of Augusta was very problematic for the Catawba Nation; in any case, the General Council decided to wait before electing a successor. Instead of beginning the process of selecting a leader from members of the ruling family, the General Council named Colonel Ayers as ruler.[11] As the newly elected leader, Colonel Ayers accompanied representatives of the Catawba General Council to Augusta where they voted to re-affirm the Treaty of 1760 to occupy a surveyed reservation smaller than their previously held lands. The vote was unanimous and likely also reflected the wishes of King Haigler. Following the ratification of the Treaty (1763), the Catawba retained sovereignty on the fifteen miles square of land in the face of an overwhelming tide of European settlers.[12]

Two years after the treaty was ratified, the General Council ended Colonel Ayers's tenure as regent and elected Frow, a descendent of King Haigler, as the representative of the Catawba Nation. Frow accepted and remained in office until 1775. In 1775, Frow abdicated and disappeared from the pages of history.[13]

From this point on until 1839, the Catawba Nation was represented by a succession of generals and a group of headmen who held military titles. The final decision in all matters, however, remained with the Catawba Nation General Council, the tribe's legislative body. The prestige of this string of generals rested on the fact that they were all members of the Catawba ruling family. The last to hold this office in this manner was General William Harris. Unfortunately, Harris lived only long enough to be in office for just a few months in 1838. The General Council then elected James Kegg as general. Of Pamunkey descent, he was not a direct descendent of the ruling family. His claim to legitimacy lay in the fact that his wife was a member of the ruling line and descended directly from King Haigler. General Kegg wanted the Treaty of Nation Ford signed, thus giving Catawba patrimony to the State of South Carolina.

Half of the tribe's members were living among the Cherokee in Heyward County, North Carolina, and the other half were holding on in York County, South Carolina.[14] The General Council or legislative body continued to meet from time to time. The rules of procedure were based on tribal custom and tradition. In 1848, the Catawba Nation had dropped military titles for its leaders, and William Morrison was named chief. A period of relative political stability began in 1852, when the General Council elected Allen Harris as chief. In 1859, at the direction of the General Council, Chief Harris led a delegation from the Catawba Nation in South Carolina to the Choctaw Nation in Indian Territory (now Oklahoma). The objectives of the trip were to see if the Choctaw would welcome the Catawba to join them and if the land in Indian Territory was good for farming. Should Chief Harris return to the General Council with a positive report, the entire Catawba Nation planned to migrate to Indian Territory and incorporate with the Choctaw.[15] The concept of incorporation has enjoyed a long tradition among Southeastern American Indian tribes. Incorporation has meant that weaker tribes could enter into a close alliance with stronger tribes for protection. In this case, the weakened Catawba Nation sought to incorporate with the land-rich Choctaw.

Chief Harris failed in his mission. He died in 1860 in the Choctaw Nation and was buried there. Just before his death, however, he was able to send word home that the Choctaw were open to a Catawba migration and that the land the Choctaw offered was good. This information reached the Catawba Nation around the time of Chief Harris's death. The General Council was delighted with the report. All members of the Catawba nation with the exception of one family (the now extinct Quash family) agreed to relocate in Indian Territory.

However, another problem had to be faced by the Catawba Nation: the impending war among the states. South Carolina was preoccupied with its own political conflicts. As a result, the migration was cancelled, and the entire male population of the Catawba Indian Nation joined the Confederate States Army.[16]

The next chiefs to be elected by the General Council were Confederate veterans. It took twenty years for the Catawba Nation to recover from its war losses and the traumas of Reconstruction. As soon as they were able, the Catawba renewed their ancient land claims against South Carolina. The new generation went to work in 1886 under Chief Thomas Morrison, who collaborated closely with his successor Chief James Harris, elected in 1892.

The supreme importance of the Catawba General Council may be studied in a different light during the period from 1904 to 1905. At this time, the Catawba could not decide on a new chief. The General Council appointed a Committee of Three from its ranks. The Committee handled all tribal affairs while a chief could be decided upon. Apparently, the confusion concerned two chief candidates who were brothers: James Harris and David Adam (Toad) Harris. The eventual selection rested on David Adam Harris. He represented the Catawba Nation for the next twenty years.

In the 1943 *Memorandum of Understanding Agreement*, the State of South Carolina united with the Federal Government and adopted a Constitution (see Appendix B). E. Fred Sanders refers to the years between 1943 and 1959 as the era of the "musical chairs." Sanders served as Assistant Chief from 1975 to 1993, and most recently, as councilman under the Chief William Harris administration. During the 1940s and 1950s, a total of eight different administrations attempted to settle the issue of the termination of the tribe's assets. Some, like Chief Nelson Blue and Chief Idle Sanders, were opposed to termination. Others, like Chief Samuel T. Blue and Chief Albert Sanders, wanted the tribe's assets divided, including land resources. Neither faction could stay in power for long.[17] During this entire period, the Catawba General Council met as needed to hold elections in spite of a constitution which called for four-year terms. Not only did chiefs resign, but other Executive Committee members such as Secretary/Treasurer Garfield Harris quit in frustration as well. In the midst of these political storms, Bureau of Indian Affairs (BIA) agents publicly campaigned to promote the idea of private land ownership to the rank and file Catawba. The efforts of the BIA agents were against the law, but they continued despite General Council objections.

Although the BIA agents eventually won the day, the Catawba Nation and its ancient General Council did not vanish. The Catawba termination statute ended federal recognition in 1962, yet the Catawba remained recognized by South Carolina. Contrary to all predictions, the General Council remained dear to the hearts of the Catawba people and continued to function during the fourteen years between Federal Termination and restoration. Soon after the Tribe reorganized in the summer of

1973, the General Council, freed from any outside influence, promulgated the Constitution of 1975 (Appendix C).

This constitution and the activities of a General Council have been relied upon until today. Both constitutions combine long-standing tribal law and the 1934 Indian Reorganization Act. If the Catawba find it to their advantage to promulgate a constitution to replace that of 1975, it too will grow from old and deep democratic roots. Like its predecessors, it will be a testimony to the resilience of the Catawba Nation.

According to the Settlement Act of 1993, the Catawba Indian Nation Constitution of 1975 would remain in effect until a new constitution would be promulgated by the General Council. In 1994, the Director of the Eastern Area office of the Bureau of Indian Affairs, Bill Ott, upon studying a draft of the new constitution, declared it could serve the Catawba well for years to come with only a few general modifications. However, the new 1994 Constitution has not yet been made public to the Catawba people as a whole to become ratified. Its content reflects the constitutions of 1944 and 1975 and thus ancient Catawba tradition (see Appendices B & C).

Before the Settlement Act of 1993, the then current administration of Gilbert Blue understood that the 1975 Constitution needed improvement. As a consequence, the General Council formed a Constitution Committee to draft a new constitution. Almost to a person, the Constitution Committee members refused to abandon the democratic principles taught them by the "old Indians." Just before the Settlement Act was approved, Wanda George Warren was named the Chair of the Constitution Committee. In 1994, while working as a tribal employee, Warren disbanded the Constitution Committee and locked its members out of its working space. Soon after the approval of the Settlement Act, the Blue Administration began to look for additional ways to abandon the traditions of the General Council. On October 4, 1996, without consultation with the tribe as a whole, the Blue Executive Committee sent a secret request to the Secretary of the Interior for a "Federal Charter of Incorporation" form of government. Federal Law states that any American Indian tribe may resort to a business Corporate Charter entity, but this may be done only with full tribal approval. In the case of the laws of the Catawba Nation, the public approval of tribal voters must be sought to ratify such significant change. Tribal members did not learn of the Corporate Charter until it was made public in a newspaper article in 2001—long after the Blue Administration had submitted the Charter to the Bureau of Indian Affairs. The document was signed into force by Ada E. Deer, Assistant Secretary of Indian Affairs, on September 8, 1997. Considering that established Catawba legal procedures were ignored, it has to be concluded that Deer signed the document into law without appropriate tribal approval. From a General Council point of view, the Federal Charter of Incorporation thus holds no validity in the Catawba Indian Nation, and until a new constitution has been approved, the 1975 Constitution must still be complied with in all tribal Indian affairs.

Almost immediately after the "Corporate Charter" form of Catawba government was federally established in 1997, serious changes began to take place. Land was bought and sold. Trust accounts were squandered or mismanaged. While the Settlement Act of 1993 called for a 4,200 acre increase in reservation lands, and the tribe had set aside a 12.5 million dollar trust account to purchase new lands, only 299 remote acres were added to the reservation. Transactions were not made public, even though the Settlement Act and the General Council required a regular schedule of reports and an annual audit. The only source of information for tribal General Council members continued to be occasional notices in the *Herald* newspaper.

"WITHOUT ANY JARS AND WRANGLING": WHERE WE ARE TODAY

Many years ago, Lawson observed about the General Council that "after every Man has given his Opinion, that which has most Voice, or, in Summing up, is found the most reasonable, that they make use of without any Jars and Wrangling, and put it in Execution, the first Opportunity that offers."[18] Are we still conducting tribal business today without "any jars and wrangling"? No doubt, the Catawba are making a strong effort to resolve the current tribal governance conflict. As called for by traditional Catawba Law, and demanded by the Constitution of 1975, the Catawba have held regular General Council meetings. Unfortunately, the tribal administration has refused General Council members the use of the Catawba Long House, a building paid for with Catawba tribal funds. Departing from long-standing custom, meetings, democratically called assemblies, have instead been held in the Long House parking lot, the York County Law Center, and the Catawba Civic Center. In 2002, the General Council called for tribal elections in accordance with the Constitution of 1975 (see Appendix C). It was the first election since the Settlement Act of 1993 went into effect, although the Catawba Constitution of 1975 calls for two General Council meetings a year and provides for a regular schedule of elections. In the summer of 2002, a full slate of Catawba tribal members was nominated for chief, assistant chief, secretary/treasurer and two positions of councilmen. The election was held by secret ballot. It was open to any Catawba tribal member who wished to run for office. All Catawba over the age of eighteen were encouraged to vote.

As of 2007, the Catawba Nation remains sadly divided between a traditionally elected government and a tribal administration under siege. However, in spite of all difficulties, the General Council tradition retains a clear presence among the Catawba—as it has been for time immemorial.

APPENDIX A
Catawba Rulers Documented from the Sixteenth Century to the Present

1540	Lady of Cofitachique, hostess for Hernando de Soto; taken captive and escaped.
1670	Canos of Cofitachique
1717	Whitmanmatangtghee, taken captive at Fort Christiana, Virginia, by the Seneca and escaped.
1739	Onato
1740	Iscountgonita, recorded to 1741, may have ruled longer
1746	Yanabe Yalengway, recorded to 1753.
1754	King Haigler (Arantaswa), recorded to his murder in 1762, had reserved 2,000,000 acres to the Nation, Treaty of Pine Tree Hill in 1760.
1763	Regent Colonel Ayers, reserved 144,000 acres at the Treaty of Augusta, approved by the Catawba General Council, Ayers remained regent to 1764.
1765	Frow, approved by the Catawba General Council, abdicated in 1775 and the Catawba Republic was founded.
1776	General New River (Scott family) became general of the Catawba Indian Nation by virtue of the fact that his wife Sallie New River was the granddaughter of King Haigler. Ruled until his death in 1802.
1803	General Jacob Scott, a member of the ruling family, ruled until 1821. During his reign, South Carolina began negotiations to take the 144,000 acre reservation but could not do so as long as the ruling family remained in power.
1822	General Jacob Ayers, a member of the ruling family, ruled until 1837.
1838	General William Harris, the last member of the ruling family, did not reign for a full year by the time of his death.
1839	General James Kegg was a Pamunkey Indian who had married into the ruling family. Lacking loyalty to Catawba tradition, he signed the Treaty of 1840 and fled to Cherokee from which place he tried to obtain the money promised by the Treaty.

1841	Confusion over who was the ruler of the Catawba Nation. This confusion lasted until 1852. William Morrison claimed to be chief in 1848 and James Kegg entered into the picture from 1850 to 1852. Confusion was fostered by the fact that the bulk of the Catawba General Council was split between Cherokee and the New Reservation in York County.
1852	Chief Allen Harris ruled firmly to his death in the Choctaw Country in 1860, just before the War between the States.
1861	Chief John Scott ruled until 1868. His last official act was to circulate a petition authorized by the General Council.
1869	Chief John Harris, Confederate States Army veteran, ruled until circa 1873.
1874	Chief John Scott ruled until circa 1884.
1885	Chief James Harris.
1886	Chief Thomas Morrison ruled until circa 1891. Began a suit against South Carolina which lasted until the Settlement of 1993.
1892	Chief James Harris ruled until 1895 and continued the suit against South Carolina under the direction of the Catawba General Council.
1896	Chief Robert Lee Harris ruled for one year.
1897	Chief Lewis Gordon ruled until 1900 and possibly to 1903.
1904	Chief William Harris (Billy Bowlegs Harris) ruled until a General Council committee took over the running of the government.
1905	Committee of Three ruled for one year.
1906	Some confusion over who was the legal chief: David A. Harris or his brother James Harris.
1907	Chief David A. Harris ruled possibly until circa 1927. He died in 1930.
1927	Chief Samuel T. Blue ruled until 1939.
1940	Chief Robert Lee Harris ruled from the beginning of the Federal Wardship period possibly until 1943.
1944	Chief Albert Sanders ruled for a few months.
1944	Chief Douglas Harris ruled until 1946.

1946	Chief Raymond Harris, World War II Veteran, ruled to 1951.
1952	Chief Ephraim George ruled for a few months.
1952	Chief Nelson Blue ruled for a few months.
1953	Chief Ephraim George possibly ruled to 1955.
1956	Chief Samuel T. Blue ruled for a few months.
1956	Chief Idle Sanders ruled for a few months.
1957	Chief Samuel T. Blue ruled for a year.
1958	Chief Nelson Blue ruled for a few months and resigned.
1959	Chief Albert Sanders ruled during the Termination Period and claimed office until his death.
1973	Chief Gilbert Blue was elected by a small Catawba General Council meeting held to reorganize the tribe. About forty Catawba citizens attended and voted in spite of a lack of a quorum. Chief Blue was consistently kept in office during the entire Settlement Period by the Catawba General Council to maintain consistency in the face of the Federal Court system. After the Settlement, he looked for ways to stay in office and eventually refused to allow Catawba General Council meetings knowing that he would be deposed.
2000	Chief William Harris nominated for chief during a Catawba General Council meeting which met all legal requirements according to the Catawba Constitution of 1975. Chief Blue refused to recognize Harris's legal election and continued to look for ways to stay in power. In spite of Blue's opposition, the General Council continues to meet.

APPENDIX B

Constitution and By-Laws of the Catawba Indian Tribe of South Carolina Approved June 30, 1944

Preamble

We, the members of the Catawba Indian Tribe of South Carolina, in order to set up a more effective tribal organization, to improve our social and economic welfare, and to secure to ourselves and our posterity the benefits of organization, do hereby establish and ordain this constitution and by-laws for the Catawba Indian Tribe.

Article I—Territory

The jurisdiction of the Catawba Tribe shall extend to the land within the boundaries of the present Indian reservation in South Carolina, and to such other lands as may hereafter be acquired for the mutual benefit of its members.

Article II—Membership

Section 1. The Membership of the Catawba Tribe of South Carolina shall consist of:

(a) All persons of Indian blood whose names appear on the tribal roll of July 1, 1943, as recognized by the State of South Carolina.
(b) All children born to any member of the Catawba Tribe, who is a resident of the State of South Carolina at the time of the birth of said children.

Section 2. The General Tribal Council, hereinafter provided for, shall have the power to pass ordinances, subject to the approval of the Secretary of the Interior, covering future membership and the adoption of new members.

Article III—Governing Body

Section 1. The governing body of the Catawba Tribe of South Carolina shall be the General Tribal Council which shall be composed of all qualified voters of the Catawba Tribe.

Section 2. All enrolled members of the Catawba Tribe, male and female, who are 21 years of age or over shall be qualified voters at any tribal election.

Section 3. The General Tribal Council, by secret ballot, shall elect from its own members (a) a Chief, (b) an Assistant Chief, (c) a Secretary-Treasurer, and (d) two Trustees who shall, ex officio, serve as an Executive Committee of the Tribe, as provided by Section 5 of this Article and Section 3, Article I of the bylaws.

Section 4. The General Tribal Council shall meet on the first Saturday of January and July of each year. Within 30 days after the ratification and approval of this constitution and bylaws, a General Tribal Council of the Tribe shall be called by the present Chief for the purpose of electing the officers named herein, and it shall transact such other business as may be necessary. The officers elected at this meeting shall thereupon take office and serve until the July 1946 meeting, at which time their successors shall be chosen. Thereafter, officials shall be chosen at the July meeting every even year. The Chief or 25 per cent of the qualified voters of the Tribe, by written notice may call special meetings of the General Tribal Council. Thirty-five qualified voters of the Tribe shall constitute a quorum at any special or regular meeting.

Section 5. There shall be an Executive Committee consisting of the Chief, Assistant Chief, Secretary-Treasurer, and the two Trustees provided for in Section 3 of this Article, which Committee shall perform such duties as may from time to time be conferred on it by the General Tribal Council.

Article IV—Powers of the General Tribal Council

Section 1. The General Tribal Council of the Catawba Tribe shall exercise the following powers, subject to any limitations imposed by this constitution and by the statutes or the Constitution of the United States:

    (a)   To negotiate with the Federal, State, and local governments;

    (b)   To employ legal counsel, the choice of counsel and fixing of fees to be subject to the approval of the Secretary of the Interior;

    (c)   To veto any sale, disposition, lease, or encumbrance of tribal lands, interests in lands, or other tribal assets of the Tribe;

    (d)   To advise the Secretary of the Interior with regard to all appropriation estimates or Federal projects for the benefit of the Tribe prior to the submission of such estimates to the Bureau of the Budget and to Congress;

    (e)   To pass and enforce ordinances, which shall be subject to the approval of the Secretary of the Interior, providing for the supervision and management of tribal lands, including provisions for assignments of tribal lands to the members;

    (f)   To protect and preserve the property, wildlife, and natural resources of the Tribe;

    (g)   To adopt resolutions regulating the procedures of the Tribal Council itself and of other tribal agencies and tribal officials;

    (h)   To regulate the use and disposition of tribal property and funds.

Section 2. The General Tribal Council may exercise such further powers as may hereafter be delegated to it by the Secretary of the Interior, by any duly authorized official or agency of the State or Federal government, or by members of the Tribe.

Section 3. Reserved Powers. —Any rights and powers heretofore vested in the Catawba Tribe of South Carolina, but not expressly referred to in this constitution, shall not be abridged by this Article, but may be exercised by the people of the Tribe through the adoption of appropriate bylaws and constitutional amendments.

Article V—Vacancies and Removal
Section 1. In case of a vacancy of any office caused by death, resignation, permanent removal from the State, or expulsion from office, such vacancy shall be filled at the next council meeting of the Tribe.

Section 2. In case of misconduct, immorality, or neglect of duty by any tribal officer, 35 members of the Tribe may, by written petition, prefer charges against any such official at a regular or special meeting of the General Tribal Council. The accused shall be notified in advance of such meeting of the charges and shall have an opportunity to defend himself at such meeting. A two-thirds (2/3) vote of those present shall be necessary to remove an official from office.

Article VI—Amendments
Amendments to this constitution and by-laws may be proposed by a majority vote of the Catawba General Tribal Council and may be ratified and approved in the same manner as this constitution and by-laws.

BY-LAWS OF THE CATAWBA INDIAN TRIBE OF SOUTH CAROLINA

Article I—Duties of Officers
Section 1. The duties of officers of the General Tribal Council shall be as follows:

(a) The Chief of the Tribe shall preside at all meetings of the General Tribal Council. He shall also be the presiding officer at any public meeting which may be duly called in accordance with this constitution. He shall at all times have general supervision of the affairs of the Tribal Council and Executive Committee and such matters as naturally pertain to the general welfare of the community. It shall also be the duty of the Chief to countersign all checks drawn against any funds of the organization by the Treasurer.

(b) The Assistant Chief in the absence of the Chief shall preside at all meetings of the General Tribal Council and shall act in his stead in all matters pertaining to the office of Chief.

(c) The Secretary-Treasurer of the General Tribal Council shall conduct all the Tribal correspondence and shall keep an accurate record of all matters transacted at General Tribal Council meetings and Executive Committee meetings. It shall be his duty to send promptly to the Superintendent of the jurisdiction and the Commissioner of Indian Affairs copies of all minutes of regular and special meetings of the General Tribal Council and the Executive Committee.

He shall accept, receive, receipt for, preserve and safeguard all tribal funds or special funds for which the Council is acting as trustee or custodian. He shall deposit all funds in such depository as the Council shall direct and shall make and preserve a faithful record of such funds, and shall record all receipts and expenditures and the amount and nature of all funds in his possession and custody at each regular meeting of the General Council. An audit of accounts shall be made once a year and at such time as the General Tribal Council or Commissioner of Indian Affairs may require. He shall not pay out or otherwise disburse any funds in his possession or custody except in accordance with a resolution duly passed by the General Tribal Council. He shall be required to give a bond satisfactory to the General Tribal Council and to the Commissioner of Indian Affairs whenever in the opinion of the General Tribal Council or the Commissioner of Indian Affairs sufficient funds have accumulated in the tribal treasury to justify the need for such bond.

Section 2. The duties of all officials of the General Tribal Council and the Executive Committee shall be clearly set forth by resolution of the General Tribal Council at the time of their creation and appointment. Such officers and committees shall report to the General Tribal Council from time to time as required.

Section 3. The Executive Committee. – It shall be the duty of the Executive Committee, established pursuant to Section 3, Article III of this constitution, to act on behalf of the General Tribal Council at such times as said Council is not in session and to have charge of all routine matters which shall arise during such recess, including the administration of ordinances concerning lands under this constitution and such other matters as may be delegated to it by the General Tribal Council. It shall designate the time and place of its meetings and it shall determine the rules of its proceedings and keep a journal thereof, which shall be open to members of the Tribe at all reasonable hours. The Executive Committee shall make a report at each regular and special session of the Council.

Article II—Adoption

This constitution and by-laws, when adopted by a majority vote of the voters of the Catawba Tribe of South Carolina, voting at a special election called by the Secretary of the Interior, in which at least 30% of those entitled to vote shall vote, shall be submitted to the Secretary of the Interior for his approval, and shall be in force from the date of such approval.

Certification of Adoption

Pursuant to an order, approved April 13, 1944, by the Assistant Secretary of the Interior, the attached constitution and by-laws was submitted for ratification to the members of the Catawba Indian Tribe of South Carolina and was on May 20, 1944, duly ratified by a vote of 54 for and 0 against, in an election in which at least 30 per cent of those entitled to vote cast their ballots, in accordance with Section 16 of the Indian Reorganization Act of June 18, 1934 (48 Stat. 984), as amended by the act of June 15, 1935 (49 Stat. 378).

Albert Sanders

Roy Brown

Nelson Blue

C. M. Blair,

Superintendent, Cherokee Indian Agency.

I, Oscar L. Chapman, the Assistant Secretary of the Interior of the United States of America, by virtue of the authority granted me by the act of June 18, 1934 (48 Stat. 984), as amended, do hereby approve the attached constitution and bylaws of the Catawba Indian Tribe of South Carolina.

All rules and regulations heretofore promulgated by the Interior Department or by the Office of Indian Affairs, so far as they may be incompatible with any of the provisions of the said constitution and by-laws are hereby declared inapplicable to the members of the Catawba Indian Tribe of South Carolina.

All officers and employees of the Interior Department are ordered to abide by the provisions of the said constitution and by-laws.

Approval recommended:

William Zimmerman, Jr.,

Assistant Commissioner of Indian Affairs.

Oscar L. Chapman

Assistant Secretary of the Interior

Washington, D.C., June 30, 1944.

APPENDIX C

Constitution and By-Laws of the Catawba Indian Nation of South Carolina

Approved August 30, 1975

Preamble

We, the members of the Catawba Indian Nation of South Carolina, in order to set up an effective tribal organization, to improve our social and economic welfare, and to secure to ourselves and our posterity the benefits of organization, do hereby establish and ordain this constitution and by-laws for the Catawba Indian Nation.

Article I—Territory

The jurisdiction of the Catawba Nation shall extend to the land within the boundaries of the present Indian reservation in South Carolina, and to such other lands as may hereafter be acquired for the mutual benefit of its members.

Article II—Membership

Section 1. The membership of the Catawba Nation of South Carolina shall consist of:

(a) All persons of Indian blood whose names appear on the tribal roll of July 1, 1943, as recognized by the State of South Carolina, and all those whose names appear on the February 7, 1962, final roll as recognized by the Bureau of Indian Affairs and the U. S. Department of Interior.

(b) All children of blood descended born to any enrolled member of the Catawba Nation.

Section 2. The General Council, hereinafter provided for, shall have the power to pass ordinances, covering future membership, subject to approval of the State of South Carolina.

Article III—Governing Body

Section 1. The governing body of the Catawba Nation of South Carolina shall be the General Council which shall be composed of all qualified voters of the Catawba Nation.

Section 2. All enrolled members of the Catawba Nation, male and female, who are 18 years of age or over shall be qualified voters at any tribal meeting.

Section 3. The General Council, by secret ballot, shall elect from its own members (a) a Chief, (b) an Assistant Chief, (c) a Secretary Treasurer, and (d) two Committee men who shall ex officio, serve as the Executive Committee of the Nation, as provided in Section 5 of this Article and Section 3, Article I of the by-laws.

Section 4. The General Council shall meet on the first Saturday of January and the first Saturday of July each year. Within 30 days after the ratification and approval of this constitution and by-laws, a General Council of the Nation shall be called by the present chief for the purpose of electing the officers named herein, and it shall transact such other business as may be necessary. The officers elected at this meeting shall thereupon take office and serve until the _____ meeting, at which time their successors shall be chosen. Thereafter, officials shall be chosen at the July meeting of every four years. The Chief or 15 per cent of the qualified voters of the Nation, by written notice may call special meetings of the General Council. Eighty-six qualified voters of the Nation shall constitute a quorum at any special or regular meeting.

Section 5. There shall be an Executive Committee consisting of the Chief, Assistant Chief, Secretary-Treasurer, and the two Committeemen provided for in Section 3 of this Article, which Committee shall perform such duties as may from time to time be conferred on it by the General Council.

Article IV—Powers of the General Council
Section 1. The General Council of the Catawba Nation shall exercise the following powers, subject to any limitations imposed by this constitution and the statutes of the Constitution of the United States:

(a) To negotiate with Federal, State, and local governments;
(b) To employ legal counsel, the choice of counsel and fixing of fees;
(c) To veto any sale, disposition, lease, or encumbrance of Catawba lands, interests in lands, or other Catawba assets of the Nation;
(d) To pass and enforce ordinances providing for the supervision and management of Catawba land, including provisions for assignments of Catawba lands to the members;
(e) To protect and preserve the property, wildlife, and natural resources of the Nation;
(f) To adopt resolutions regulating the procedures of the General Council inself and of other Catawba agencies and Catawba officials;
(g) To regulate the use and disposition of Catawba property and funds.

Section 2. [This section was omitted in 1975 because the tribe at that time had no legal contact with South Carolina or the United States. The section was not necessary.]

Section 3. Reserved Powers—Any rights and powers heretofore vested in the Catawba Nation of South Carolina, but not expressly referred to in this constitution, shall not be abridged by this Article, but may be exercised by the people of the Nation through the adoption of appropriate by-laws and constitutional amendments.

Article V—Vacancies and Removal

Section 1. In case of a vacancy of any office caused by death, resignation, permanent removal from the State, or expulsion from office, such vacancy shall be filled at the next General Council meeting of the Nation, or by special meeting called by Executive Committee.

Section 2. In case of misconduct, immorality, or neglect of duty by any tribal officer, eight per cent of members of the Tribe may, by written petition, prefer charges against any such official at a regular or special meeting of the General Council. The accused shall be notified in advance of such meeting of the charges and shall have an opportunity to defend himself at such meetings. A majority vote of all eligible voters shall be necessary to remove an official from office.

Article VI—Laws Enforced By Executive Committee

1. The General Council resolves that the existing reservation cannot be reduced in size or terminated.
2. The General Council resolves that Catawba General Council and Executive Committee Record is the property of the General Council and not of any member or officer.
3. The General Council resolves that residences placed on Catawba property must be at least 300 yards from other residences not separated by roads, and does not effect the existing residences.
4. The General Council resolves that non-Indian spouses of deceased or divorced Catawbas who do not have children may not reside on the reservation longer than six months and may be compensated for water systems or residences left as incurred costs to that spouse and the deceased.
5. The General Council resolves that residents of and visitors to the Catawba Reservation are subject to the constitution, by-laws and resolutions of the Catawba Nation. Authority of enforcement is vested in the Executive Committee.

6. The General Council resolves that applications have to be presented to the Executive Committee and approved before new home sites and facilities can be claimed and utilized on the reservation. Such residences <u>must</u> be registered to enrolled members.

7. The General Council resolves that reservation property can only be claimed and utilized by application for one year, home and small acreage, approved by the Executive Committee.

8. The General Council resolves that members claiming Reservation property must furnish proof of that property utilized on a regular approval basis or the control of that property reverts back to the control and supervision of the Executive Committee.

9. The General Council resolves the authority to Executive Committee to developing and controls of new residences on the reservation in compliance to existing laws.

BY-LAWS OF THE CATAWBA INDIAN NATION OF SOUTH CAROLINA

Article I—Duties of Officers

Section 1. The duties of officers of the General Council shall be as follows:

(a) The Chief of the Nation shall preside at all meetings of the General Council. He shall also be the presiding officer at any public meeting which shall be only called in accordance with this constitution. He shall at all times have general supervision of the affairs of the General Council and Executive Committee and such matters as naturally pertain to the general welfare of the community. It shall also be the duty of the Chief to countersign all checks drawn against any funds of the organization by the Treasurer.

(b) The Assistant Chief in the absence of the Chief shall preside at all meetings of the General Council and shall act in his stead in all matters pertaining to the office of Chief.

(c) The Secretary-Treasurer of the General Council shall conduct all the Nation correspondence and shall keep an accurate record of all matters transacted at General Council meetings and Executive Committee meetings.

He shall accept, receive, receipt for, preserve and safeguard all tribal funds or special funds for which the Council is acting as trustee or custodian. He shall deposit all funds in such depository as the Council shall direct and shall make and preserve a faithful record of such funds, and shall record all receipts and expenditures and the amount and nature of all funds in his possession and custody at each regular meeting of the General Council. An audit of accounts shall be made once a year and at such time as the General Council may require. He shall not pay out or otherwise disburse any funds in his possession or custody except in accordance with a resolution duly passed by the General Council. He shall be required to give sufficient bond satisfactory to the Tribal Council.

Section 2. The duties of all officials of the Tribal Council and the Executive Committee shall be clearly set forth by resolution of the Tribal Council at the time of their creation and appointment. Such officers and committees shall report to the General Tribal Council from time to time, as required.

Section 3. The Executive Committee—It shall be the duty of the Executive Committee, established pursuant to Section 3, Article III of this Constitution, to act on behalf of the General Tribal Council at such times as said Council is not in possession and to have charge of all routine matters which shall arise during such recess, including the administration of ordinances concerning lands under this constitution and such other matters as may be delegated to it by the General Council. It shall designate the time and place of its meetings and it shall determine the rules of its proceedings and keep a journal thereof, which shall be open to members of the nation at all reasonable hours. The Executive Committee shall make a report at each regular and special session of the Council.

Article II—Adoption

This constitution and by-laws, when adopted by a majority vote of the voters of the Catawba Nation of South Carolina, voting at a special election called by Elected Chief, in which at least 15 per cent of those entitled to vote shall vote, and shall be in force from the date of such approval by a majority vote.

CERTIFICATE OF ADOPTION

Pursuant to an order approved August 30, 1975, by the Tribal Council, the attached constitution and by-laws was submitted for ratification to the members of the Catawba Nation of South Carolina and was duly ratified by a vote of 48 for and 0 against, in an election in which at least [15] per cent of those entitled to vote cast their ballots in accordance with Section 1b of the Indian Reorganization Act of June 18, 1934 (48 Stat. 984) as amended by the act of June 15, 1935 (49 Stat. 378).

Names of the Executive Officers

Gilbert B. Blue, Chief

Samuel Beck, Asst. Chief

Frances Wade, Sec.-Tres.

Carson T. Blue, Committee

Hayward Canty, Committee

NOTES

1 See J. H. Merrill, *The Indians' New World: Catawbas and Their Neighbors from European Contact Through the Era of Removal* (Chapel Hill: University of North Carolina Press, 1989). The authors wish to thank Judy Leaming Sanders for collaborating on an earlier unpublished version of this essay and for her comments on this essay.

2 Thomas Blumer, *Catawba Nation: Treasures in History* (Charleston, SC: The History Press, 2007), 36–64.

3 Douglas Summers Brown, *The Catawba Indians: People of the River* (Columbia: University of South Carolina Press, 1966), 226–27.

4 Thomas J. Blumer, *Catawba Indian Pottery: Survival of a Folk Tradition*, Tuscaloosa: University of Alabama Press, 2004.

5 John Lawson, *A New Voyage to Carolina* (Chapel Hill: The University of North Carolina Press, 1967), 204–5.

6 Lawson, 46.

7 Douglas Summer Brown, *The Catawba Indians: People of the River* (Columbia: University of South Carolina Press, 1966), 226–27.

8 Brown, 240–41.

9 William L. McDowell, Jr., *The Colonial Records of South Carolina, Documents Relating to Indian Affairs, September 20, 1710-August 29, 1718* .(N.p.: South Carolina Department of Archives and History, 1955).

10 Brown, 246–48.

11 See Appendix A and Brown, 254.

12 Brown, 254–56.

13 Brown, 276.

14 See Appendix A and Brown, 314.

15 Thomas J. Blumer, *Bibliography of the Catawba* (Metuchen, NJ: Scarecrow Press, 1987), entry 1227.

16 Thomas J. Blumer, "Record of the Catawba Indians' Confederate Service," *South Carolina Historical Magazine,* July 1995, 221–29.

17 See Thomas Blumer, *Images of America: The Catawba Indian Nation of the Carolinas* (Charleston, SC: Arcadia Publishing, 2004), 109–15.

18 Lawson, 204–5.

BIBLIOGRAPHY

Blumer, Thomas J. *Bibliography of the Catawba*. Metuchen, NJ: Scarecrow Press, 1987.

————. *Catawba Indian Pottery: Survival of a Folk Tradition*. Tuscaloosa: University of Alabama Press, 2004.

————. *Images of America: The Catawba Indian Nation*. Charleston, SC: Arcadia Publishing, 2004.

————. *Catawba Nation: Treasures in History*. Charleston, SC: The History Press, 2007.

————. "Record of the Catawba Indians' Confederate Service." *South Carolina Historical Magazine* July 1995, 221–29.

Brown, Douglas Summers. *The Catawba Indians: People of the River*. Columbia: University of South Carolina Press, 1966.

Lawson, John. *A New Voyage to Carolina*, edited with an Introduction and Notes by Hugh Talmage Lefler. Chapel Hill: University of North Carolina Press, 1967.

McDowell, Jr., William L. *Colonial Records of South Carolina: Documents Relating to Indian Affairs, September 20, 1710–August 29, 1718*. N.p.: South Carolina Department of Archives and History, 1955.

Merrill, J. H. *The Indians' New World: Catawbas and Their Neighbors from European Contact Through the Era of Removal*. Chapel Hill: University of North Carolina Press, 1989.

6 RECLAIMING HEALTH AS AN ACT OF SELF-DETERMINATION: TOBACCO ADDICTION RESISTANCE

Lawrence Shorty

INTRODUCTION

Yá'át'ééh! Shí éí Lawrence Shorty yinisheyé. Nashashe éí nishłį dóó Mississippi Choctaw báshíshchíín. Áádóó Táachíni éí da shichei dóó Mississippi Choctaw éí da shinálí. Kót'éego éí dine nishlí!

My name is Lawrence Shorty. I am Nashaashe born for the Mississippi Choctaw people. My maternal grandfather is Táachíni i, and my paternal grandfather is Mississippi Choctaw. These things are what make me a man.

My work in health promotion and fighting against Indigenous tobacco addiction is also what makes me a man. The promotion of health asserts our individual and collective self-determination as we exercise our rights to be healthy as Indigenous people. Knowing about my ancestors informs my identity. My identity and ancestry thus shape the relationships I can have. Likewise, my people's ways of addressing illness as much as my knowledge of other medical models continue to form my views of how to promote healthy Indigenous communities.

My essay will focus on the range of tools we have currently available in health promotion and disease prevention. I will offer critical reflections on public health research and the political and economic aspects of American Indian tobacco use. I will argue for the incorporation of Traditional Indigenous Knowledge to render available frameworks culturally inclusive and dynamic.[1] What gives me this right to speak, to write, and to engage in culturally based wellness promotion? From my own Indigenous perspective, being part of the Diné/Navajo/Indian tribal/Indigenous community gives me some rights. Having a deep understanding of the processes that have propelled Indigenous nations into a situation where we suffer the greatest potential for addiction, disease, and death requires that I participate in wellness work. This knowledge endows me with the right and the responsibility to do my work. My desire, too, to be a part of an informed and participatory process of healing gives me the right to do my work. I thus assert that there is an inherent right and responsibility to work for the well-being of my community and to participate in influencing the direction of the tribal leadership that precedes any United States legal basis for tribes and tribal members to be able to assert their will.

OVERVIEW OF UNITED STATES FEDERAL GOVERNMENT FRAMEWORK: INDIAN SELF-DETERMINATION AND EDUCATION ASSISTANCE ACT, PUBLIC LAW 93–638

United States legal frameworks underscore the right of Indian tribes to control how their health needs will be met. In 1975, United States President Nixon signed into law the Indian Self-Determination and Education Assistance Act, Public Law 93–638. It was a reaffirmation of the primacy of the United States of America and Indian Tribal Nations' government to government relationship, a relationship between sovereigns. This Act provided federally recognized Indian Tribes with the opportunity to administer and operate programs and health services to their communities or to remain with the Department of Health and Human Services Indian Health Service, an administered direct care health system. With this affirmation of self-determination, Indian Tribes now had three options for receiving their health care:

- health care directly delivered by the Indian Health Service;
- contracted with the Indian Health Service, yet with the administrative control, operation, and funding for health programs transferred to American Indian and Alaska Native tribal governments;
- health care delivery through compacting with the Indian Health Service with tribes assuming even greater control and autonomy for the provision of their own health care services.[2]

Amendments to the Indian Self-Determination and Educational Assistance Act enabled and strengthened Tribes' abilities for self-governance and health delivery, including the establishment of a permanent Tribal Self-Government Program at the Indian Health Service. According to the Indian Health Service (Web page cited below), a total of seventy-two government-to-government compacts encompassing ninety-three funding agreements have been negotiated. In all, three hundred and twenty-two Indian tribes or 57.4% of all federally recognized tribes are participating in the Tribal Self-Governance Program through the Indian Health Service.

The reasons for tribes to autonomously manage their health concerns are compelling. According to national statistics, American Indian and Alaska Native communities suffer the following health disparities[3]:

- Cardiovascular disease is now the leading cause of mortality among Indian people, with a rising rate that is significantly higher than that of the U.S. general population.

- American Indians and Alaska Natives have the highest prevalence of Type Two diabetes in the world. The incidence of Type Two diabetes is rising faster among American Indians and Alaska Native children and young adults than in any other ethnic population, and is 2.6 times the national average.

- Rates of substance dependence and abuse among persons age twelve and older is highest among American Indians and Alaska Natives (14.1%). Rates of illicit drug use (10.1%), alcohol (44.7%) and binge alcohol use (27.9%) are among the highest in the nation.

- American Indian and Alaska Natives die at higher rates than other Americans from alcoholism (770%), tuberculosis (750%), diabetes (420%), accidents (280%), homicide (210%) and suicide (190%).

- American Indians and Alaska Natives born today have a life expectancy that is almost six years less than the U.S. population (70.6 years to 76.5 years).

- Infants in American Indian and Alaska Native communities die at a rate of eight per every thousand live births, as compared to 7.2 per thousand for the U.S. population.

- Injuries cause 75% of all deaths among American Indians and Alaska Natives age nineteen and younger, and are the leading cause of death for American Indians and Alaska Natives one to forty-four years of age. Deaths from car crashes, pedestrian accidents, fire, and drowning have decreased over the last decade, but the overall death rate from preventable injuries remains nearly twice as high for Native people than it is for the general population.

This list of health disparities indicates the fields in which we must do our work. It requires not only claims for increased health servicing, but the informed and involved action of tribal health leadership to increase prevention policy development on behalf of our community's health. Moreover, the Indigenous public in promoting public health also plays an intricate part. Even so, there is a serious omission to this list. Tobacco use is a major problem in Indigenous communities, especially in the United States.

INDIGENOUS NATIONS, TOBACCO USE, AND UNITED STATES LAW

While working on my advanced degree in Public Health, I sought to describe the politics of American Indian tobacco control within the sphere of tribal sovereignty and associated issues.[4] I was especially curious about the impact of what has come to be known as the Master Settlement Agreement (MSA) and the result of Indian tribal lawsuits against the tobacco industry. The Master Settlement Agreement established procedures for settling lawsuits against tobacco companies between states and United States territories and tobacco manufacturers. It included forty-six states,[5] the United States Virgin Islands, American Samoa, Puerto Rico, the Northern Mariana Islands, Guam, and the District of Columbia.[6] The tobacco manufacturers listed in the agreement include Brown and Williamson Tobacco Corporation, Lorillard Tobacco Company, Philip Morris Incorporated, R. J. Reynolds Tobacco Company, Commonwealth Tobacco, and Liggett and Myers. The total payout to the states and these territories was two hundred and six billion dollars to recover healthcare costs related to smoking. In addition to providing payouts to states, the MSA established prohibitions on advertising targeting youths, a state mechanism for the enforcement of guidelines, and provisions for the establishment of a National Foundation and a Public Education Fund. In addition, the MSA provided guidelines for changing the corporate culture of tobacco manufacturers. It required corporate commitment to reducing youth access and consumption, opening industry records and research to the public, and to restrict industry lobbying.[7]

My research focused on the omission of American Indian health concerns in crafting the settlement agreement. The agreement emerged from a failed national tobacco legislation proposal to recover the costs of treating illnesses associated with tobacco product usage. This legislation would have included Indian tribes. Tribal leadership and American Indian issue opinion leaders provided testimony to guide the proposed national legislation. In contrast to the failed proposal, the state attorney generals and tobacco manufacturers did not include Indian tribal testimony or input in the MSA negotiations.

During the national tobacco legislation discussions, some Indian tribes recognized the harm caused by tobacco on their peoples' health and began to file lawsuits. The year 1997 marked the first lawsuits brought forth by Indian tribes against the tobacco industry. The Muscogee Nation in Oklahoma, the Lower Brule Lakota in South Dakota, the Crow in Montana, and the Chehalis in Washington filed lawsuits against tobacco companies. They asserted that the tobacco companies manufactured an addictive, defective, and dangerous product and marketed the product on their reservations. The lawsuits sought the following:

- Compensation for treating tobacco related disease
- Cessation of tobacco companies marketing to youths
- The funding and implementation of anti-smoking education programs
- The funding of an educational campaign on reservations about the health hazards of smoking.[8]

Other tribes filed lawsuits when a review of the Master Settlement Agreement revealed that Indian tribes were excluded from the settlement. The omission was argued along the lines of both state sovereignty and Indigenous sovereignty. This may be one of the few times that states acknowledged Indian tribes' sovereignty. State attorney generals and attorneys for the tobacco companies negotiated the MSA, with state attorney generals asserting that they could not negotiate on behalf of Indian tribes. They argued that negotiation on behalf of Indian tribes would constitute a violation of tribal sovereignty. It was their position that the MSA was worded such that it did not exclude tribes from filing their own claims against the tobacco companies. Section XII (6) of the MSA document stated that it did not "purport to waive or release any claims on behalf of Indian Tribes."[9]

Subsequently, two major lawsuits representing fifty-four tribes were filed against the tobacco industry. The first lawsuit, entered in Albuquerque, New Mexico, on 17 June 1999, sought compensation from tobacco companies to repay the costs of treating tobacco related illnesses for thirty-four Indian tribes.[10] This lawsuit alleged that five and a half billion dollars had been spent on Indian health care since 1962. It sought reimbursement and punitive damages for "fraud, intentional and negligent misrepresentation, negligence, civil conspiracy and prima facie tort" and also accused the defendants of manufacturing and marketing 'unreasonably dangerous products'" to tribal members and "of concealing and misrepresenting the dangerous nature of these products." The lawsuit was dismissed. The court agreed with the defendants, the tobacco manufacturers, that tribes had no right to recover the monies spent on Indian health care, because they were federal funds, and that tribes could not recoup money on behalf of individual members.[11] This decision was in keeping with previous federal rulings that dismissed attempts by organizations to sue on behalf of their members for tobacco related diseases.[12]

The second lawsuit, filed in San Francisco, California, on June 3, 1999, alleged that tobacco companies, in addition to creating a public health problem, had specifically "targeted Native Americans," which contributed to the current high tobacco use rates. According to the lawsuit, tobacco companies that provided incentives to tribes to establish smoke shops on reservations targeted Native Americans. Native American youths were targeted by tobacco advertising that featured Indian images and symbols. A major argument of this lawsuit highlighted the fact that American Indian population numbers had been used in the forty-six state MSA settlements, all derived from the U.S. Census, to determine the amount of MSA compensation to states, but that Indian tribes had no mechanism to receive MSA money. This omission was a violation of tribal sovereignty.[13]

INDIGENOUS NATIONS, TOBACCO USE, AND THE INDIAN HEALTH SERVICE

Until 1997, tobacco had not been identified as a priority issue by tribal governments or national American Indian leaders.[14] Reasons for this lack of prioritization are manifold. Economic issues include tribal reliance on tobacco smoke shop sales, a lack of infrastructure and leadership for tobacco control, and a lack of resources for culturally appropriate tobacco research and public health education. Cultural issues range from the ceremonial use of tobacco to the targeting of American Indians by the tobacco industry as barriers to tribal participation in the emerging tobacco control movement.[15] In terms of pressing health and political issues, tribal governments instead focused on American Indian mortality due to alcoholism, accidents, suicide, homicide, and challenges to tribal sovereignty.[16] Tribal governmental choices of health priorities reflect the data provided by the Indian Health Service (IHS). IHS has identified the three leading causes of death for American Indians and Alaska Natives ages five to fourteen to be accidents, homicide, and suicide. For ages fifteen to twenty-four, the leading causes of death are identified as accidents, suicide, and homicide. For ages twenty-five to forty-four, the leading causes of death are determined to be accidents, chronic liver disease and cirrhosis, and suicide.[17] Through the Indian Health Service (IHS) data and its tribal consultation mechanisms, tribal leaders learn to identify health priorities such as diabetes, unintentional injuries, alcoholism, and substance abuse as health priorities (Indian Health Service, 2003). Alcoholism and its contribution to accidents were issues that could be more easily identified and that had greater, more public visibility than the detrimental consequences of tobacco addiction. These health priorities have been characterized as being at "crisis levels" and as being "unacceptable" to tribal leaders.

Limited funding for tribal health care issues has added to the pressure to prioritize health crisis responses. For example, half of the IHS system is provided less than sixty percent of the funding needed to approach mainstream funding levels for similar non-Indian programs. Due to budget shortcomings, contracted services not provided by IHS are available only for the most severe cases. To lessen these disparities, tribal leaders continually seek a federal health budgetary increase.[18]

For American Indian and Alaska Native organizations as well as for states, tobacco control thus is a relatively new challenge. However, there are important differences between states and Indian tribes for moving tobacco control to the top of their political and social agenda. Unlike participating states, there has been no mechanism for Indian tribes to be included in settlements between tobacco manufacturers and states. Given their size, tribes do not have the incentive that comes with multimillion dollar settlements to participate in emerging tobacco control activities. Furthermore,

Indian tribes may not have been well informed on legislative affairs by legal organizations that represent them collectively, or by national organizations such as IHS that could focus specifically on tobacco control activities for American Indians and Alaska Natives. For all these reasons, it is important to utilize a multidisciplinary framework that is capable of identifying and explaining the cultural, economic, and social politics associated with the public discourse of tobacco addiction. The following section offers a brief overview of these three dimensions.

CONTEMPORARY AMERICAN INDIAN TOBACCO CULTURE, TRIBAL SOVEREIGNTY, AND ECONOMIC DEVELOPMENT

Tobacco's role in Indigenous culture ranges from ceremonial tobacco use to habitual and addictive tobacco use to its status as an important supplement for tribal economies. American Indian and Alaska Native adults and youths smoke at higher rates than other populations. Tobacco sales provide necessary funding for tribal programs.[19] In addition to tobacco's historical role in religious and ceremonial activities and its use for medicinal purposes in many Indian tribes' pharmacopoeia, other cultural aspects affect Indigenous behavior with respect to tobacco use. For example, American Indian values include behavior that encourages group harmony and non-interference and an ethic that nurtures a sense of tribal belonging and the respect for the rights of individuals. One researcher thus concluded on the use of cigarettes that "American Indians are not disposed to interfere with the behavior of fellow Indians even when that behavior is self-destructive or causes inconvenience or harm to others" and that

> a study among Northern California Indians found that although awareness was high regarding the harmful effects of tobacco, this knowledge had little impact on attitudes and smoking behavior. Over ninety percent of the Indians sampled knew that smoking harms pregnant women and their fetuses, and yet, over fifty percent were reluctant to interfere with smokers even in the presence of a pregnant woman.[20]

Having one's peers, friends, siblings, and family smoke is a significant predictor for smoking initiation among American Indian and Alaska Native teenagers. Research indicates that reasons to smoke were to alter one's mood, "to get a buzz," to "get mellow," and to feel good to avoid sadness. Other reasons include image enhancement and addiction.[21] Teens shared that siblings and extended family members such as uncles and cousins were instigators and accomplices for their smoking.

On the political level, the importance of tribal sovereignty and the acknowledgment of the potential effect of state tobacco control legislation on tribes are fairly obvious. The issue is mentioned in American Indian and Alaska Native tobacco control materials as a topic that requires careful consideration, especially in conjunction with traditional spiritual practices. For example, the Independent Task Force on Advancing Parity and Leadership for Priority Populations writes that "it is vital to address tobacco issues, including the traditional, ceremonial use of tobacco, in our native communities across the United States within the context of respecting the sovereign status of American Indian/Alaska Native tribes and villages, since Native Americans have a higher prevalence of tobacco use than any other group."[22] This statement and similar others identify a threefold basis for engaging in Indigenous tobacco control work: sovereignty, health, and spirituality. Slogans that guide work with American Indians and Alaska Natives include "Keep Tobacco Sacred," "Tobacco: Use It in a Sacred Way,"[23] "Many Voices One Message: Keep Tobacco Sacred."[24] The rhetorical strategy implicit in the slogans is to create a distinction between "commercial tobacco" and "traditional/ceremonial tobacco" and to work against "commercial tobacco." Respect for tribal sovereignty complements an emphasis on spirituality.[25]

Economic development is defined as a function of tribal self-determination.[26] A contemporary example of the nexus between tribal self-determination and economic development are smoke-shop ventures. Fuel and tobacco product sales by tribes create an advantage because these products are not subject to state excise taxes.[27]

The link between tobacco use and tribal sovereignty is riddled with difficulties. According to tribes, economic ventures such as smoke shops and other economic development activities, including Internet tobacco sales, were and are necessary. Indian tobacco control advocates, individual Indian entrepreneurs, and American Indian business and economic development organizations agree. Tobacco commerce seems to offset decades of fiscal shortage, poor health (diabetes being paramount), extremely high accidental death rate, failed termination and assimilation policies, few local economic opportunities, and weak tribal governments.[28] Donations from entrepreneurial Indian tobacco marketers to the needy and the revenue from tribal Internet sites to support underfunded local programs may also contribute to positive perspectives on tobacco commerce. This evocation of economic and social development via tobacco's commercial potential may explain a barrier to participation in tobacco control activities by many American Indian communities.[29] For example, Omaha tribal chairman Gary Lasley presented testimony in a 1998 U.S. Senate Hearing to address his Indian tribe's role as a sovereign tribal government and as a cigarette manufacturer. His statement creates a symbolic link, past and present, between tobacco, economics, sanctity, and sovereignty.

> Before the Omaha Tribe even signed treaties with the United States, the Tribe cultivated and
> manufactured tobacco for trade and cultural use. That tobacco was used in a reverent and sa-

cred manner by the Tribe, and used by the Omaha Tribe when signing our Treaty with the United States. Today, the Omaha Tribe operates an ATF licensed cigarette manufacturing plant located on land in Nebraska held in trust by the United States for the benefit of the Tribe within the exterior boundaries of the Omaha Indian Reservation.[30]

Many tribes sell tax free cigarettes to address the need for economic development.[31] From another point of view, however, tax-free cigarettes sales are also described as a form of tax evasion.[32] One study concluded that states lost over two hundred million dollars from tax evasion activities in 2003, such as purchasing cigarettes from Internet vendors, and estimated that this number would increase. Unfortunately, this type of information may create a tendency of holding Indian tribes and Indian people responsible for state budgetary shortcomings and for the existence of non-Indian tobacco-related illness, disease, and death.

As tribes try to navigate between the pressing economic needs and the tremendous burden of tobacco related health concerns, some tobacco control methodologies create additional challenges. On the one hand, there are tobacco control/anti-tobacco advocates who attempt to influence state and federal legislation, challenge existing laws in state and federal courts, and use media advocacy to create a tobacco free world. On the other hand, we find Indian tribes interested in increasing economic development and preserving and expanding tribal sovereignty by using tobacco as a tool. From the onset, there are competing agendas. Threats to tribal sovereignty come from Congress, states, courts, the public, and the media, the very same arenas with which tobacco control works to create policy change.[33] Any of these challenges can be characterized as "anti-Indian." Implicitly, control over tobacco may be viewed as control over all things related to tobacco, including Indian tribal interests. For example, control over tobacco may constitute control over economic development because smoke shops were some of the earliest and "traditional" economic ventures for some tribes.[34] Tobacco control may also mean control over tribal sovereignty, particularly if federal legislation were to impose increased taxation. This policy change would leave tribes unable to seek a jurisdictional remedy, because Congress has plenary power over Indian tribes.[35] Tobacco control may also usher in a renewed threat to Indian religious practices for Indian tribes that use tobacco products ceremonially.[36]

If these topics comprise the agenda for American Indian tribes and the American Indian public, use of a strict tobacco control methodology may contribute to agenda competition that will permit the perpetuation of high tobacco use rates and resultant disease because energies will focus on the agenda's conflicts and not on creating change to reduce tobacco use rates.

CURRENT AMERICAN INDIAN TOBACCO CONTROL PRACTICES

Given the complexities of the tobacco issues as outlined above, current acceptable characterizations and methodologies to address the "tobacco problem" may not be able to create the necessary change to reduce tobacco use rates and the resultant disease and death. As identified earlier in this essay, slogans that guide work with American Indians and Alaska Natives include "Keep Tobacco Sacred," "Tobacco: Use It in a Sacred Way," and "Many Voices One Message: Keep Tobacco Sacred." The primary focus is to inform the individual through education. To be culturally specific, a distinction is made between "commercial tobacco" and "traditional/ceremonial tobacco." Policy development is encouraged with an emphasis on addressing tribal leadership to make the changes once key leaders have reviewed and provided input on the proposal. Any resultant tribal tobacco resolutions or policies (or lack thereof) are considered "culturally appropriate" and an expression of tribal sovereignty. Respecting tribal sovereignty is the most important principle in working with American Indians and Alaska Natives on tobacco control.

The current approach, however, suffers from serious limitations. It advocates a low level of action. It does not encourage the formation of independent groups to demand environmental change. Some of its methods are not open to debate or criticism. For an example, consider the slogan of "Keep Tobacco Sacred." This is a message for American Indians that is not controversial and that can easily be agreed upon by most as an important message. Even so, it is also an ambiguous message. It may mean that "traditional" usage of tobacco is important and that knowing how tobacco is used "traditionally" will reduce the likelihood a person will use it inappropriately or "commercially." It may mean that a person does not need to act unless another person is doing something that makes tobacco not be sacred. As an action message, it thus suffers from a lack of specificity to how one can keep tobacco sacred. An Indian person can keep tobacco sacred by doing nothing. As a result, the public may not be encouraged to participate and to create change. Of course, doing nothing helps the perpetuation of high tobacco use rates and resultant disease and death. "Keep Tobacco Sacred" is also a message that can be easily subverted by smokers who can justify their smoking as being ceremonially related, thus complicating American Indian tobacco control practice. Similarly, it is a message that the tobacco industry would promote.

Another tactic is to be "against commercial tobacco" because it is important to make a distinction between "commercial tobacco" and "ceremonial tobacco" or "traditional tobacco." Another way may be to describe "commercial tobacco" as being capable of causing disease and death. This distinction appears to enable tobacco control initiatives to focus on "commercial tobacco" and simultaneously to respect the way tobacco is used for ceremonial purposes and thus not to offend ceremonial tobacco users and ceremonial leaders. Some American Indian advocates have spoken out against how sacred medicines, such as sweet grass, sage, and tobacco have been commercialized. However, this tactic has neither developed into greater action to focus on how Indian tribes and American Indians have contributed to the commercialization of tobacco nor has this strategy been conducive to helping tobacco control leadership in the dissemination of information that American Indian tobacco marketers do the majority of tobacco marketing by using American Indian symbols. In addition, this strategy has not focused on reducing the exposure to "commercial tobacco" from Indian tribal tobacco smoke shops and/or Internet tobacco vendors. An example of this oversight is seen in a poster developed by the California Rural Indian Health Board and the California Department of Health. The poster shows the stereotypes of "the Indian" used by tobacco manufacturers and marketers. The main message for this poster is "Don't Buy the Stereotype." Some products represented are *Red Man*, *Geronimo*, and Santa Fe Natural Tobacco's *American Spirit*. None of these products that utilize these stereotypes are from American Indian manufacturers.

Further, the message of "respecting tribal sovereignty" or those attributes that enhance sovereignty, such as the sale of tobacco products by Indian/tribally owned smoke shops and Internet vendors, act as barriers to limit criticism of "commercial tobacco" and the role that American Indian culture contributes to the perpetuation of its use.

Finally, there has been reluctance to acknowledge that in identifying the importance of making the distinction between "commercial tobacco" and "ceremonial tobacco" or "traditional tobacco" that in many instances "commercial tobacco" is the "ceremonial tobacco," or rather, that it is the tobacco used for ceremonial purposes. Paradoxically, there is also an insistence that the terms "commercial tobacco" be used to describe the "harmful" tobacco. Therefore, there is a reluctance to discuss critically how the "commercial tobacco" or manufactured tobacco came to be the "ceremonial tobacco" replacing the many Nicotiana species or other botanicals originally used by Indians who had a religious smoking tradition.

First of all, not only do American Indians have limited discursive and action tools for tobacco control practice, but these tools are also perfectly suited for subversion by smokers and tobacco marketers. Again, a smoker can justify smoking as being religious in context. Second, a smoker could justify smoking as being supportive of tribal sovereignty and against tobacco control activities that have worked against tribal economic development and sovereignty interests.[37]

American Indian tobacco control programs should take care that they are not providing the savvy smoker with the information as to how to invoke the holy trinity

of Indian issues to justify and protect their right to smoke: religious freedom, economic development, and tribal sovereignty.

RECOMMENDATIONS FOR PRACTICE: THE CONCEPT OF TOBACCO ADDICTION AND TOBACCO AS KILLER OF INDIAN PEOPLE

If the acceptable methods for American Indian tobacco control enable the perpetuation of an Indigenous community's high tobacco use rates and create a perceived
agenda conflict with tobacco control advocates, an effort needs to be made to identify
the intersection of agendas by the public, Indian opinion leaders concerned about
Indigenous health, and public health and tobacco control practitioners. The following
section presents new tools and descriptions of the process used in their development.

To resolve the difficulties in implementing activities based on the identification of
the problem (the concept of "commercial tobacco") and the guidelines established by
mainstream "tobacco control" activities, we must create, repeat, and disseminate
characterizations that have meaning and enable community based action within
American Indian/Alaska Native communities. My recommendation is to identify the
problem as "tobacco addiction" or "nicotine addiction" and to clearly describe its impact on American Indians and Alaska Natives. While the notion of tobacco and nicotine addiction is not new and is frequently used in descriptions of prevention and
cessation materials and in pharmacologic research, these terms, until now, have not
found favor and have not been used to create a rallying cry for Indigenous populations. Notions of substance abuse and addiction already exist in American Indian and
Alaska Native communities. Alcohol addiction is a well-established priority. Sobriety
and wellness activities are available for those afflicted by alcohol addiction. Models to
address addiction and to identify the causes and perpetuation of addiction are available.

The emphasis on tobacco or nicotine addiction constitutes an extension of these
models. A thorough multidisciplinary examination of enabling factors, perhaps most
importantly the development of tobacco advertising discourse within United States
history that assisted manufactured tobacco to become "ceremonial tobacco" and the
most widely available tobacco for all populations would help explain the high prevalence rates of commercial tobacco. This would include an examination of the historical development of tobacco products from plant to products designed to increase the
addictive properties of nicotine to create addiction needs. Linkages with better
funded and arguably more influential wellness and sobriety programs can help raise
tobacco addiction to greater priority. "Tobacco abuse," another acceptable term,
should be updated to emphasize that it is manufactured tobacco (formerly "commer-

cial tobacco"), which creates addiction, disease, and death. Repeated and consistent exposure to "manufactured tobacco" creates and perpetuates tobacco or nicotine addiction within American Indian and Alaska Native communities. Defining the problem as "tobacco addiction" and focusing on cessation (quitting smoking) can be a way to allay fears that "tobacco control" movements exist to control Indians and are, by association, anti-Indian/anti-Indian religious/anti-Indian sovereignty. Questions from the American Indian public about whether activities will inform Indians that their religious practices are "bad" can be addressed by identifying Indigenous wellness resources for individuals who want to quit their tobacco addiction. The goal of smoking cessation can be used to increase the individual's locus of control. This approach is in keeping with American Indian tobacco control leadership opinion that American Indians do not want to infringe on the rights of others who want to smoke.[38] Additionally, identifying the problem as "tobacco addiction" provides needed clarity in American Indian tobacco control that has encumbered itself with terms that are not compatible with mainstream terms and may further give the impression that this programming is deficient.[39]

The author has also created a Diné (Navajo) specific example of focusing on tobacco addiction through visual art. I have always been intrigued by the representation of "the Indian" in tobacco marketing. Typically, the image of "the Indian" with tobacco products is one that is solemn, peaceful. In representations of Indian ceremonialism, artists create images of Indian people making offerings with a "sacred pipe" holding it with reverence before them. Tobacco marketers have also used these types of images of "the Indian" to promote their products. You may have an image in your mind as you read these descriptions. The art that I have created developed in response to these representations. These stereotypes have been used to flaunt tobacco companies' products and their use in the colonization and subjugation of Indigenous peoples. My counterimage is part of a prevention message in a poster format. There is a picture of me holding a cigarette in my outstretched hand looking dead into the camera with a serious look that accompanies the following message:

> This is a Diné Killer. This is Bíligáana bi' nát'oh—White Man's Smoke or Commercial Tobacco. Cigarettes are designed to create addiction in its user. Tobacco addiction is imprisonment. Our rates of using White Man's Smoke are growing, making our people addicted. This addiction helps cancer, diabetes, heart disease, and stroke to kill Diné. We must fight. Create and enforce a Bíligáana bi' nát'oh smoke free policy.

I have created similar messages with Maori and with other Indigenous people from Hawai'i and the continental United States, tailored from their experiences, and employing salient topics that appeal to their activism for protecting themselves, their families, and their nations. These messages include statements about how tobacco was used against their people in power and treaty negotiations,[40] about how their words for sacred beings were used for products designed to create addiction, and how tobacco was used as a tool to make communities addicted so that their work and property could be exploited through colonial processes. In each instance, my collaborators were willing to say "this product is a killer of the people to whom I belong."

Using the word "this" operates as an opportunity for people to craft their own definition of what this word represents. For some, it may be that they are able to say "commercial tobacco." Others may take a more policy specific approach and identify the product in the way the United States Department of Alcohol Tobacco and Firearms does in regard to "manufactured tobacco." Some may be able to speak their Indigenous language as I have and say that "this" represents "Bíligáana bi' nát'oh" or white man's smoke. Finally, some may be able to say simply, "tobacco." In my opinion and with the tools I utilize, these definitions are synonymous and may provide an important opportunity for tribes and individuals to express more fully and with a broad range of input their self-determination and sovereignty over their health and wellness. At the very least, they are an American Indian tobacco use prevention message that will not be mistaken by anyone as a message from the tobacco industry.

My next example works with a story of an Indigenous tobacco addiction resistance leader and with the fact that the year 2007 marked the 400th anniversary of the settlement of Jamestown in Virginia. I offer this story as a way to demonstrate how Indigenous people can take descriptions and definitions from mainstream initiatives and indigenize them on behalf of their community. The American Indian fight against tobacco addiction began in the early seventeenth century with Powhatan, father of Pocahontas. He was the first to recognize that tobacco—and the desire to grow more of it in response to increasing European consumption—would create great problems for his people. Powhatan's daughter, Pocahontas, wed John Rolfe, the planter responsible for bringing tobacco to the Virginia colony. Reportedly, Powhatan said, "Is this what you wish? To marry a coat wearing man? One who is stealing our land to plant tobacco on it? Are you sure you are not being tricked?"[41]

Important questions should be asked at this point: How is it possible that an Indian could be against tobacco and the growing of tobacco? How could tobacco create a problem for Indian people when it is so revered? How can it be that tobacco was introduced to Virginia when conventional wisdom claims that tobacco has always been a part of America?

Botanists classify plants that contain nicotine as "true tobacco." In contrast, many people consider any of the plants or mixtures that were used for ceremonial smoking as "tobacco." While this generality works well, it can be sharpened or indigenized as a tool to help in tobacco addiction resistance work.

My recommendation is therefore that the word "tobacco" should only be used when talking about the plant *Nicotiana tabacum*. This is the plant introduced into the Virginia colony by John Rolfe after he had stolen it from the Spanish. Products manufactured from this plant only would form the backbone of the tobacco industry. The people responsible for introducing these products into North American Indigenous societies called their product "tabac," "tabak," "tabaco," and, yes, tobacco. Before Powhatan knew the word "tobacco," however, he and his people reportedly employed the word *uppowomoc* for the plant they used. Botanists assigned the Latin name *Nicotiana rustica* to this plant. By definition and through the model I use, *Nicotiana rustica* is not *Nicotiana tabacum*. Similarly, *uppowomoc* is not "tobacco."

This shift affirms Indigenous wellness and sovereignty through the reminder that Indigenous languages describing plants and herbal mixtures were gifts of their Creator(s). Indigenous names and the knowledge coded in the naming are as strong as the Latin classification system. Indigenous language and plant knowledge can be used to identify what was replaced when *Nicotiana tabacum* was introduced as a trade item into Indigenous communities. This shift in language and knowledge may be a powerful tool against tobacco addiction.[42]

A simple re-contextualization of tobacco history can also be helpful. Navajos and others can view addiction as a type of illness that has the potential to re-establish itself in an individual and a community. In short, an illness never really goes away. In 1612, the English in the Virginia colony grew their first commercial crop of tobacco. British tobacco addiction developed when Virginia colonists discovered that they could profit far greater by being tobacco planters than by being employed in the job they were originally hired to perform in the colony. So great was the response to European tobacco addiction that colonists began to plant tobacco in all areas in Jamestown, including its roads. The demand for tobacco in Britain was so extensive that planters demanded more land, which led to increased tension and war. The pattern of land trade or theft, as some would call it, appears to repeat itself throughout the globe with tobacco being a major trade item, thus making it possible for tobacco addiction to flourish.

Fourth, a global study of the spread of tobacco addiction throughout Indigenous communities is yet another strategy that will help in this fight against oppression through the spread of addictive products. One of the ways I am doing this is to ask people around the world, Indigenous and non-Indigenous, when their ancestors learned the word "tobacco" or one of the other similarly pronounced words. I ask them to describe what the value through time has been for tobacco, in trade and, more recently, in exchange for money. I am interested, too, in how they describe illness and whether not being able to quit the use of tobacco can be considered an illness. I am also curious about how the illness manifests itself in people and in the culture. What is the culture of tobacco use in a given community? How is it maintained? Who promotes its existence? What have been patterns of resistance, if any? How staunch is the resistance? How has tobacco changed the culture? Answers to these questions can help to describe the overall impact of tobacco addiction on a people.

As a commentary on political jargon and the Indigenous experience of colonialism, I organized these considerations into a pedagogical model I have been calling the *Tobacco Addiction Treaty*, the modus operandi for how tobacco addiction operates.

Tobacco Addiction Shall:

Dominate culture, language, leaders, and people.

> *How has tobacco become integral to a culture and the life ways of a people?*
> *Why do we revere the word "tobacco" and tobacco products more than the aboriginal words and the botanicals that tobacco replaced?*
> *How does tobacco addiction affect our people?*

Incorporate sacred symbols and things seen as beautiful.

> *What symbols and symbolic acts do we associate with tobacco?*

Disrupt community economies.

> *In what ways did tobacco help to change our means of making a living?*
> *What role did tobacco among other trade goods help to make fur traders out of some Indian people?*
> *Before we had smoke shops, upon what did we base our economies?*

Change concepts of geography.

> *How have Indigenous people's lands changed as the result of tobacco being used as a trade item?*

Make it impossible for people to speak negatively about tobacco.

> *Why do we revere the word "tobacco" and tobacco products more than the aboriginal words and the botanicals that tobacco replaced?*
> *Why has it been so hard for many American Indians to say anything critical about tobacco?*

Make it impossible for people to create action against tobacco.

> *How has the way tobacco and tobacco addiction embedded itself in our communities that makes it difficult to act against it?*

Make it impossible for people to quit tobacco.

> *How has tobacco been manufactured to enable its addictive properties to work best?*

Create a community tradition where adults reinforce one another and teach children to smoke.

> *Why is it that one can ask any number of children how they would smoke a cigarette, and they can readily show us?*

Create a cycle of oppression that cannot be well described and thus, addressed.

> *How do all of the above contribute to oppression and keep us from articulating action plans?*

The first time I had presented this model, I was challenged to provide proof beyond my own opinion. I had just purchased a cartoon from 1878 that described how

Blackwell's Durham was used to help colonize and subjugate the Indian. In the cartoon, there is a wild, free Indian who is causing trouble where he lives. A tobacco executive, the gentle drummer, reads about the situation in the newspaper and is determined to help. The gentle drummer goes west and is nearly killed by the Indian. The Indian stops his attack when he sees that the tobacco executive is carrying with him Blackwell's Durham product. The Indian says "If that's the stuff you white men smoke, I'll tell you what I'll do. I'll wash the war-paint off my face and be a pale-face too." Then the executive and the Indian smoke for over three days and when all the tobacco has been used, they walk arm in arm toward the tobacco executive's home in the East. Blackwell's Durham tobacco later became known as Bull Durham. Bull Durham was one of the products used as a ceremonial tobacco by my grandfather, a Native American Church practitioner.

This information, coupled with my work on the historical and colonial processes that introduced *Nicotiana tabacum* to Indigenous Peoples made it possible for me to construct and articulate these provocative questions: What if what we embrace is not the gift of our Creator, but a gift of our colonizer? Similarly, what if our Creator is our Colonizer?

In contrast, I also created another treaty. I call it *A Personal Treaty Against Tobacco Addiction*. The treaty text reads as follows:

I will learn the language of resistance.
I will challenge those who create tobacco addiction.
I will fight how tobacco products are marketed to my people.
I will identify and destroy barriers that keep tobacco addiction in my community.
I will help people quit their tobacco addiction.
I will work to create policies to protect my people.
I will teach people what I know.
I will protect my people from this oppression.

CONCLUSION

The fact that Powhatan recognized tobacco addiction's harm to his community makes him the first American tobacco resistance leader. As such, the notion about being against tobacco or tobacco addiction should not be a foreign concept for American Indian and other Indigenous peoples. A multidisciplinary approach to fight against tobacco addiction, incorporating Indigenous languages, tobacco history, and a review of the original plants vis-à-vis *Nicotiana tabacum* can be a powerful tool to help American Indians fight for increased self-determination in the promotion of their community's health and economic freedom.

For future work, it will be important to continue exploring the ways we describe the problem of tobacco addiction in Indigenous communities. By honestly evaluating the contradictory ways we communicate about its harm to our well-being, we will increase our health, protect our sovereignty, and improve our ability to be responsive to the ever changing tactics of the tobacco industry. Doing these things is an act of tobacco addiction resistance.

NOTES

1 According to Leanne R. Simpson in her article, "Anticolonial Strategies for the Recovery and Mainte-nance of Indigenous Knowledge," *American Indian Quarterly* 28.3 and 4 (summer & fall 2004), recover-ing and maintaining Indigenous worldviews, philosophies, and ways of knowing and applying those teachings in a contemporary context represents a web of liberation strategies Indigenous peoples can employ to disentangle themselves from the oppressive control of colonizing state governments.

2 Indian Health Service Web site, <*http://www.hhs.gov/news/press/2003pres/fsindian90803.html*> (ac-cessed March 26, 2007).

3 United States Department of Health and Human Services, *Eliminating Health Disparities in the American Indian and Alaska Native Community,* <*http://www.hhs.gov/news/press/2003pres/fsindian90803. html*>.

4 I received an exemption from the University of New Mexico Institutional Review Board, research project number HRC 02–221 in 2003, to conduct key informant interviews with executive directors or public relation officers for the organizations that inform health policy development for American Indians.

5 Florida, Minnesota, Mississippi, and Texas had implemented their own agreements.

6 Race, Healthcare, and the Law, 2002 Master Settlement Agreement Overview, <*http://www.dayton .edu/~health/syllabi/tobacco/summary.htm#Glance*> (accessed May 22, 2002).

7 Race, Healthcare, and the Law, 2002 Master Settlement Agreement Overview.

8 Marguerite Carroll, "Coming to Grips with the Downside of Tobacco," *American Indian Report* Septem-ber 1997, 12–15.

9 Branch Law firm Web site 2003, "Indian Nations Tobacco Litigation," <*http://www.branchlawfirm.com/cases_of_note.shtml#indiantobacco*> (accessed July 5, 2003).

10 Branch Law Firm Web site 2003, "Acoma Pueblo vs. American Tobacco in the United States District Court for the District of New Mexico." <*http://www.brownandwilliamson.com/APPS/LitigationArchives/Index.cfm?ID=633*> (accessed May 17, 2003).

11 Brown and Williamson Web site (2003), "Acoma Pueblo vs. American Tobacco in the United States District Court for the District of New Mexico."

12 NO SMOKING Web site (2003), <*http://www.no-smoking.org/sept01/09-05-1.html*> (accessed June 17, 2003). On a historical note, it is important to acknowledge that Native Americans, like others serving in the military, were exposed to cigarettes during World War II when these products were included in their government issued rations.

13 Associated Press, "Tribes to Sue Tobacco Industry," *Joplin Globe,* June 16, 1999, <*http://www. joplin-globe.com/archives/1999/990616/business/story1.html*> (accessed August 23, 1999).

14 Carroll, 12–15.

15 F. Hodge, "Tobacco Control Leadership in American Indian Communities," in *Tobacco and Health,* edited by K. Slama (New York: Plenum Press), 375–78.

16 Hodge, 375–78.

17 Indian Health Service, "Trends in Indian Health 1998–1991," 2001. *<http://www.ihs.gov/publicinfo/ publications/trends98/trends98asp>* (accessed April 26, 2002).

18 Indian Health Service, "Priorities and Partnerships," 2003. *<http://www.ihs.gov/ PublicInfo/ PublicAffairs/Director/index.asp>* (accessed September 7, 2003).

19 Research on the high tobacco use rates by American Indians and Alaska Natives adds to our understanding of American Indians' contemporary tobacco culture. While Hodge and C. M. Pego et al., "Tobacco—Deer Person's Gift or Columbus's Curse?" *Winds of Change* 12 (1996): 3 identified cultural and economic issues being important to tribes, neither article provided an in-depth analysis of how these issues affected policy decisions.

20 Hodge.

21 Steven Schinke, Michael Moncher, Gary Holden, Gilbert Botvin, and Mario Orlandi. "American Indian Youth and Substance Abuse: Tobacco Use problems, Risk Factors, and Preventive Interventions," *Health Education Research* 4.1 (1989): 137–44; Peg Allen, Sally Davis, Lawrence Shorty, and Cheryl Mason, "Rural New Mexico Teen Views," *On Target: New Mexico Project ASSIST Quarterly Newsletter,* October 1997; Cheryl Alexander, Peg Allen, Myra Crawford, and Laure McCormick, "Taking the First Puff: Cigarette Smoking Experiences among Ethnically Diverse Adolescents," *Ethnicity and Health* 4.44 (1999): 245–57; Robin Mermelstein and The Tobacco Control Network Writing Group, "Explanations of Ethnic and Gender Differences in Youth Smoking: A Multi-Site, Qualitative Investigation," *Nicotine & Tobacco Research* 1 S91-S98, 1999; Michelle Kegler, Vicki Cleaver, and Beverly Kingsley, "The Social Context of Experimenting with Cigarettes: American Indian 'Start Stories,'" *American Journal of Health Promotion* 15.2 (2000): 89–92.

22 Independent Task Force on Advancing Parity and Leadership for Priority Populations, 2002. This task force developed with input from members of the National Tribal Tobacco Network, sponsored by the Centers for Disease Control. The National Tribal Tobacco Network emerged as a Center for Disease Control and Prevention initiative to fund national networks for tobacco control work. It has been argued that tobacco control, especially on a large scale, for American Indians emerged from the Northwest Portland Area Indian Health Board in the late 1980s, home of the National Tribal Tobacco Network with its tobacco policy project. For more information on the Tribal Tobacco Policy Project see: R. E. Glasgow, E. Lichtenstein, D. Wilder, R. Hall, S. Gilbert McRae, and B. Liberty, "The Tribal Tobacco Policy Project: Working with Northwest Indian Tribes on Smoking Policies," *Preventive Medicine* 24, 434–40.

23 Used by the California Rural Indian Health Board and California Joint Ethnic Tobacco Network. These messages were among the first prevention messages determined to be culturally appropriate. It is an important message that emphasizes the teaching of respectful tobacco use for ceremonial purposes as a tool to help retain Indian tribal customs and traditions.

24 A Montana initiative comprised of Indian tribes, the University of Montana, and non-Indian partners.

25 According to the National Conference of State Legislatures, tribal sovereignty and economic development are the two most crucial issues for Indian tribes. See J. Reed and J. Zelio, *States and Tribes: Building New Traditions.* National Conference of State Legislatures, November 1995. The rights to have self-determination and exercise their sovereignty are the most important legal principles and rights that tribal nations possess. See, Indian Health Service, 2002. The following definition of tribal

sovereignty is utilized by the Indian Health Service. "The Indian Health Service, a division of the Federal Department of Health and Human Service provides health services to federally recognized American Indian and Alaska Native tribal governments. These health services are based on treaty agreements, legal judgments, and Congressional Acts that reflects the government-to-government relationship between tribes and the Federal Government. It provides the following description of tribal sovereignty and its relationship to health affairs" (see Indian Health Service, 2003). "Tribal sovereignty is the ability for Indian tribes to govern their territory and internal affairs. For Indian tribes, possessing sovereignty means the United States and Indian tribes must interact in a government-to-government relationship, though the U.S. Congress can control this interaction. Self-governance and self-determination, tenets of sovereignty, determine how tribes that have contracted or compacted with the United States can have their health services delivered. For example, tribes can redesign their health programs if they choose to enter into a contract/compact under the provisions of the Public Law 93–638, the Indian Self-Determination and Education Assistance Act" (see Indian Health Service, 2003).

26 S. Cornell and J. Kalt, "Sovereignty and Nation-Building: The Development Challenge in Indian Country." The Harvard Project on American Indian Economic Development. <*http://www.ksg.harvard.edu/hpaied/pubs/pub_003.htm*> (accessed June 6, 2003).

27 S. Cornell and J. Taylor, "Sovereignty, Devolution, and the Future of Tribal-State Relations." Malcolm Wiener Center for Social Policy. Harvard University, John F. Kennedy School of Government, <*http://www.ksg.harvard.edu/hpaied/res_main.htm*> (accessed June 6, 2003).

28 Harvard, 2002 (Web site, 2003).

29 Hodge. This trinity comprises the major tobacco issues identified by tribal leaders and American Indian advocates in testimony about a proposed national settlement in 1998 (United States Senate 1998). These are issues that are considered non-negotiable. See Shorty, field notes, 1998 and L. New Breast, *Presentation on tribal sovereignty at 2003 Many Voices, One Message Conference.*

30 1998 U.S. Senate Hearing. Thomas LeClaire testimony at hearing before the Senate Committee on Indian Affairs on Indian Provisions contained in Senate Bills 1414, 1415, and 1530, <*http://www.senate.gov/`scia/1998hrgs/021298.htm*> (accessed May 23, 2001).

31 Idaho Indian Commission 2003. Minutes from February 18, 2003. <*http://www2state.id.us/legislat/ind0218min.html*> (accessed November 2, 2003).

32 Matthew Farrelly, Christian Nimsch, and Joshua James, *State Cigarette Excise Taxes: Implications for Revenue and Tax Evasion* (Research Triangle Institute, RTI Project Number 08742.000, 2003).

33 Cornell and Taylor.

34 Tom Wanamaker, "Economics Special: Indian Gaming Is Healthy and Growing," *Indian Country Today*, September 5, 2003, <*http://www.indiancountrytoday.com/?1062782144*> (accessed September 6, 2003).

35 I.e., the power to overturn lawmaking at the tribal level with a majority vote; cf. U.S. Senate Hearing 1998. An example of this conflict comes from the proposed Prohibit All Cigarette Trafficking (PACT) or Senate Bill 1177 (S.1177). States and tobacco companies could sue and have enforcement over Indian tribes, weakening tribal sovereignty. Reports from *Indian Country Today* (J. Adams, "One Nation Prepares Stealth Attack for Hatch's Cigarette Trafficking Bill," *Indian Country Today*, September 8, 2003) and a key informant from the National Congress of American Indians identify a perceived partnership between Philip Morris, a major tobacco manufacturing company, the Campaign for Tobacco Free Kids (<*http://www.ctfk.org*>), a tobacco control advocacy group, petroleum and grocers'

associations concerned about the advantage of excise tax free sales by Indian tribes, and One Nation, an organization dedicated to limiting the expansion of tribal authority and the "inequities created by sovereignty-based policies" (Adams). According to Adams, Homeland Security and the threat of terrorism is a tactic being used to advocate for S. 1177's passage. For example, monies from an Internet tobacco vendor located on Indian lands were reportedly being used to finance Hezbollah (Adams), frequently described as a terrorist group (Council on Foreign Relations, "Terrorism: Questions & Answers," 2003). This dynamic creates additional complexities with the 2003 National Congress of American Indians' and the National Indian Health Board's focus on accessing Homeland Security funding for Indian tribes (National Indian Health Board, 2002), "Letter to Senator Joe Lieberman, September 5, 2002, <http://www.nihb.org/docs/ homeland_sec_NIHB-NCAI_lieberman_ltr.pdf> (accessed April 8, 2003).

36 Gerry Raining Bird, Discussion at American Legacy Foundation Native American/Alaska Native Forums, 2000.

37 These issues came up in discussion with leadership of Alaska Native tobacco control programs in 2001.

38 Felicia Hodge, "Tobacco Control Leadership in American Indian Communities," in *Tobacco and Health*, edited by K. Slama (New York: Plenum Press, 1995).

39 The author co-authored the following examples of using "tobacco addiction" as a key phrase in statements by non-Indian and Indian tobacco control programs to increase clarity and to demonstrate a means for its ability to be indigenized. "This strategic plan addresses the effects of addictive use of manufactured tobacco. It is not for the purpose of challenging some populations' use of tobacco for (cultural) ceremonial or religious purposes. Instead, this strategic plan focuses on promoting health. It serves as a compass to guide communities that want to reduce the health impact of tobacco by promoting services for those who want to quit the addictive use of tobacco products as well as educate communities on tobacco use to prevent further addiction in the community" as described in "Achieving Parity: A Strategic Plan to Identify and Eliminate Tobacco-Related Disparities in North Carolina." Similarly, for an American Lung Association American Indian Not on Tobacco (AINOT) Cessation Guide: "This cessation program addresses the effects of addiction on American Indian youth caused by the use of manufactured tobacco. The program activities are not intended to challenge the use of tobacco for ceremonial or religious purposes. Instead, voluntary program activities focus on promoting health and helping youth who want to stop their tobacco addiction." Finally, as the mission statement for a Native tobacco policy advocacy organization: "To serve as a resource to promote healthy Native communities and to address the impact of tobacco addiction, disease, and death through policy advocacy."

40 Maori are perhaps best able to articulate how tobacco was used as a major trade good to persuade Indigenous leadership into participating in the signing of the Treaty of Waitangi, *Te Reo Tiriti*. So strong is the understanding of tobacco's role in the colonization of Maori that modern political leadership, especially from the newly formed Maori Party, are staunch anti-tobacco advocates and have spoken out most eloquently on Indigenous people's leadership responsibility.

41 Philip L. Barbour, *Pocahontas and Her World* (Boston: Houghton Mifflin Company, 1970).

42 In my presentations I have started to teach additional elements of what I call the Language of Tobacco Addiction Resistance. I assert, "When we fight against tobacco addiction, we are fighting against oppression. Addiction is oppression. When we fight against tobacco addiction we fight against the forces

that keep it in our community. When we fight against tobacco addiction we fight for our community's wellness. When we fight against tobacco addiction, we fight for the return of the plant(s) that *Nicotiana tabacum* (tobacco) replaced for our ceremonies." I also ask the following questions: "Can you imagine what it would be like to be in a ceremony with all the sacred paraphernalia and all the proper, original plants? I wonder what it must have been like for our ancestors who had to decide whether to allow the use of White Man's Smoke into their ceremonies. I wonder what the arguments sounded like."

BIBLIOGRAPHY

Adams, Jim. "One Nation Prepares Stealth Attack for Hatch's Cigarette Trafficking Bill." Published September 8, 2003. <http://www.indiancountrytoday.com/?1062165713> (accessed September 8, 2003).

Alexander, Cheryl, Peg Allen, Myra Crawford, and Laure McCormick. "Taking the First Puff: Cigarette Smoking Experiences among Ethnically Diverse Adolescents." *Ethnicity and Health* 4.44 (1999): 245–57.

Allen, Peg, Sally Davis, Lawrence Shorty, and Cheryl Mason. "Rural New Mexico Teen Views." *On Target: New Mexico Project ASSIST Quarterly Newsletter,* October 1997.

Associated Press. "Tribes to Sue Tobacco Industry." *Joplin Globe*, June 16, 1999. <http://www.joplinglobe.com/archives/1999/990616/business/story1.html> (accessed August 23, 1999).

Barbour, Philip L. *Pocahontas and Her World.* Boston: Houghton Mifflin Company, 1970.

Branch Law Firm Web Site. "Indian Nations Tobacco Litigation." <http://www.branchlawfirm.com/cases_of_note.shtml#indiantobacco> (accessed July 5, 2003).

Brown and Williamson Web Site. "Acoma Pueblo vs. American Tobacco in the United States District Court for the District of New Mexico." <http://www.brownandwilliamson.com/APPS/LitigationArchives/Index.cfm?ID=633> (accessed May 17, 2003).

Caroll, Marguerite. "Coming to Grips with the Downside of Tobacco." *American Indian Report*, September 1997, 12–15.

Centers for Disease Control and Prevention. Fact Sheet. "American Indians and Alaska Natives and Tobacco." <www.cdc.gov/tobacco/sgr/sgr_1998/sgr-min-fs-nat.htm> (accessed June 14, 2001).

Cornell, Stephen, and Jonathan B. Taylor. "Sovereignty, Devolution, and the Future of Tribal-State Relations." Malcolm Wiener Center for Social Policy. Harvard University, John F. Kennedy School of Government. <http://www.ksg.harvard.edu/hpaied/res_main.htm> (accessed June 6, 2003).

Cornell, Stephen, and Joseph Kalt. "Sovereignty and Nation-Building: The Development Challenge in Indian Country." The Harvard Project on American Indian Economic Development. *<http://www.ksg.harvard.edu/hpaied/pubs/pub_003.htm>* (accessed June 6, 2003).

Council on Foreign Relations. "Terrorism: Questions & Answers." *<http://www.terorismanswers.com/groups/hezbollah.html>* (accessed September 16, 2003).

Department of Health and Human Services, 2003. *<http://www.hhs.gov>* (accessed November 15, 2002).

Farrelly, Matthew, Christian Nimsch, and Joshua James. *State Cigarette Excise Taxes: Implications for Revenue and Tax Evasion.* Research Triangle Institute, RTI Project Number 08742.000, 2003.

Glasgow, Russell E., Edward Lichtenstein, Doni Wilder, Roberta Hall, Suzanne Gilbert McRae, and Bryson Liberty. "The tribal tobacco policy project: working with Northwest Indian tribes on smoking policies." *Preventive Medicine* 24 (1995): 434–40.

Hall, Roberta, et al. "Tobacco Use Policies and Practices in Diverse Indian Settings." *American Indian Culture and Research Journal* 19.3 (1995): 165–80.

Hodge, Felicia. "Tobacco Control Leadership in American Indian Communities." In *Tobacco and Health*, edited by K. Slama. New York: Plenum Press, 1995.

Idaho Council on Indian Affairs.. Minutes from February 18, 2003. *<http://www.2state.id.us/legislat/ind0218min.html>* (accessed November 2, 2003).

Indian Health Service Congressional and Legislative Affairs Office. "IHS Congressional Testimony." *<http://www.ihs.gov/AdminMngrResources/legislativeaffairs/legaffairs-ihs_testimony.asp>* (accessed July 20, 2003).

Indian Health Service. "Trends in Indian Health 1998–2001." *<http://www.ihs.gov/publicinfo/publications/trends98/trends98asp>* (accessed April 26, 2002).

Indian Health Service. "Indian Health Service—An Agency Profile: Health Care Provide & Advocate for Indian People." *<http://www.info.ihs.gov/IHSProfile.pdf>* (accessed April 8, 2003).

Indian Health Service. "Priorities and Partnerships." *<http://www.ihs.gov/PublicInfo/PublicAffairs/Director/index.asp>* (accessed September 7, 2003).

Kegler, Michelle, Vicki Cleaver, and Beverly Kingsley. "The Social Context of Experimenting with Cigarettes: American Indian 'Start Stories.'" *American Journal of Health Promotion* 15.2 (2000): 89–92.

Lasley, Gary . "Statement to 105 Congress." *<http://www.senate.gov/~scia/1998hrgs/0212_1~1.htm>* (accessed September 28, 1999).

Locke, Michelle. "Tribes Sue Tobacco Industry." Associated Press. June 4, 1999. <http://www.junkscience.com/jun99/tribes.htm> (accessed September 28, 1999).

Mermelstein, Robin, and The Tobacco Control Network Writing Group. "Explanations of ethnic and gender differences in youth smoking: A Multi-Site, Qualitative Investigation." *Nicotine & Tobacco Research* 1 S91-S98, 1999.

National Indian Health Board. "Letter to Senator Joe Lieberman." September 5, 2002. <*http://www.nihb.org/docs/homeland_sec_NIHB-NCAI_lieberman_ltr.pdf*> (accessed April 8, 2003).

New Breast, L. Paper presented at Many Voices, One Message Conference, 2003.

NO SMOKING Web site. <*http://www.no-smoking.org/sept01/09-05-1.html*> (accessed June 17, 2003).

Pego, Christine, et al. "Tobacco—Deer Person's Gift or Columbus's Curse?" *Winds of Change* (1997): 12, 3.

"Race, Healthcare, and the Law." Master Settlement Agreement Overview. <*http://www.dayton.edu/~health/syllabi/tobacco/summary.htm#Glance*> (accessed May 22, 2002).

Reed, James, and Julie Zelio. *States and Tribes: Building New Traditions.* National Conference of State Legislatures, November 1995.

Schinke Steven, Michael Moncher, Gary Holden, Gilbert Botvin, and Mario Orlandi. "American Indian Youth and Substance Abuse: Tobacco Use Problems, Risk Factors, and Preventive Interventions." *Health Education Research* 4.1 (1989): 137–44.

United States Senate Committee on Indian Affairs. Thomas LeClaire testimony at hearing before the Senate Committee on Indian Affairs on Indian Provisions contained in Senate Bills 1414, 1415 and 1530. <*http://www.senate.gov/`scia/1998hrgs/021298.htm*> (accessed May 23, 2001).

Wanamaker, Tom. "Economics Special: Indian Gaming Is Healthy and Growing." *Indian Country Today,* September 5, 2003. <*http://www.indiancountry to-day.com/?1062782144*> (accessed September 6, 2003).

II. EDUCATION, CULTURE, AND THE ARTS

7 *'IKE PONO:* PROMOTING LEARNING FROM A NATIVE HAWAIIAN PERSPECTIVE

David Kekaulike Sing

While the issue of sovereignty for Native Hawaiians in this century, at least from the U.S. government's perspective, sits in the hands of its congressional processes,[1] there are various efforts in Native Hawai'i by Native Hawaiians to encourage sovereignty in ways that are not contingent on political decisions.[2]

The pedagogy implemented by Nā Pua No'eau, a Hawaiian education center for Native Hawaiian students in grades kindergarten through grade twelve at the University of Hawai'i, is designed within a Native Hawaiian context. Both the content and the process of teaching and learning are built on concepts and values derived from Indigenous roots with the goal of optimizing learning for Native Hawaiians.[3]

Hawaiian educational demographics demonstrate a system that has failed Native population of Hawai'i. It has neglected to provide information on Indigenous history, language, and culture at both the lower and higher education level.[4]

Recent federal initiatives continue colonial attitudes by dictating goals and standards that remove the personal and cultural dimensions of education between Hawaiian students and teachers and fall short of providing educational services in an effective way to Native Hawaiians. As research has grown in describing the failures of the education system, there is, however, sufficient evidence of Indigenous pedagogies promoting the successful schooling of Native Hawaiians.[5]

A university-based center in operation for fifteen years, Nā Pua No'eau demonstrates how culturally appropriate pedagogy promotes and supports Native Hawaiian students in learning their language, culture, and history and at the same time raises their achievements and aspirations in a European American-based curriculum. Its pedagogy frees Native Hawaiians of an educational framework caught in the political web of colonialism. The Hawaiian concept *'ike pono* best describes this pivotal path in Hawaiian education. *'Ike* refers to knowledge. *Pono* means correct, right or just. Thus, *'ike pono* in this case refers to using knowledge in a just or correct way. We have not always seen the content and process of teaching and learning as *pono* for Native Hawaiians. The Center's work attempts to provide a pedagogy that is *pono* or just.

Nā Pua No'eau's philosophy optimizes learning conditions that are congruent with Indigenous home and community experiences, perspectives, and values.[6] This philosophy moves beyond attitudes that devalue home and community experiences. The "baby boom" generation of Native Hawaiians grew up being told to leave their "Hawaiian-ness" at home. Indigenous behaviors, language, and values were held in check. This policy deeply impaired the range and possibilities of Native Hawaiians' participation in the classroom and in society. In my experience with European-American based pedagogy and education, programs and activities are designed to use frameworks that are narrowly responsive to certain ways of accomplishing tasks. In most cases, the assessment of effectiveness is based on frameworks that originate from this one cultural perspective exclusively. For example, some of the initiatives formulated by the U.S. Department of Education's "No Child Left Behind" policy leave me with a sense of imposition on Indigenous Hawaiian values and perspectives that were first brought to Hawai'i by missionaries. Stated simply, such policies of imposition have defined what we as Native Hawaiians did and how we engaged in our activities as "different" and "inferior" to European American practices. As a result, it was demanded that Native peoples needed to learn everything in a more "civilized" way. There have been many influences that steered Hawai'i and its people away from Hawaiian beliefs, customs and practices. One of the most significant was the arrival of the missionaries in 1778. Their arrival led to the opening of Hawai'i to Western influences and the abolishment of traditional Hawaiian religious practices in 1821.

It amazes me that our public school system in Hawai'i continues to accept the standardized European American tests and measurements to assess learning, when many of our Native children do not demonstrate their abilities and achievements in the context of these tests. In a society where cultural diversity has never been more publicized than today, we still continue to disregard and devalue the diversity of how we think, how we behave, and how we learn, and the diversity of topics possible in instruction.[7]

The educational model introduced below provides sovereignty in the sense that its curriculum and its philosophy are designed for Native Hawaiians, by Native Hawaiians and with Native Hawaiians in the context of our own goals, needs, and resources. While we recognize the importance of the preservation of our language and culture, the education program that drives Nā Pua No'eau is based on what the Hawaiian people envision as the skills, attitudes, and knowledge essential for Native Hawaiian youths in today's and tomorrow's Hawai'i and the world at large.

In previous generations, the discussion of Hawai'i in the context of teaching and learning would represent what people believed to be Hawaiiana and later Hawaiian Studies. This represented studying Hawaiian matters in isolation and from a Western perspective as objectified "culture," "language," and "crafts." This approach constituted merely superficial teaching and learning, or what I would categorize as Hawaiian crafts. On the university level, Hawaiian Studies were taught as a separate content area. Today, the growing field of Native Hawaiian education speaks beyond fragmented and objectified categories such as "culture." It addresses all aspects of the process of teaching Hawaiian people and its inherent philosophical perspective—that is, the complex ways in which Hawaiians see things, understand things, and do things. The field of Native Hawaiian education recognizes the richness of how we think and perceive things and the development of those elements within our culture through generations. Committed to a system of education from a Native Hawaiian perspective, Nā Pua No'eau is building a stronger connection between the classroom and the culture of the people it serves.[8]

We are witnessing a global awakening to the foundation of knowledge by Native educators. Research and publications are defining the essence of Native people's thinking and their body of knowledge.[9] Along with the recognition of the failure of Western systems of education in serving Native populations, we are creating a new understanding of "equal education opportunity." The challenge is that, although there is "talk" and discussion, we have few examples of education models that successfully demonstrate the integration of Native knowledge in a system of European American established education.

To begin with, an educational model like Nā Pua No'eau aligns both teachers and activities to the way Indigenous Hawaiians learn best. While some may suggest that we cannot necessarily generalize about the process and content that works best for Hawaiian students, I believe that the fact that Native Hawaiians as a group achieve at lower levels at both the kindergarten to grade twelve and higher education levels indicates a group response related to the cultural context of learning. Low attendance and retention in higher education represent a lack of providing education that addresses the needs and interests of Native Hawaiians. Thus, the first building block for a foundation of Indigenous education is the insight that, "Hawaiians have not failed, the education system has failed Hawaiians."[10] Sociological and cultural patterns of learning among Native Hawaiians and other Indigenous peoples worldwide suggest that a Western educational system lacks a pedagogy and a social climate that connects the Indigenous student to teaching and learning, and thus fails to respond to the vision and needs of an Indigenous population.

Native Hawaiians' educational practices embrace respect, spirituality, education, family, and Hawaiian life ways. While Hawaiian families see education as a top priority, they place it in the context of family and culture. Representatives of a Western system of education assume that Native Hawaiians do not value education as a priority, but cannot perceive the role Hawaiian family life plays in learning and teaching. The complexities of life for Hawaiians in balancing the bond of family and relationships with the demands of survival in a challenging society that has not treated them well is not as simple as discussing whether "education is a top priority or not" for Indigenous people.

As Native Hawaiians, we need to wonder about such misinformation joined with the fact that our population has enjoyed very limited access in the classroom to knowledge about our own history, culture, language, and perspective. The Center's effort to solve this problem and optimize the learning of Hawaiian students begins by looking at ways to design and change the educational climate and to provide access to accurate knowledge.[11]

NURTURING THE GIFTS OF ALL STUDENTS

Initially, the Center's funds came through monies allocated to conduct gifted and talented youth programs. While our Center has evolved to provide educational enrichment beyond the concept and funding of gifted and talented youths, the initial conceptual framework provided a valuable guiding point. Our belief is that "giftedness lies not in determining who is gifted and who is not, but rather in nurturing the gifts of all children and students."[12] The conventional perspective of gifted and talented tends to set exclusive parameters and limits participation. Nā Pua No'eau found the assessment measures to be limited and designed its application and programs to recognize potential, the diversity of giftedness, and the ways students exhibit their giftedness. Nā Pua No'eau nurtures the gifts of all its students and is open to all who are interested in the Center's resources.[13]

Understanding the role of culture in the development of Native Hawaiians is an essential part of designing learning frameworks. The kite metaphor illustrates their philosophical foundation.

The kite metaphor depicts a graphic representation of how Nā Pua No'eau sees the development of the students served by the Center. As the Center promotes the wide range of topics/ disciplines and the depth of educational experiences it provides for its students, three factors are kept in mind that link the topics and experiences. These are: the self or the person and how he/she views himself/ herself; the family or 'ohana, i.e., the notion of having responsibility within a family and that all parts are important for success; the Hawaiian culture, the history, culture, technology of each topic or discipline needs to integrate Hawaiian perspectives, culture, and/or history into the lesson/curriculum.

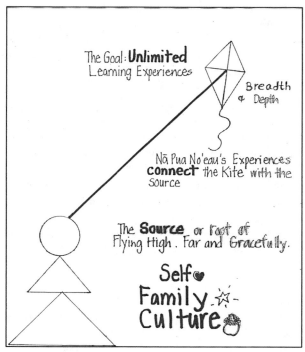

The Goal: **Unlimited** Learning Experiences

Breadth & Depth

Nā Pua No'eau's Experiences **connect** the Kite with the Source

The **Source** or root of Flying High. Far and Gracefully.

Self
Family
Culture

Fig. 1. Kite Metaphor of Nā Pua No'eau Pedagogy

A second foundation of the Center is the congruency of the learning process with home/community values/cultural relevance. Center curricula purposefully integrate appropriate aspects of Native Hawaiian culture, history, and values to enrich the student with a deeper appreciation of being Native Hawaiian. Students need a strong affective as well as academic base. Research indicates that members of more functional Native Hawaiian families have a better understanding of and attitude toward "self" and achieve higher than those who have a poor attitude toward "self."[14]

The literature on Native Hawaiian education suggests that classroom strategies integrating culturally relevant learning processes also raise student achievement. Such instructional strategies are planned and integrated into the classroom and are an important part of the Center's research activities. Teacher training and evaluations are an integral part of the Center's activities to enhance classroom learning for Native Hawaiians.

INSTRUCTIONAL APPROACH

We do not want to repeat the failures of our current educational system. Rather, we develop our practices to reflect the research and efforts successful in raising the aspirations and achievements of our Hawaiian students. The following Hawaiian values can guide the teacher in developing culturally appropriate lessons and activities:

Lokahi (unity)

The idea of utilizing the concept of *lokahi* as an instructional strategy is consistent with the Hawaiian perspective of seeing things and consequently, learning. The worldview of Indigenous Hawaiians draws upon an understanding of the relationship between things and the balance of these relationships. We should understand that learning of new concepts or ideas can best be understood in relationship to concepts or ideas students are familiar with and within the context of their surroundings.

Na'auao (learned, intelligent)

The concept of *na'auao* refers to gaining knowledge through synchronizing the mind, heart, and body. Activities should involve an understanding and sensitivity to the learning process that draws upon the *na'au* (guts or feeling). Students should see, feel, know, and have an emotional understanding of the subject matter they are learning. This will build upon a deeper understanding of the topic.

The Hawaiian concept of Na'auao represents a philosophical foundation of the model. The concept refers to being able to attain knowledge when all of one's senses are engaged in the learning process. *Na'au* in Hawaiian refers to guts, heart, and emotion. *Ao* refers to the attainment of knowledge. Thus, instruction should always incorporate the mind, the body, the spiritual, and the emotional. Many of the classes in the Center are taught around a theme as opposed to being western discipline-based, i.e., mathematics, English. Classes revolve around creating authentic learning environments and providing "hands-on" experiences. Developing a model that uses these ideas reinforces the concept of *na'auao*. "Voyaging," "Rocks and Rolls" (Geology and Hawaiian Studies wrapped together), are two important examples of classes conducted during the summer residential program. "Voyaging" incorporates traditional Hawaiian protocol, developing a sail plan that requires learning how to read the sky, the stars, the sun, the wind, the water currents, the geography of the land and ocean, and sailing techniques. The students learn through all of their cultural and personal elements. The outcomes of such a class consist in an appreciation of the application of science in a traditional and contemporary endeavor; strengthening their pride in their Hawaiian-ness; gaining a depth of knowledge in a particular area; raising their awareness of possible career endeavors related to the area of voyaging.

Aloha (love, compassion)

Our *kupuna* (elder) shares this value, which calls upon us to connect our "breath" to each other. Expressing *aloha* brings depth to interacting with other people. The *maka* or eyes, the *honi* or kiss, the *ho'opili* or embrace are various ways to express *aloha*. The specialness that other people see in people from Hawai'i stems from the depth of our relationships built around the value of *aloha*.

Students indicate that the stronger the spirit that exists between them and the teacher, the more likely their attitude will be positive toward the teacher, the class, their peers, and learning. Instruction should build upon the concept of *aloha* in developing the classroom climate.

Mālama kou piko (take care of/protect your *piko*)

I would like to illustrate this value with a personal story. My Mom passed away suddenly on April 24, 2004. Her thoughts, especially to her grandchildren, were shared in a phrase she often conveyed—*mālama kou piko*. My mother was the matriarch of our family and not until she left us, did we realize how significant her lessons were in building the lives of all whom she touched.

The *piko* is commonly known to Native Hawaiians as the navel. However, those closely connected to the culture interpret the reference to *piko* in varied ways. These different interpretations are based on their understanding of *piko* as a connection to their ancestors, their parents, children, and those yet to be born family members.[15] There is reference to three *pikos*, one on the top of the head that connects one to one's ancestors, *'aumākua, ke Akua*. Another *piko* is the umbilical cord that connects parents to children. The third *piko* refers to the genitals that connect us to the future generation of family, our children and the yet to be born.[16] *Mālama* is a common phrase used to mean take care of. By *mālama kou piko* my Mom talked about the caring for one's *piko*. She was speaking about keeping a connection to those from the past, connection to the present, and connection to the future. The *piko po'o* is the connection to the past. The past is your family, your culture, your beliefs, your *'aumakua* and your spiritual understandings. The *piko* navel is your building of strong relationships with your family, your parents, your children, those around you, and the environment you are in. The *piko* genitals refer to your future, those yet unborn—procreation. How does this differ from people talking about the past, the present and the future? In several ways, it talks about caring for or protecting. It also talks about relationships. Thus, as we talk about *mālama kou piko,* we are talking about caring for, protecting, and building strong relationships with the people and the beliefs of your past, your present, and the future. My niece mentioned that when her *tutu* (grandparent) said *mālama kou piko* to her, she sensed that it was about the relationships she was having and that she needed to take care of herself, her womanhood, and to be strong within herself. Mom made connections to our past through the stories she told, and the actions she took. As the youngest sibling, even up to the age of eighty, she still felt responsible to take care of her older siblings. She showed great respect and commitment to them.

CONCLUSION

Since my mother has passed on, I have learned that the work that we have been doing in *Nā Pua No'eau,* the program model that we designed to orchestrate the activities to "optimize learning" can be articulated more clearly through this cultural understanding of *mālama kou piko*. It is the acknowledgment of those who have come before us, the spiritual world that embraces their soul; it is the acknowledgment of knowing who we are and that awareness is essential in developing and sustaining ourselves as individuals and as part of a great cultural heritage; it is the acknowledgment of the legacy that we are held to, in spite of the political and cultural challenges that are presented to us. It expresses our sovereignty as Native Hawaiians.

NOTES

1 Senate Bill 147, United States Congress. "Native Hawaiian Government Reorganization Act of 2005," <*http://www.nativehawaiians.com*>(accessed July 2005).

2 D. K. Sing, L. A. Hunter, M. Meyer, "Native Hawaiian Education: Talking Story with Three Hawaiian Educators," *Journal of American Indian Education* 39.1 (Fall 1999).

3 Nā Pua No'eau Center for Gifted and Talented Children, *Program Booklet* (University of Hawai'i at Hilo, 1999). See also D. E. Martin, D. K. Sing, and L. A. Hunter, "Nā Pua No 'eau: The Hawaiian Perspective of Giftedness," in *Underserved Gifted Populations* (Cresskill, NJ: Hampton Press, 2002).

4 Nā Pua No'eau; S. M. Kana'iaupuni and K. Ishibashi, "LEFT BEHIND? The Status of Hawaiian Students in Hawai'i Public Schools," prepared by PASE REPORT (020–03:13) <*http://www.ksbe.edu/pase*> (accessed July 2005).

5 D. E. Martin, D. K. Sing, and L. A. Hunter, "Nā Pua No'eau: The Hawaiian Perspective of Giftedness," in *Underserved Gifted Populations* (Cresskill, NJ: Hampton Press, 2002).

6 D. K. Sing, "Raising the Achievement Level of Native Hawaiians in the College Classroom through the Matching of Teaching Strategies with Student Characteristics" (PhD diss., Claremont Graduate School, 1986). See also D. K. Sing, "Creating an Educational Model That Promotes Learning, Maintains Cultural Identity," in *Ka Wai Ola o OHA* (Honolulu: Office of Hawaiian Affairs, 2000), 13.

7 M. Dudoit and D. K. Sing, "Mahealani Dudoit and David Kekaulike Sing—Interview with David Kekaulike Sing," *'Ōiwi* 3 (2003): 62–64.

8 A. J. Kawakami and K. K. Aton, "KeAʻo Hawaiʻi (Critical Elements for Hawaiian Learning): Perceptions of Successful Hawaiian Educators," *Pacific Educational Research Journal,* 11.1 (2001): 53–66.

9 R. Barnhardt and A. O. Kawagley, "Culture, Chaos and Complexity: Catalysts for Change in Indigenous Education," *Cultural Survival Quarterly* 27.4 (2003): 59–64. See also M. A. Meyer, "Native Hawaiian Epistemology: Contemporary Narratives" (PhD diss., Harvard University, 1998).

10 Nā Pua Noʻeau Center *Program Booklet*

11 Sing, "Creating an Educational Model That Promotes Learning, Maintains Cultural Identity."

12 Martin, 1998. See also Nā Pua Noʻeau Center for Gifted and Talented Native Hawaiian Children, "Curriculum Guidelines, Native Hawaiian Curriculum Development Project," University of Hawaiʻi at Hilo, Spring 1999.

13 Dudoit and Sing, "Mahealani Dudoit and David Kekaulike Sing—Interview with David Kekaulike Sing."

14 Sing, *Raising the Achievement Level of Native Hawaiians in the College Classroom through the Matching of Teaching Strategies with Student Characteristics* . PhD. Diss., Claremont Graduate School, 1986.

15 M. K. Pukui, E.W. Haertig, and C. A. Lee, *Nānā I Ke Kumu, Queen Liliʻuokalani* (Honolulu: Children's Center, 1972).

16 Native Hawaiian Education Council and *Ka HakaʻUla O Keʻelikolani, Nā Honua Mauli Ola, Hawaiʻi's Guidelines for Culturally Responsive Learning Environments* (Hilo: University of Hawaiʻi, 2002).

BIBLIOGRAPHY

Barnhardt, R., and A. O. Kawagley. "Culture, Chaos and Complexity: Catalysts for Change in Indigenous Education." *Cultural Survival Quarterly* 27.4 (2003): 59–64.

Benham, Maenette K. P., and Ronald H. Heck. *Cultural and Educational Policy in Hawaiʻi.* Mahwah, NJ: Laurence Erlbaum Associates, 1998.

"Curriculum Guidelines, Native Hawaiian Curriculum Development Project." Center for Gifted and Talented Native Hawaiian Children (Nā Pua Noʻeau), University of Hawaii at Hilo. Hilo, Spring 1999.

Dudoit, M., and D. K. Sing. "Mahealani Dudoit & David Kekaulike Sing—Interview with David Kekaulike Sing." *ʻŌiwi—A Native Hawaiian Journal* 3 (2003): 62–64.

Kanaʻiaupuni, Shawn. "Kaʻakālai Ku Kanaka: A call for strength-based approaches from a native Hawaiian Perspective." *AERA Research News and Comment,* 2004. <http://www.ksbe.edu/pase>.

Kanaʻiaupuni, S. M., and K. Ishibashi. "LEFT BEHIND? The Status of Hawaiian Students in Hawaiʻi Public Schools," prepared by PASE REPORT 02-03: 13. Published June 2003. <http:// www.ksbe.edu/pase>.

Kanaʻiaupuni, S. M., N. J. Malone, and K. Ishibashi. "Ka huakaʻI I mua... Findings from the 2005 Native Hawaiian Education Assessment." 2005. <http://www.ksbe.edu/pase>.

Kawakami, A. J., and K. K. Aton. "KeAʻo Hawaiʻi (Critical Elements for Hawaiian Learning): Perceptions of Successful Hawaiian Educators." *Pacific Educational Research Journal* 11.1 (2001): 53–66.

Martin, D. E. *Towards an Understanding of the Native Hawaiian Concept and Manifestation of Giftedness.* PhD diss. University of Georgia, 1996.

Martin, D. E., D. K. Sing, and L. A. Hunter. "Nā Pua Noʻeau: The Hawaiian Perspective of Giftedness."In *Underserved Gifted Populations*, edited by J. Smutny. Cresskill, NJ: Hampton Press, 2002.

Meyer, M. A. "Native Hawaiian Epistemology: Contemporary Narratives." PhD diss., Harvard University, 1998.

Nā Pua No'eau, Center for Gifted and Talented Native Hawaiian Children. Program Booklet. Developed for staff and teachers. Hilo: University of Hawaii at Hilo.

"Nā Honua Mauli Ola, Hawaii's Guidelines for Culturally and Responsive Learning Environments." Native Hawaiian Education Council and Ka HakaʻUla O Keʻelikolani. University of Hawaii at Hilo, 2002.

Pukui, M. K., E. W. Haertig, and C. A. Lee. *Nānā I Ke Kumu,* Queen Liliʻuokalani Children's Center. Honolulu, 1972.

Senate Bill 147, United States Congress. "Native Hawaiian Government Reorganization Act of 2005." Washington, DC. *<http://www.nativehawaiians.com>.*

Sing, D. K. "Creating an Educational Model That Promotes Learning, Maintains Cultural Identity." *Ka Wai Ola o OHA.* Office of Hawaiian Affairs, Honolulu, February 2000, 13.

Sing, D. K. "The Hawaiian Connection." *Journal of Aging and Identity* 2.4 (1997), 285-293.

Sing, D. K. *Raising the achievement level of Native Hawaiians in the college classroom through the matching of teaching strategies with student characteristics.* PhD diss., Claremont Graduate School, 1986.

Sing, D. K., L. A. Hunter, and M. Meyer. "Native Hawaiian Education: Talking Story with Three Hawaiian Educators." *Journal of American Indian Education* 39.1 (Fall 1999), 4-13.

Task Force, World Indigenous Peoples' Conference, *The Coolangatta Statement on Indigenous Rights in Education,* Unpublished document, Coolangatta: New South Wales, 1993.

8 FOUNDATIONS OF LAKOTA SOVEREIGNTY

Harry Charger, Ione V. Quigley, and Ulrike Wiethaus

INTRODUCTION

In March of 2007, the South Dakota state legislature voted for Lakota language and culture to be taught in all public schools.[1] This is a decision of great significance, given the history of federal and state orchestrated efforts to assimilate and/or annihilate Lakota culture, language, economic, and spiritual practices.[2] As several of this volume's essays have described in some detail, full sovereignty depends on a thriving culture and language, practiced across generations. Legal solutions alone are not enough. In responding to a study by Thomas Biolsi on legal dimensions of Lakota-Euro-American interactions on the Rosebud reservation, Vine Deloria Jr. asserted that "history has nearly vanished from law, culture is being torn apart by law, religion stands outside law for the most part. Without a context in which law can function, it is a farce and resolves issues by brute force."[3]

The present chapter features two conversations with Lakota elders on the traditional foundations of Lakota sovereignty. We chose the interview format to acknowledge the importance and culturally appropriate protocol of oral communication in traditional contexts to assert truth, teach values, and share view points. This choice, an evocation of intellectual sovereignty in dialogue with Euro-American scholarship, is one of several models to work against discursive displacement strategies. As the discipline of the humanities transforms itself to become multi-perspectival and inclusive, academic discourse by necessity is broadened to include a wealth of meta-academic discursive styles.[4] Both Lakota contributors to this chapter grew up as fluent Lakota speakers, learned English as a second language while removed from their families, and have taught Lakota language classes.[5] Harry Charger (Sans Arc Lakota) works as a ceremonial leader, cultural educator, and wisdom keeper in Eagle Butte, South Dakota. Ione V. Quigley (Sicangu Lakota) is the chair person of the Department of Lakota Studies at Sinte Gleska University in Mission, South Dakota. Trained as an anthropologist, she teaches numerous courses on Lakota history, geography, biology, and culture, and is actively involved in revitalizing Lakota governmental structures through her participation in the process of rewriting the Sicangu Oyate (Sicangu Nation) constitution and by-laws. Both elders stress the meaning of sovereignty not as an abstract concept, but as a lived reality expressed through distinct values, spirituality, and behaviors. It is manifest in an education for personal independence and a sense of communal responsibility capable of supporting the well-being of the Lakota nation. The participants underscore the contributions of Lakota women in the struggle for sovereignty, and address contemporary themes such as the historic role of AIM

(American Indian Movement), efforts to move towards a model of restorative justice, and spiritual and environmental revitalization.[6]

SOVEREIGNTY IS OUR THOUGHTS, OUR WORDS, OUR CEREMONIES: A CONVERSATION WITH HARRY CHARGER

UW: How would you like to begin?

HC: This is about sovereignty. You know, to a lot of Lakota, it is something that is kind of strange to us because we are already sovereign. If you want to use the word sovereign… it is god given: it is our thoughts, our words, our ceremonies. Everything is free. We did not feel that we had to satisfy anybody when we were sovereign. We were just a very strong, balanced, harmonized people. Then of course with the coming of the people that did not belong on this continent, or came to this continent from other countries, they brought something with them that was not sovereign in this sense, it wasn't even— they were tied to their religion, you know. So that wasn't sovereign in our understanding. They were tied to their language, which wasn't our definition of being sovereign. They were tied to their culture. That was not an expression of sovereignty either in that they did not recognize everybody as brother and sister. They did not recognize kinship obligations—they called each other John, Bill, Joe, and Bob, but they did not call each other Little Brother, Older Brother, Little Sister, Big Sister and Uncle, Grandfather, Grandmother, something like that, you know. There was a big gap we noticed right away—how they did away with their relationships, even in their families. They called their boys Joe, Bob, Bill, or sometimes they would call them son, but it seemed like it had a hollow ring to it, instead of recognizing a real son or a real grandson. The deeper meaning was not there. Oh, that's my grandson over there, or that's my son. As if he was just a piece of property or a thing, not very important. Our relationships to each other were very important. They were one of the bases of our culture, our freedom.

The same contrast holds true for religion. Although the newcomers talked about the Great Spirit, which they called God, it did not sound real. They only went to church one day, one hour a week. That is how they tried to do everything, cram it all in at once. But when they got out of church, they were the same old people again, you know, showing the same old greed—how to cheat your neighbor, how to nibble at your neighbor so you can get some money or some material gain out of it. Well, we were not like that. When we came out of a ceremony, we were at peace. We felt deeply, deeply conscious of our relationship to one another, but also to the Great Spirit. And we had to do that and be that way, because we knew, too, that we were not anything, we were nothing.

Without spirituality, there is no sovereignty. To us, sovereignty exists in spirituality. And spirituality is an expression of sovereignty, a god-given innate freedom, that feeling that you have that hey, I am a part of things, I am a part of something – but still a part of something, instead of wanting to be all of it. We pray as we do, being part of something. We were satisfied with that, you know.

So sovereignty to us is not a form of government, but yet it expresses itself in a form of government. When you are free, you can freely interact with your neighbors, freely, for real, instead of having to reenact shallow rules. For example, I know that this is an expression of respect, but people will see the governor or the president, and they fall all over themselves. It is truly happening, but it is not real. These men and women do not know that governor, that president that much. I don't. I have heard of him, but I don't know him that much. Whereas all of my relatives, my uncle, my dad, my relatives, my brothers, my cousins—I take time to talk to them. You know that we are genuinely—I don't know if you can see that or not, but we are genuinely glad to see one another. If we weren't cowboys, we'd probably cry [chuckles]. So anyway, I am just touching very briefly, very lightly on what sovereignty means to me.

And sovereignty is something you have to not just talk about, or read about, or write about, but you have to live it. And that is one of the big aspects of it, you have to live it. And if you don't, then you have got something else. You have another kind of control, or government, and it is not good.

UW: What needs to be said to the next generation of Lakota?

HC: It would be a message of different meanings, or different points, because all of those things that we just talked about have to be strengthened and in some cases rediscovered. Take our ceremonies as an example. Whatever ceremony it is, it has to be rediscovered and it's a little bit difficult when you don't speak the language. So that brings up the point of language, which is all important. And before we get into that, we have to practice compassion. I mean full compassion, not just good acts or good deeds, and that kind of thing, but full god-given compassion—love, unrequited love for your fellow man and woman and all things god-given or god-created.

And then there is the respect for these things, these people, these relatives, and everything created. And related to it are responsibility and accountability. We have to be responsible for our self. This is me; I have to be responsible for my words, my actions, as they have to as well. This is what relationship, kinship, responsible interaction means. And accountability refers to my person as well. And if I am trying to hold myself to be responsible and accountable, then of course the other fellow should be expected to do the same. When they do that, we are all at the same level, we feel good, we do not feel fear of one another, we do not feel resentment. Rather, we feel comfortable in each other's presence, and we feel we are real; he is real; she is real. And I know that he or she is real, as real as we can get.

And it is no longer that way. We are just a little bit leery of one another, even relatives. So there is not much of that original sovereignty there. I do not know if it is really even the same word anymore, if we can apply it to that or not, but sovereignty to me is god-given freedom of equality. That is very important, equality, because I am equal to everybody, but no better and no worse. I feel that. And that is the message that I have to give to our young people, because we not only have to give it to them, we have to show them how.

We must show them how to be free, or it would be just that much more talk. So somehow we have to get up groups, maybe in school. Maybe the American Indian classes that they have in the schools nowadays could pick up on that, or American Indian Studies groups at universities. Instead of just teaching a block system type of Indian Studies, they should really get into it and do these things, if they really want to get the concept of sovereignty across. Otherwise it's just a stuffy old class.

Of course, young people were all important [in traditional Lakota society]. *Wakanheja,* children, means that 'sacred they, too, are', or, 'mysterious they, too, are' because of their innocence and inexperience. So everything belongs to them, or must belong to them. And as far as political maneuvering goes, it existed not in the western sense, if you will, or in the European sense of politics. Politics did exist, but only in kind of a fun way. My brother-in-law's a chief, so you know that I will make a play of getting away with mischief. In actuality, I am still just as subject to any of the rules and regulations. The mischief is a way to tease him and for him to tease me.

Governance is based on respect. Respect people, do not turn them one way or another, because that is disrespectful. You can tell them about some things, but let them make up their own mind. And I think that was where we differed in our definition of sovereignty: we had a choice. We had a choice to make our own decisions, good or bad, and we made them. And we were given that respect, you know. And so I think that we did not practice "politics." We learned that when organized government came on the scene. And they divided our people to gain power. To be in power. To gain a vote. There was no voting back in those days when we were free. There was mutual consent as to who was going to be the thinker of thinkers, the *naca*, the chief, for example. And he was chosen because of his compassion, respect, responsibility, and accountability. He had to live those values, you see. And he was chosen on those merits.

And then of course there are derivatives. Compassion means to be able to share things, and never expect anything in return. And the people depended on him so much that when they made him a *naca,* then for four days there was grieving because they had done him a terrible injustice. He was no longer his own man. He belonged to the people, everything that he is, and owned, and knew belonged to the people, forever. It was not just a four-year term, a five year term, but forever. And they were men who could make these decisions for the people. But it goes back further than that even. From the time that he was born until the time that he died, there were rules to follow in each corner of his life as in the four different directions. Each corner had 111 rules of behavior. So in all there were 444 rules of behavior for how the individual ought to behave toward god's creations. And if that person lives accordingly, he is then noticed by the elders and by the people, who say, hey this guy might be worthy of being a *naca*. And so if that's politics, we knew it was superior to what was brought over here.

UW: I am interested in women's roles.

HC: The women, let me see now, who are they? [laughs] No, the women are very important. They were not possessions, certainly; they were partners; they were a part of everything; they were equal. Yet they did not have the masculine kind of voice, but they had the feminine voice. Because the Lakota were very aware of that—the male and female energy, and that one cannot do without the other. They have to complement one another, in a family circle, in decisions as a camp, decisions that affect teaching, many decisions. Although there are some decisions that are made by men only, for example, when to go to war or when to go on a raiding party, or on the hunt. But the women accompanied them on these journeys for other purposes, to tend to them or to do the butchery. Yet they did not do it alone, but the men helped. In the hunt the men killed a buffalo, and they helped with the butchery, but the women did the refined work, if you will. They decided who would get what—if a hunter killed four buffalo, for example, each woman would think of the welfare cases back home, the elderly, the young, the orphan, and they would set aside, this one here, and this and this, for those in need. In other words, it was kind of a welfare system, to take care of those people. And the women would decide this hide here will make a teepee for old stick-in-the-mud, or whoever he is, you know, an old guy who is not able to hunt anymore. And he might even be a relative. So we would put these hides aside and prepare them for him and make him a teepee, so he can take care of his grandchildren or himself or even other villagers. It took a whole camp to raise youngsters. It was not just one family, although you knew which family you belonged to. If you happened to be at a certain family's camp during the night, then you slept there, but everyone knew it was normal. It took the whole camp to raise youngsters. And this was how our sense of extended family responsibility came about. Everybody cared for everybody else.

And all of these kids listened, and they learned from this uncle, that uncle, and all of the relatives. What was happening then was that each youngster would have several doctors, several masters, several professors, teachers, and so on. They did not have a degree and did not want one. They passed on what they knew to this child. And then as they got older, these young people got older, the old ones passed away, and they in turn passed it on. There was a continuance of knowledge that was shared, which was very good. There was no need for books. They did not have to put their knowledge in books. They taught everything in tellings, in words, and in songs. The women played a big part in this; they passed on many of the finer points of camp life, of personal life, interactive knowledge, stories, all that was the women's job to do in addition to keeping and holding the family together. So they were very important; they were partners; they were not possessions, like in some societies, but they were equal partners. And then of course like everyplace else, there were abusers. But they were dealt with by the laws of the Lakota. They were banished.

UW: Or killed.

HC: Or killed. If somebody mistreated my sister badly, or even struck her or cut her, it was my right to stand up for her and to kill the abuser. The camp was not going to say anything. It happened on occasion, but rarely, because of our belief in compassion. You first went to talk to him and ask him to leave; if he resisted, then you took other measures.

Of course, compassion, respect, responsibility, and accountability are just human characteristics or attributes. They govern any human being, or should, but some human beings choose not to. The reason lies in their upbringing, geography maybe, culture, religion, government maybe, and education. All of these might have steered them away, and were replaced by negative things. The most important are greed, anger, and guilt. Why do you think in some parts of the world, especially here in South Dakota, do white men hate us? Now why is that? Is that because of guilt? Is that because of greed? That hatred, that stupidity, that ire against the Lakota still exists among these people. And I often wonder is that because they feel guilty? Because this land for which they have a piece of paper saying it's theirs is not theirs? Do they know that intuitively? The land that was given to the white people on our reservation has been declared "surplus" by a foreign government, the United States government, and given to their citizens.[7] That is a crime against humanity, against the treaties that were written. Is this what European Americans feel? What is it? We are the only nation in the world where a foreign government says, hey, your land is surplus. We will give it to our own people—in our own country. It is for the Lakota to determine what constitutes "surplus land" because it is our land. European Americans came into our land uninvited. The language of the treaty stipulates only three white people on any reservation, especially on the Cheyenne River Reservation. This includes a superintendent, the chief clerk, and a member of the clergy. And a clergy member is to only teach the English language. The treaty did not say to educate the Lakota, it did not say to convert the Lakota. We already had our educational and religious resources in place, and we already had our Black Hills, which is rich in mineral resources. You name it, and it was there. Our land was our storehouse and they stole it. And it's still stolen. The Black Hills are still stolen now.[8] No matter how long, no matter who has title to it, the title belongs by law to the Lakota.

UW: Can there be sovereignty without the land?

HC: Can you grow without your mother? It would be very hard. But with land *and* spirituality, not either one or the other, it takes those two main ingredients, big ingredients. I should say, spirituality and *unci maka,* Mother Earth. Land, like you use the word, is a possession type of thing, but we look at it as Mother Earth, *unci maka.* And the great essence, you know, is spirituality. And without those two, it would be pretty hard, almost impossible. Without those two it would be hard, hard to have sovereignty because I think people would be suffering for a lack of those two. In fact, we are lost when we kick spirituality aside and only take it up one hour a week. It would be awfully hard. When we tear up Mother Earth, that's like hurting your mother, you take knives and tear her open. It's what we're doing today to Mother Earth. You do that too many times to your Mother and she will die. This is what Mother Earth is beginning to feel—the destructiveness that we are imposing upon her. The air is getting bad, the water is not very good any more. The land is not very good anymore. The animals are not very good anymore. The people are not very good anymore. The plants are not very good anymore. The fliers, the crawlers, the borers are not very good anymore. They are losing their strength. And when you come to that point, it brings you up against a whole new chapter of history which, if you are without spirituality, you are not going to believe.

UW: Today, over sixty-five percent of American Indians live in cities and not in the countryside.[9]

HC: Well, when they live in cities, they went perhaps out of necessity, or perhaps to get a job and make a living for their families. So necessity might be a part of being in a city. The other part is perhaps due to some kind of attraction that city life might hold for them. Some might be there because of a loss of identity, but some made a free choice to go there, to live there. And of course the sovereignty is not taken away from them, the innate sovereignty, the god-given sovereignty that they have within them. Collectively, if they try to form something, perhaps they can arrive at some peace. But it is hard in the city. I have had a brother in a city—I have even lived in big cities myself for a while. I have lived in Cleveland, Ohio, I have lived in Indianapolis, Terre Haute, Indiana, Portland, Oregon. I lived in Austin, Texas, different places. When you get in that hectic mainstream, it is hard to maintain any sort of spirituality, because you are going for a fast ride. And it is just almost impossible for spirituality to emerge out of that. You got to slow down and there is no time for that in the big city. I have heard people say that so many times when they come to South Dakota. All of a sudden, an old guy says, "[sighs] I feel so good, what is it about this place here?" I respond, "nothing." It is slower, a slower place. The clock is not king anymore. It is, but not controlling every second of your life, you know. So if the Indians in the big cities, those urbans, if they would slow down … I think that's why a lot of them come back to the rez for a few days to catch their breath [chuckles], but then they go right back into that. Because there is something there that attracts them, I don't know what it is, but a lifestyle that they see or live there attracts them. They have to go back to it. But they come back every now and then to strengthen themselves.

UW: AIM activism began in the city. What is your view of its legacy in support of sovereignty?

HC: Of course, Wounded Knee number two in the 70s did one thing. It drew attention to the plight. It showed the world that all was not a bed of roses for the

American Indian here in America. We were forgotten, we were abused, we were all of these things. There again, because of guilt, I don't know what it is, but there was hatred for us. So then the movement started to retaliate, maybe avenge. And of course the beginning of it was perhaps to come back to the rez and learn whatever you need to know, perhaps. And I think maybe most of all spirituality, because they did not know anything about spirituality. But like their Caucasian brothers, they just wanted it in a lump sum. They did not care to be patient, there was not much respect there because they did not take the time to learn the language. So then they cut across a lot of these things I spoke of earlier. And then when you realize that this quick fix is not the real thing, you are going to get angry. You are getting mad at somebody, at yourself perhaps, at your brothers, for not knowing. And you know that what you are pursuing was real for a while to you, but then you found out that it was not all that real after all. The reason is that now, you are doing ceremonies, or whatever you will call it, in English.[10] It was not intended that way. This caused a lot of confusion back in those days and still does to this day. Pipes are a good example. People are saying that [ceremonial] pipes are for Indians only, Sun Dances are for Indians only. At one time, when there were only Indians on this continent, that might have been true. But now we got relatives who are half this and half that, and yet we are still blood relatives, you see. What does that indicate to me? It indicates that we are all relatives and that all things are intended to be shared. But it must be grounded in the Lakota language, in the Lakota life ways.

LAKOTA STUDIES AS SOVEREIGNTY STUDIES: A CONVERSATION WITH IONE V. QUIGLEY

The vision of Lakota Studies at Sinte Gleska University embraces seven areas vital to the strengthening of Lakota sovereignty, thus following the definition of sovereignty as developed by the United Nations.[11] Of premier importance is an intimate knowledge of the homeland, *otiwota*, both as the place of birth and the home to which a human spirit returns after death. Language revitalization and preservation programs include the development of online courses, immersion language camps, and regular classes ranging from the introductory level to Lakota oratory. The Lakota Studies Department sponsors several major ceremonies throughout the year, including the "Welcoming Back the Thunders" ceremony at every spring equinox at Harney Peak in the Black Hills. Meals, meetings, and other gatherings are begun with a Lakota prayer. Leadership training across the university analyzes and encourages the practice of the traditional four Lakota values of bravery, *woohitika*, generosity, *wacantognaka*, wisdom, *woksape,* and fortitude, *wowacintanka.* Lakota Studies classes are offered on the topic of tribal social systems with particular instruction in Lakota educational and family support systems, past and present. Sinte Gleska University has also become a leader in the economic development of tribal resources by offering courses and research in traditional tribal economic systems, economic values, and their relationship to the environment. A consistent effort is being made to apply traditional practices, principles, and insights to contemporary problems.[12]

Finally, Lakota Studies supports the development of tribal self-governance and self-determination by offering courses on traditional forms of Lakota government and the history of the IRA government, especially as it relates to the *Sicangu Oyate,* the Sicangu Nation. Lakota citizens are thus empowered to work toward positive changes in tribal self-governance. Non-Lakota students benefit from Lakota Studies by learning holistically about regional and national history in the midst of a vibrant Lakota educational environment that offers cultural and spiritual windows into the Lakota past, present, and future. In the following conversation, Ione Quigley presents her view of the relationship between the seven Lakota Studies themes and the issue of Lakota sovereignty for the *Sicangu Oyate.*

UW: How would you like to begin addressing the issue of sovereignty in the context of Lakota Studies at Sinte Gleska University?

IQ: I gave the issue of sovereignty a lot of thought. I have been looking at it from every angle that I could think of. Sovereignty is an issue that every one of us faces, no matter who we are or where we come from, no matter what background and history we have. We all face this. Even as we speak, the United States faces the issue of sovereignty. Are we a true sovereign nation? I have my own thoughts on that issue. But for now, I would like to focus on Lakota sovereignty and how we view it.

   To understand sovereignty, we must start at the individual level. As individuals, we should ask, are we truly sovereign? Can we answer that question on an individual level and ask ourselves, am I happy? Do I have enough? Am I completely responsible for my own self, for my emotions, for my mental well-being, and for my physical well-being? Am I comfortable with my life, which is truly the time that I am to live on the land that I was born on? Am I truly living a sovereign life where I am my sole sovereign, and am I able to let others be sovereign in the same sense?

   At one time, over one hundred years ago, we were a strong and sovereign nation. Each individual, each social unit, each band or nuclear family unit was actually given the choices implicit in the questions posed above. So we look at sovereignty as actually having the freedom of choice.

I have also given thought to the counter or opposite of sovereignty. What is that? I have begun to think of the different ways in which you are not free to choose. On the opposite side of your right to choose we find oppression, which takes away the right to make choices.

UW: The Lakota Studies Program at Sinte Gleska University is rooted in a long struggle to regain sovereignty.

IQ: We actually started with a movement of our own right here. We started trying to find out what land and resources we actually have. Before we began our own search, all of that information was kept from us. All of that information was kept within United States government agencies. The government declared itself a guardian of us, the Lakota, a sovereign nation. Considering themselves a guardian of our land as well, they also took it upon themselves to have the land measured and surveyed and explored for its resources. The government decided who could have access to our land and who could come in and choose to do what they pleased. What is our land worth? Where are the borders of our land base? What resources do we really have here? This information has been made publicly available more and more. And there are certain Sinte Gleska programs and departments that are increasingly addressing these questions.

The United States guardianship took away a lot of our power as a sovereign nation. For the United States government, oppression of our nation and the sovereignty of the United States go hand in hand. It is important to understand that oppression takes away power as well as responsibilities. For example, consider our society and our culture. We had to think twice whether we should speak our language. Should we allow our children to speak the language or allow them to get beaten?[13] Today, these and other destructive aspects of United States government policies are coming out into the open.

The greatest of oppression we faced, however, was the destruction of gaining our livelihood and the food, when they took that away. The threat of starvation puts people into a vise. You have them where you want them. That was only the starting point, however. The people were suffering, and then they were given this medicine that was going to make them feel better. That's when they introduced *mni wakan,* the sacred water. It is said that in the beginning, only the men of our people drank. Yet like any kind of disease that spreads, drinking spread to everybody. This particular tool, alcohol, was probably the strongest weapon that the government had.[14]

Another tool that it used against us was education. The United States imposed a completely new language upon us. It imposed a completely new system of education upon us. Yet we already had a fully functioning system of education. Our mothers, grandmothers and grandfathers, they were our educators. All of a sudden, a completely different system was forced on us. Instead of family members, strangers educate us. The Western system is impersonal and hierarchical. You get children into a classroom and tell them that this is the way it is. Our family-based system of education was different. We were taught lessons through life experiences, and then we were given the choice to interpret, explore, and apply our lessons. In the rigid education system that we have now, we are learning abstractly. We are given only one version of the way things are, even when it comes to history. This is what happened, and we were never really given any other option.

UW: The Lakota encountered Western education first in religious schools.

IQ: The education that was imposed on us was rigid and impersonal. From there we move on to the question of spirituality. We have had the Catholic Church and the Episcopal Church, but the major church coming in was the Catholic Church.[15] Personally speaking, I have always thought that Catholicism is not a system of teaching about the good things in life. And these are the important matters. Life is to be loved and appreciated. Life is to be lived. You know, these are the rules to live by. That was always my ideal. Lakota spirituality teaches that through living life fully, you will have many experiences. All of these experiences are your own immersion into the process of creation. In contrast, in Catholicism you look for external attributes and symbols that everybody recognizes. We still look for those attributes and confuse them with spiritual values. For example, consider the belief that you are not a good person until you have a good job, a nice home, beautiful children—the ideal family, the ideal Mr. and Mrs. Jones if you like. The Lakota people say no to this view. Enjoy life, live life—even if society is concerned with materialism.

Our social systems at one time worked in harmony with our spirituality. We lived in a kinship system in which relatives were never addressed by their name. When you address a person through our kinship terms, the person knows her responsibilities and how she will be taken care of by her relatives. I never quit using kinship terms. I still say to my children, "tell your grandfather, go visit your grandmother." In the past, we lived our lives with each other in camps where we were able to take care of each other. Now we have to cope with another culture's social system. I am forced to drive across town to where my mother lives, and she has to live by herself. We have been living with this foreign system for the past one hundred years, adjusting to a program of education and values that the United States government has forced on us. What does that do to the spirit, what does that do to the family?

When you have relatives, you will always have care, you will always have that. Our social systems are still intact in that we care for each other. So we do have a course on the kinship system here at Sinte Gleska's Lakota Studies. It's called *LS 221: Lakota Social Systems*. The instructors have done a wonderful job of having everybody learn and appreciate what behaviors are appropriate for each kinship role and how to fully participate in the family unit and beyond. This knowledge allows our children to feel that they belong and that they are an important part of the family. It is one of several cultural projects we have created. It is exciting to be a part of it all, because it is going to be a good thing for the people. Kinship ways were so natural and they are still meaningful today.

When the *canupa* (sacred pipe) was brought to us by White Buffalo Calf Woman, the pipe came with responsibilities. The goal was to live in peace with all people.[16] You know there are always stories within the families, within the kinship that you know and belong to. Where language is concerned, at one time, our language was such that it carried the larger cultural, social, and spiritual meaning in all these specific kinship terms. At the time of the worst oppression of our culture, our language came to almost a standstill. And because of that we have had to work hard on not only teaching the language, but on the meaning behind the words. This affects all that we face in trying to revitalize our culture. So we actually have multiple bumps.

In the Lakota system, kinship relations are deeply connected to economic survival and well-being as well.[17] The United States government tried to destroy this link as well. If you are allowed welfare benefits, for example, it amounts to yet another form of oppression. We have a lot of lost people out there because of state welfare. If you are on welfare, it can quickly happen that a social worker looks into whether a child needs to be placed outside of her biological family. The child grows up without learning who she is in the larger kinship system and what it means to be Lakota.

Take another example, the Native American Graves Repatriation Act.[18] It allows us to bring home our relatives, our ancestors. The flip side of that is that it is only applied to federal travel, and not regionally. That restriction actually helps keep us oppressed. True sovereignty will not come about until we can educate and unite the Lakota who live here.

UW: To accomplish all of this takes a strong group effort.

IQ: We actually have a group of women who have begun all of this, one of the best things that could have happened to us.[19] It was a group of women that finally stood up and said, "we want positive change for ourselves and for our children." The women actually went about to start the change by gathering information. They started a movement within the tribe. They are also one of several groups that I have been working with in writing our constitution. During our work on the constitution, we have accepted several proposed amendments. With all of the decisions we make, we have to remember that we are not making them for ourselves. For example, we are working to set up our own judicial system. You know, having the understanding that "this is wrong, let's fix it," not, "this is wrong, let's put him away for two years and let him think about it." Rather, "this is wrong, let's fix it, right here." At the university, Marlise Whitehat leads a movement called "Restorative Justice."[20] We had a judge who made all the decisions without allowing us to apply our own justice system. He said, in top-down fashion and without knowing the community, "ok you're wrong and you're not and you're the one that needs to go sit in jail." It is another form of oppression to not be allowed to fully deal with legal issues through our own justice system. I think we need to work with a model to allow everybody involved to resolve the crime and to give everybody a sense that this is what needs to be done. This is where the government courts fail. It has brought a lot of grief, a lot of anger. And it is just another example of denying sovereignty to the Lakota.

I truly believe that we can be economically sovereign. When people do not have something they need, it constitutes an imbalance. It is in the nature of things that are unbalanced that they attract that which will bring back balance. That is possible for economic sovereignty as well. What we need to do is take an inventory of what we have here on the reservation and say, "okay, this is what we each have. Now what do the tribes in Montana have, what do the tribes in Arizona have?" We practiced a bartering system in the past that worked. Many archaeologists have said that our area was a trade center. A bartering system can be brought back today. It is happening for our language, our justice system, and our kinship system.

CONCLUSION

In her study of the origins of the Lakota Nation, Ione Quigley writes that Lakota oral traditions point to the emergence of the Lakota during the Pleistocene Period about

20,000 to 40,000 years ago. An ice age bison kill in Colorado from about 13,000 years ago suggests strong similarities with a Lakota buffalo hunt/kill site in the 1600s, thus suggesting ancestral links.[21] At the other end of the historical spectrum, efforts are being made to heal the trauma of boarding schools,[22] relocation, and other forms of colonial oppression through culturally appropriate means that center on the reappearance of *Pte Oyate,* the buffalo nation, traditional ceremonies, and other cultural and economic activities.[23]

Both Lakota elders affirm the viability of their traditions in shaping the necessary conditions for a full exercise of sovereignty now and in the future. Both work with the knowledge that the process will not be a "quick fix," that it will take the patient labor of many to heal and revitalize legal systems in tandem with cultural, economic, and spiritual systems. The fact that the State of South Dakota has made one significant step toward supporting the efforts of tribal colleges such as Sinte Gleska University and the teachings and ceremonial work of elders such as Harry Charger render their conversations timely and relevant to their students, their communities, and other tribal nations.

NOTES

The notes are intended to guide the reader to further information on the subjects discussed in the chapter.

1 "Public schools in South Dakota to include American Indian education" posted March 19, 2007 by David Melmer, *Indian Country Today* Web site. "PIERRE, S.D.—Students in South Dakota will hear different approaches to the state's history in the next school year: [T]hey will be exposed to American Indian culture and the language of the Lakota. Much like Montana, which has implemented an Indian Education for All program, South Dakota will attempt to bridge educational achievement gaps between American Indian and non-Indian students, lower dropout rates, and bring about a better understanding of the cultures. Gov. Mike Rounds has signed a bill into law that will include curriculum changes that will teach about American Indian culture and language, and require teachers to upgrade their skills with American Indian studies courses. The new law also officially creates the office of American Indian Education."

2 For an introduction to the many cultural strategies to undermine Indigenous sovereignty in European-American contexts, especially in the academy, see Elizabeth Cook-Lynn, *Anti-Indianism in Modern America: A Voice from Tatekeya's Earth* (Champaign: University of Illinois Press, 2001). On the impact of boarding schools, see Debra K. S. Barker, "Kill the Indian, Save the Child: Cultural Genocide and the Boarding School," in *American Indian Studies: An Interdisciplinary Approach to Contemporary Issues,* edited by Dane Morrison (New York: Peter Lang, 1997), 47–69.

3 Thomas Biolsi, "Bringing the Law Back in: Legal Rights and the Regulation of Indian-White Relations on Rosebud Reservation," *Current Anthropology* 36.4 (August-October 1995): 543–71, quotation p. 561.

4 For an academic analysis of the inherent tensions involved in negotiating a relationship between Indigenous and non-Indigenous discursive practices, see Chadwick Allen, *Blood Narrative. Indigenous Identity in American Indian and Maori Literary and Activist Texts* (Durham: Duke University Press, 2002), and Thomas W. Cooper, *A Time before Deception: Truth in Communication, Culture, and Ethics* (Santa Fe: Clear Light Publishers, 1998).

5 On the resurgence of oral knowledge and traditions in American Indian Studies, see Donald L. Fixico, *The American Indian Mind in a Linear World: American Indian Studies and Traditional Knowledge* (New York: Routledge, 2003), especially chapter two, "Oral Tradition and Traditional Knowledge," 21–41.

6 For background information on Lakota women, see, for example, Marla N. Powers, *Oglala Women: Myth, Ritual, and Reality* (Chicago: The University of Chicago Press, 1986) and Mark St. Pierre and Tilda Long Soldier, *Walking in the Sacred Manner: Medicine Women of the Plains Indians* (New York: Touchstone, 1995); on AIM, see Joane Nagel, *American Indian Ethnic Renewal: Red Power and the Resurgence of Identity and Culture* (New York: Oxford University Press, 1996); on Lakota history and political structures, see *Unit Three: Makoce,* and *Unit Five: Itancan, Curriculum Materials Resource Units,* designed by Vivian One Feather, Oglala Sioux Culture Center, Red Cloud Indian School, Inc., Pine Ridge, South Dakota, 1972–1974.

7 For a survey on the constitutional foundations of the relationship between United States Federal Government and Tribal Nations, see Vine Deloria Jr. and David E. Wilkins, *Tribes, Treaties, and Constitutional Tribulations* (Austin: University of Texas Press, 1999).

8 See Edward Lazarus, *Black Hills, White Justice: the Sioux Nation Versus the United States, 1775 to the Present* (New York: Harper Collins, 1991).

9 See Susan Lobo and Kurt M. Peters, *American Indians and the Urban Experience* (Walnut Creek, CA: Altamira Press), 2001. On the multiple dimensions of exile for American Indians, see Vine Deloria, Jr., "Out of Chaos," in D. M. Dooling and Paul Jordan-Smith, *I Become Part of It: Sacred Dimensions on Native American Life* (New York: Harper San Francisco, 1989), 259–70.

10 On Lakota vocabulary used in ceremony, see William K. Powers, *Sacred Language: The Nature of Supernatural Discourse in Lakota* (Norman: University of Oklahoma Press, 1986).

11 Thanks to several global initiatives, including efforts by the United Nations, the concept of a "Fourth World" of Indigenous Peoples is steadily gaining momentum. For an overview, see Jeffrey Sissons, *First Peoples: Indigenous Cultures and Their Futures* (London: Reaktion Books, 2005).

12 For an example of the culturally appropriate integration of all these elements, see Ronald Goodman, *Lakota Star Knowledge: Studies in Lakota Stellar Theology* (Mission, SD: Sinte Gleska University, 1992).

13 The scholarship on the vital link between Indigenous languages and environmental and ecological health is steadily growing, thus supporting Sinte Gleska's holistic vision. See, for example, Daniel Nettle and Suzanne Romaine, *Vanishing Voices: The Extinction of the World's Languages* (Oxford: Oxford University Press, 2000).

14 Indigenous Sobriety and Wellness Programs are spreading; for an academic contextualization of intergenerational trauma and culturally appropriate healing, see Eduardo Duran and Bonnie Duran, *Native American Postcolonial Psychology* (Albany: State University of New York Press, 1995).

15 On the cultural and theological dynamics of missionary activity among First Nations, see George E. Tinker, *Missionary Conquest: The Gospel and Native American Cultural Genocide* (Minneapolis: Fortress Press, 1993).

16 See D. M. Dooling and Paul Jordan-Smith, "White Buffalo Woman," in *I Become Part of It: Sacred Dimensions on Native American Life,* edited by D. M. Dooling and Paul Jordan-Smith (New York:

HarperSanFrancisco, 1989), 204–6, and James R. Walker, *Lakota Belief and Ritual*, edited by Raymond DeMallie and Elaine A. Jahner (Lincoln: University of Nebraska Press, 1980, 1991), 109–12.

17 See Dean Howard Smith, *Modern Tribal Development: Paths to Self-Sufficiency and Cultural Integrity in Indian Country* (Lanham, MD: Altamira Press, 2000) for a succinct and optimistic model of integrating culture and economic development.

18 See Winona LaDuke, "Quilled Cradleboard Covers, Cultural Patrimony, and Wounded Knee," in *Recovering the Sacred. The Power of Naming and Claiming,* edited by Winona LaDuke (Cambridge, MA: South End Press, 2005), 87–113.

19 For further discussion of women's contributions to the reclamation of full sovereignty, see Andrea Smith, "Native American Feminism, Sovereignty, and Social Change," *Feminist Studies* 31.1 (Spring 2005): 116–32.

20 The concept of restorative justice is gaining global momentum in and beyond Indigenous communities. See Elizabeth Elliott, Robert M. Gordon, eds., *New Directions in Restorative Justice: Issues, Practice, Evaluation* (Portland, OR: Willan, 2005). For a Canadian First Nations comparison, see Wayne Warry, *Unfinished Dreams: Community Healing and the Reality of Aboriginal Self-Government* (Toronto: University of Toronto Press, 2000), chapter five, "Restoring Justice: Conflict with the Law," 163–205. Warry concludes that at least for the Canadian context, "the idea that alternative justice programs can serve as a locus for community healing and development is greatly underestimated by non-Native policy-makers who continue to compartmentalize law" (p. 202).

21 Ione V. Quigley, "An Evaluation of True Sovereignty of the Rosebud Sioux Tribe," unpublished paper, n.p.

22 Sharon Waxman, "Sioux Allege Abuse at Church Boarding Schools," *Washington Post*, June 2, 2003, <http://www.rickross.com/reference/ckergy/clergy164.html> (accessed October 18, 2004).

23 See Winona LaDuke, "Buffalo Nations, Buffalo People," in *All Our Relations. Native Struggles for Land and Life* (Cambridge, MA: South End Press, 1999), 139–67.

BIBLIOGRAPHY

Allen, Chadwick. *Blood Narrative: Indigenous Identity in American Indian and Maori Literary and Activist Texts*. Durham: Duke University Press, 2002.

Barker, Debra K. S. "Kill the Indian, Save the Child: Cultural Genocide and the Boarding School." In *American Indian Studies: An Interdisciplinary Approach to Contemporary Issues,* edited by Dane Morrison. New York: Peter Lang, 1997.

Biolsi, Thomas. "Bringing the Law Back in: Legal Rights and the Regulation of Indian-White Relations on Rosebud Reservation." *Current Anthropology* 36.4 (August-October 1995): 543–71.

Cook-Lynn, Elizabeth. *Anti-Indianism in Modern America: A Voice from Tatekeya's Earth.* Champaign: University of Illinois Press, 2001.

Cooper, Thomas A. *A Time before Deception: Truth in Communication, Culture, and Ethics.* Santa Fe: Clear Light Publishers, 1998.

Deloria, Vine, Jr. "Out of Chaos." In *I Become Part of It: Sacred Dimensions on Native American Life,* edited by D. M. Dooling and Paul Jordan-Smith. New York: Harper SanFrancisco, 1989.

Deloria, Vine Jr., and David E. Wilkins. *Tribes, Treaties, and Constitutional Tribulations.* Austin: University of Texas Press, 1999.

Dooling, D. M., and Paul Jordan-Smith. "White Buffalo Woman." In *I Become Part of It: Sacred Dimensions on Native American Life,* edited by D. M. Dooling and Paul Jordan-Smith. New York: Harper SanFrancisco, 1989.

Duran, Eduardo, and Bonnie Duran. *Native American Postcolonial Psychology.* Albany: State University of New York Press, 1995.

Elliott, Elizabeth, and Robert M. Gordon, eds. *New Directions in Restorative Justice: Issues, Practice, Evaluation.* Portland, OR: Willan, 2005.

Fixico, Donald L. *The American Indian Mind in a Linear World: American Indian Studies and Traditional Knowledge.* New York: Routledge, 2003.

Goodman, Ronald. *Lakota Star Knowledge: Studies in Lakota Stellar Theology.* Mission, SD: Sinte Gleska University, 1992.

LaDuke, Winona. *All Our Relations. Native Struggles for Land and Life.* Cambridge, MA: South End Press, 1999.

————. *Recovering the Sacred: The Power of Naming and Claiming.* Cambridge, MA: South End Press, 2005.

Lazarus, Edward. *Black Hills, White Justice: The Sioux Nation versus the United States, 1775 to the Present.* New York: Harper Collins, 1991.

Lobo, Susan, and Kurt M. Peters. *American Indians and the Urban Experience.* Walnut Creek, CA: Altamira Press, 2001.

Melmer, David. "Public Schools in South Dakota to Include American Indian Education." *Indian Country Today*, March 19, 2007.

Nagel, Joanne. *American Indian Ethnic Renewal: Red Power and the Resurgence of Identity and Culture.* New York: Oxford University Press, 1996.

Nettle, Daniel, and Suzanne Romaine. *Vanishing Voices: The Extinction of the World's Languages.* Oxford: Oxford University Press, 2000.

One Feather, Vivian. *Unit Three: Makoce,* and *Unit Five: Itancan, Curriculum Materials Resource Units.* Oglala Sioux Culture Center, Red Cloud Indian School, Inc., Pine Ridge, South Dakota, 1972–1974.

Powers, Marla N. *Oglala Women: Myth, Ritual, and Reality.* Chicago: The University of Chicago Press, 1986.

Powers, William K. *Sacred Language: The Nature of Supernatural Discourse in Lakota.* Norman: University of Oklahoma Press, 1986.

Quigley, Ione V. "An Evaluation of True Sovereignty of the Rosebud Sioux Tribe." Unpublished paper.

Sissons, Jeffrey. *First Peoples. Indigenous Cultures and their Futures*. London: Reaktion Books, 2005.

Smith, Andrea. "Native American Feminism, Sovereignty, and Social Change." *Feminist Studies* 31.1 (Spring 2005): 116–32.

Smith, Dean Howard. *Modern Tribal Development: Paths to Self-Sufficiency and Cultural Integrity in Indian Country*. Lanham, MD: Altamira Press, 2000.

St. Pierre, Mark, and Tilda Long Soldier. *Walking in the Sacred Manner: Medicine Women of the Plains Indians*. New York: Touchstone, 1995.

Tinker, George E. *Missionary Conquest: The Gospel and Native American Cultural Genocide*. Minneapolis: Fortress Press, 1993.

Walker, James R. *Lakota Belief and Ritual*, edited by Raymond DeMallie and Elaine A. Jahner. 1980. Reprint, Lincoln: University of Nebraska Press, 1991.

Warry, Wayne. *Unfinished Dreams: Community Healing and the Reality of Aboriginal Self-Government*. Toronto: University of Toronto Press, 2000.

Waxman, Sharon. "Sioux Allege Abuse at Church Boarding Schools." *Washington Post,* June 2, 2003. <*http://www.rickross.com/reference/ckergy/clergy164.html*> (accessed October 18, 2004).

9 "FULL CIRCLE GATHERING": THE HEALING OF A NATION

J.T. Garrett

"We are who we are, but we are known by what we do and how we show respect to others. This is the Cherokee way, the Indian way of life. We live in harmony and balance with Mother Earth and give thanks to the Great One for the survival of another winter into the spring of life."

Oscar Rogers, Eastern Band of Cherokee Indians, North Carolina

SURVIVING WINTER INTO THE SPRING OF LIFE

My nation has experienced many times the survival of winter into the spring of life, at times against all odds and with terrible suffering. This essay describes past and present moments in the history of our survival as a sovereign nation. I am writing with gratitude to our elders and hope for our children.

Sitting on the worn porch of an old cabin in the Smoky Mountains was an Elder Cherokee Medicine Man. This was in 1984. The elder said,

It is a great day for the Cherokee people ... a great day to give thanks to the Great One ... a great day to remember our ancestors, for they paid the price for our past and our future ... a great day to remember that we are healing, one generation at a time. Sure, there are troubles and unrest, as there will always be these things to face as humans. We have not yet learned the secret to live and be in peace with all things. Just as the Europeans came to these shores and said, 'This is our land,' and just as greed can be called vision. These are things not for us to follow. We must always follow the Red Road to harmony and balance, and our people will celebrate in ceremony with drumming, song, and dance as we share corn with other tribes and all others in the greatest of all coming-together in the *Full Circle Gathering*. Sgi (thanks).[1]

And so our initiative of healing our nation continues. Gathering the circle of our nation, we mend the circle. American Indian people have always been a Native and sovereign people in North America, and they will always be so in mind and spirit. From an American Indian perspective, there was a time when even identifying oneself as a Cherokee or Indian could have meant the loss of one's life. However, the spirit of the Indian people and their spirituality was passed down, as an elder said, "in silent expression so as to be as much like the white people as possible." Among tribes, the Indian people understood themselves on a much deeper level, which is still true today. "The alliances among tribes will always be there in spirit," as a Cherokee Elder woman once said, "for one cannot break the bond of spirit as treaties have been broken with men." The Cherokee Elder woman was talking about the "Trail of Tears," the forced migration of over ninety percent of all Indians living east of the Mississippi River to Indian territory west of the Mississippi River.[2] The result of the Indian Removal Act, the "Trail of Tears" was carried out by President Andrew Jackson between

1830 and 1838. The removal was passed into law by Congress to force the Cherokee and other tribes to give up their homelands. As part of the forced removal, an effort was made to silence our voice and spirit as well. The people could not meet together or have ceremonial activities for fear of an uprising or conflict with the soldiers during the Removal.

In 1828, the Cherokee Tribal Council published the first issue of the *Cherokee Phoenix*, the first newspaper to be printed in an Indian language, along with English. In 1821, Sequoyah put the Cherokee language into a written format with symbols readable and understandable through the spoken language. In 1834, during the midst of the forced removal, the State of Georgia suppressed the printing and dissemination of the *Cherokee Phoenix*. As the Cherokee Elder said,

> Our words were suppressed, but our hearts and spirit have never been suppressed or defeated. With the help of some non-Indians such as Will Thomas, the Eastern Band of Cherokee Indians as a Tribe today attests to our endurance and to our determination to preserve our people and our culture so that it still survives today. [3]

William Holland Thomas (1805–1893), adopted as a boy by Chief Yonaguska (ca.1759 – 1839), bought land in the mountains of North Carolina on behalf of the Cherokee people who were allowed to stay in their homeland. They were known as the "lufty Cherokees" who lived along the Oconaluftee River known today as the Qualla Boundary or Reservation.   Together with the Cherokee Nation located in Oklahoma and Texas, the Eastern Band is a part of nearly 800,000 Cherokee Indian people. The original Cherokee language is spoken and taught in our schools and homes, as well as during ceremonial gatherings and Fall Festivals that bring the Cherokee people together once again.

In 2003, in the foothills of the Blue Ridge Mountains in North Carolina, a cross-cultural symposium, entitled "Native American Indian Sovereignty: An Interdisciplinary and Cross Cultural Symposium," provided a dynamic opportunity for tribal members and others to come together and to reflect on our past and our future. Sponsored by the National Indian Education Association, the Lilly Endowment, and Wake Forest University, the symposium offered an open environment for participation. We shared facts as much as feelings about American Indian sovereignty. A traditional ceremonial environment invited participants to experience the beauty and respect of a cultural way of life known to American Indians, but not seen so openly by the non-Indian population as a whole.

In previous centuries, Cherokee ceremonies such as the Green Corn Ceremony provided a sacred time for the nation to come together to celebrate life, family, and tribal cultural traditions. Today, every tribe practices its own cultural traditions and life ways as preserved by the ancestors and passed on to the future members of the tribe. The symposium, too, in some way was a time of *Full Circle Gathering*: a time of teaching, of "inter-tribal" ceremony, song, drumming, and American Indian and Native Hawaiian cultural sharing to more deeply appreciate and respect a way of life that possibly goes back to the beginning of time for human existence here on Mother Earth.

BEYOND THE MAYFLOWER: THE LAND OF THE BEAUTIFUL

In November of 2002, Cokie and Steven Roberts published an article entitled "Beyond the Mayflower."[4] It was a reminder that many Americans today are related to those first one hundred and two pilgrims who sailed to the "New World" on the Mayflower. The ship landed at Plymouth Rock about three hundred and eighty-five years ago. There are also many Americans living today who are related to the Native Americans who helped the pilgrims to not starve or freeze to death during their harsh first winter in Massachusetts. The first Thanksgiving celebration included the fifty or so colonists who survived the winter months to the harvest season as well as many women and men from the Wampanoag tribe.

Counting forward from those eventful encounters in 1620, a staggering number of Americans can trace some part of their genealogy and family history to American Indian ancestors of those early times. Approximately thirty-five million Americans are alive today who are direct descendents of the first Mayflower Pilgrims. Together, they constitute almost twelve percent of our American population.

We often focus on the negative and destructive experiences on both sides, of the people migrating to settle from Europe and of the Native people already here in North America. However, both shaped this "New World" that we today call the United States of America. Just look at how far we have progressed from those difficult beginnings of this "New America" that earlier American Indians referred to as "Turtle Island." My own family ancestry includes Cherokee Indian and Irish ancestry. It is probably easier for me to see both sides of a "revolutionary" past that has brought us to the powerful nation it is today. It is sometimes difficult for me to imagine a member of my Irish family in 1789 as part of a survey team marking the line between Tennessee and North Carolina as we know it today. Then I am reminded that one of the members of the survey team was a Cherokee tribal member who also is a part of my American family today and "who knew those old Indian trails like the back of his hands." Pioneer settlers *and* American Indians helped mark the lines that created the States of North Carolina, Tennessee, and Virginia shortly after the Revolutionary War.

While the past was difficult and costly with treaties, "land grabbing," and wars that reached across the seas, we still can be truly thankful for the "land of the beautiful," America.

"WE ARE KNOWN BY WHAT WE DO AND HOW WE SHOW RESPECT TO OTHERS": DOCTRINES DETERMINE TREATIES AND PUBLIC LAWS TODAY

In 1871, the U.S. Congress terminated eighty years of a precisely defined legal relationship with American Indian nations. The treaty period, defined as the decades between 1790 and 1870, is a shameful era with many failed promises then and today.[5] In the treaties, the United States used wording such as receiving American Indian nations in "friendship and protection," or "to promote the future welfare of" or even to execute an agreement "with all good faith and sincerity." This terminology is considered as a familiar expression of goodwill. Other words chosen, however, such as "agree to employ a physician … who shall furnish medicine and advice to the sick" or "agree … to erect a hospital, keeping the same in repair" are contractual agreements as millions of acres of American Indian land were taken by the United States government. The commitments did not end when Congress decided to end treaty-making with American Indian nations. The treaty-making period is based on a trust relationship and a legal responsibility still in place in the present. Were millions of acres of land lost and the lives of so many tribes destroyed only to not have those treaties fully executed with all "good faith and sincerity" extending to the present and the future? When we discussed improvements in amendments to Public Law 94–437, the Indian Health Care Improvement Act of 1976, Cherokee elder Jake Whitecrow summarized this issue from an American Indian perspective. He said,

> It is for us to look back and only reflect, but it is critical that we look forward and deflect all that was as we create our own piece of the American dream. We will call it our American Indian 'Vision.' Such a vision will keep us dreaming. We must learn to be good negotiators with the United States and mediators ourselves.[6]

As Americans, we have a commitment to carry out the intent of those treaties and to respect the sovereignty of American Indian tribal governments now and in the future. What is critical is that we as well as the U.S. Congress and state governments work with tribal governments for effective relationships in serving Indian people. There are positive examples of the United States Congress working in "consultation with" American Indian Nations as a routine activity before passing amendments to public laws affecting Indian Tribes. Examples include amendments to public laws such as the Indian Health Care Improvement Act and the Indian Self Determination and Education Assistance Act (Public Law 93–413).

"THIS IS THE CHEROKEE WAY, THE INDIAN WAY OF LIFE": TOWARD A RENEWED IDENTITY AS AN AMERICAN INDIAN

The identity of American Indians changed forever since the discovery of Columbus, lost on his voyage in search of Asia. The "Los Indios," as he called us as the Native People here, were and still are distinct groups of families and tribes. We still have clearly defined governments, ways of life, and even our own spirituality. Constitutions and Congresses, treaties and laws did not change the American Indian and tribal way of survival and protection for their own members as families. If anything, everything else has changed since the first American Indians were taken into captivity by the Spanish in the 1600s. What has most impacted American Indians is the loss of homeland, economic opportunity, and identity that has led to the high incidence of disease and destructive behaviors of American Indians today.

We can change, and we have done much through some very positive programs in education, economical development, health, and home construction on reservations. However, there is still a lot to do to take us from the earlier times of Columbus and the Vikings, who tried to "own" the land and the Native people here in what we call "the land of the free and the brave." All people are neither equal nor do they have the same advantages. This reality must be changed for American Indians to encourage a positive identity and a sense of integrity.

The impact of the loss of the American Indian homeland and "hunting grounds" or what many tribes referred to as "barrier lands" was that a sense of freedom and protection was taken away. Native Peoples were put on reservations and land reserves. A way of life was taken away that has not been fully recovered. We are struggling to survive. In terms of health, we must turn around the negative impact of alcohol and substance abuse, diabetes, and other diseases that deny individuals and families income and the opportunity for a positive way of life.

However, there is a strong ray of hope. As tribes find ways to create income and opportunities to prosper, they are able to serve their members better than the treaties and public laws of the past. These treaties and laws might have been an effort to protect American Indian health and well-being, but in essence failed the Indian people and failed the American people. This is not to say that we should not be appreciative of everything and everyone who has served American Indian populations well and who has done honorable work in the effort to raise the level of health of our nations to the rest of the American population.

History, regardless of what has happened has not altered who we are as American Indians today. We are sovereign nations of proud people called American Indians today, even though we are some 550 or more individual tribes and tribal organizations.

We have a government-to-government relationship with the United States on the basis of prior agreements. This is a part of our relationship with everything else in our environment. We are Indians as individuals and as members of a tribe. We do not ask for anything more than what is fair, than what is equitable with other populations, and what is in accordance with prior agreements and law. We have a tribal name and an identity as American Indians.

FULL CIRCLE HEALING TODAY: PRACTICING "CROSSOVER"

We are determined to be sovereign, economically secure, and confident as a tribe and a people with partnerships and alliances, and with our own religious practices and way of life. In essence, we want what every immigrant to this "New World" searched for: equality and fairness. As a Cherokee elder put it, "We only want what we had before the white man came here, but today."

The present offers an opportunity for American Indians and non-Indians alike to recognize that we are healing the wounds of history for both groups and that it is time for healing the spirit of America for American Indians. In the oldest wisdom of time, the key and the way to heal past harm is a practice that has been referred to as "crossover."[7] The traditional way was to offer our tobacco prayers in ceremonies to the Great One, cleanse our spirit with water, and share the sacred pipe for healing of the tribe in the circle and for the greater Universal Circle of life. We must continue to come together as governments and as people in a Full Circle of life. We must continue to come together as governments and as people in a Full Circle Gathering to be a "helper" for the healing of people and protection of Mother Earth. In a healing circle, we are all equal and different only by our perceived differences. These diminish with increased understanding and practice. Participants might act as "helpers" and "protectors" of our cultural traditions within our own circles as a tribe and family.

On November 6, 2000, President William J. Clinton pronounced in an executive order what so many United States presidents have said before him:

> The First Americans hold a unique place in our history. Long before others came to our shores, the First Americans had established self-governing societies. Among their societies, democracy flourished long before the founding of our Nation. Our Nation entered into treaties with Indian nations, which acknowledged their right to self-government and protected

their lands. The Constitution affirms the United States' government-to-government relationship.[8]

Like other Presidents before him, President Clinton asked the federal government to acknowledge "the importance of tribal sovereignty and government-to-government relations." In April of 1994, he was the first president since James Monroe to invite the leaders of every tribal nation to the White House. In this historic meeting, he directed all federal agencies to consult with Indian tribes before making decisions on matters affecting American Indian and Alaska Native peoples. This, too, was a full circle gathering for the healing of a nation.

NOTES

1 Personal conversation with author, 1984.
2 The "Trail of Tears" included more than 16,000 Cherokees. It was brutally enforced by 7,000 federal troops and the Georgia militia. It is estimated that one out of four Cherokee died during the journey. Cherokee were also forcefully removed from Texas during the same time period.
3 Personal conversation with author, 1984.
4 Cokie Roberts and Steven Roberts, "Beyond the Mayflower," *USA Today,* November 22–23, 2002.
5 The treaty-making period for the Cherokee nation began with the Treaty of Hard Labour (1768) and the Treaty of Lochaber (1770).
6 Jake Whitecrow, personal conversation with author, n. d.
7 For a description of the psychological and spiritual dimensions of a "crossover" cleansing of the spirit, see J. T. Garrett and Michael Tlanusta Garrett, *The Cherokee Full Circle: A Practical Guide to Ceremonies and Traditions* (Rochester, VT: Bear Company, 2002), 176–78.
8 William J. Clinton, "Executive Order 13175—Consultation and Coordination with Indian Tribal Governments." November 6, 2000.

BIBLIOGRAPHY

Clinton, William J. "Executive Order 13175—Consultation and Coordination with Indian Tribal Governments." November 6, 2000.

Garrett, J. T., and Michael Tlanusta Garrett. *The Cherokee Full Circle: A Practical Guide to Ceremonies and Traditions.* Rochester, VT: Bear and Company, 2002.

Roberts, Cokie, and Steven Roberts. "Beyond the Mayflower." *USA Today,* November 22–23, 2002.

10 SPEAKING DIFFERENCE TO POWER: THE IMPORTANCE OF LINGUISTIC SOVEREIGNTY

Thomas Belt and Margaret Bender

We argue that language is an essential component of sovereignty.[1] Maintaining and revitalizing the Cherokee language, in particular, is an important tool in the struggle to assert and defend the sovereignty of the Cherokee people. To us, sovereignty is not just a matter of political boundaries and autonomy, though those matters are crucial. It is about the radical right to be.[2] Sovereignty is the responsibility to do a particular job, to do the things you were meant to do. Sovereignty is a right, but it is not the negative right people often suppose. That is, it is not just a right to be free from impositions, to not have others tell you what to do. It is a right to do the things that make one who one is.

Why can't Cherokees just *be* in English? Growing up, Cherokees are taught that things are different for a reason. Consider a wolf, a dog, and a coyote. The skeleton of each may look the same, but the living animals are very different and serve distinct purposes. Each fulfills an important role in the totality of creation. All need to exist for the whole to maintain its integrity. Similarly, consider the nature of a person's individual fingers. Though each finger certainly has abilities, it is only when they come together as the complementary fingers of a hand that they can grasp, manipulate, threaten, and so forth, in the way that really allows them to fulfill their potential as human fingers. So it is with languages. Each community of speakers has its own language. That language would not exist if it did not serve a purpose, not only for that particular group, but for humanity as a whole. To use another metaphor, different craftsmen working on a building together—the plumber, stonemason, and the like— use different jargons. However, each recognizes the necessity of the other's speech in the service of the whole project. All languages, like all peoples, embody unique gifts that others can and should learn from. This dynamic implies that we should not only respect and support the languages of others but also that we have a responsibility to use and maintain our own.

Another reason why we should strive to retain and revitalize languages is that they are sacred. Living communities are not the inventors of the languages they speak; they are their guardians. Whether one believes that language is the product of previous generations or a gift from the creator, it is still clear that language is in some important way *not ours* to dispose of. This is particularly the way Cherokees experience sacred language, such as the language used in curative prayers or ceremonial songs. Sometimes such language is not even fully comprehensible to current speakers, showing that it has a life and a purpose beyond them.

Preserving the Cherokee language is tantamount to preserving the integrity of Cherokee thought. Cherokee ways of interpreting and categorizing experience, forms of social and political organization, and styles of interacting with one another are all encoded in and enacted through language. Cherokees have traditionally taken linguistic ability very seriously, and chose headmen for their ability to speak truthfully, artfully, with completeness, and in a way that offered comfort. Stomp ground leaders are still chosen for these gifts. The type of language traditionally used in tribal council was formal. In Cherokee, formal language is more morphologically complete than casual language, with all relevant verbal and nominal affixes included and with careful, slow pronunciation that emphasizes meaningful intonational patterns. This speaking style, or register, has a tendency to slow down the dialogue and to create a linguistic environment that signals politeness and respect. It creates for participants a social environment in which people do not speak for others, in which consensus may be given but may not be taken.

Sequoyah (ca. 1765—1843) himself, the inventor of the writing system for Cherokee, did not presume consensus in support of his invention. He first had to exercise his own autonomy in order to prove the worth of his new writing system. Consensus thus rests on a foundation of individual autonomy. Making decisions by consensus is a radically different way of being as a political entity than the dominant models operating today. In today's world of political alternatives, governing by consensus would mean not just being a distinct political entity but being a distinct *kind* of political entity. The fact that consensus is largely gone from Cherokee culture may in fact be connected to the threatened state of Cherokee sovereignty.

In addition to the formal political register, there are specific lexical and grammatical features of Cherokee that reflect a high degree of attention to social relationships and to the position of others. Cherokee grammatical categories mandate some kinds of communicative specificity that, while they are certainly possible in English, they are not mandatory in English. This linguistic specificity translates into social precision when describing past events or issuing invitations or instructions for future ones. For example, the Cherokee pronominal system (the system of pronouns) contains not only singular and plural categories as we do in English and other European languages, but also dual categories in first and second persons ('we two and you two'). First-person dual and plural are also cross-cut by a distinction between the inclusive (of the addressee) and exclusive forms. Thus, there are four Cherokee pronominal categories all of which translate as 'we' in English: 'we two, not including you,' 'we two, you and I,' 'we, three or more, not including you,' and 'we, three or more, including you.'

Another example is found in a modal distinction in Cherokee,[3] usually expressed in combination with the past tense. Speakers must choose one of two past tense endings, one of which, the assertive, informs the listener that the speaker has personal knowledge of the event described. The other past tense ending, the reportive, indicates that the speaker does not have personal knowledge of the event described. As with the pronominal categories, it is certainly possible to make this distinction in English. The difference is that it is not mandatory to do so, and it is therefore possible to remain vague about the source of one's information.

In 1829, Samuel Worcester wrote with fascination about a seventeen-syllable Cherokee word, *wini:do?di?gegina:lisgo:hldhanone:lidise:sdi*, meaning "they will, by that time, have nearly finished giving permission from a distance to you (one person) and me."[4] The precision with which social relationships, patterns of communication, and shared authority are reflected in this verb speaks volumes about the importance of these topics in Cherokee culture.

Social and economic conditions are reflected in language, and linguistic structures reinforce habitual ways of doing things. We would argue that not only does the current social order not reflect Cherokee language structure and use, but that there would be a deep conflict between speaking Cherokee and enacting some of the current troubling social and economic patterns characterizing Cherokee life. Child neglect and abuse and disparities in wealth would be difficult to think of, name, acknowledge, and (re)produce using Cherokee. If we acknowledge that language gives shape to the way in which we interpret the world, then we can say that speaking Cherokee as one's primary language would make it difficult to look out in the world and make sense of these phenomena. In Cherokee, one's child is *agwe:tsi*, 'my egg.' The child is inseparable from the speaker in two ways: first, a possessive pronoun is built into the word as a prefix (in this case, in the form *agw-*, 'my') so that no child is an abstraction but is always the child of a specific person in a conversation; second, the child's biological origin as a part of the parent is reinforced throughout life since the word for child also means 'egg.' Another Cherokee term for children, *diniyo:hli*, 'those that have been made smaller,' also reinforces the connectedness of children and adults. The word suggests that children are equal to adults, the same at a basic level. It is related to the word for carving, *ayo:tlanv*, indicating that they have been carved down from adult size. The word also speaks to the sacredness of children and their not belonging to us (adults), for clearly *we* didn't carve them. Thus, they are a part of us, connected to us, but not our property. This way of conceptualizing children conflicts with the assumptions that are necessary in order to take them for granted enough to harm them. Furthermore, a person who describes children as *digwe:tsi* ('my eggs') and *diniyo:hli* ('those that have been made smaller') and harms them must be a liar.

Social and economic inequality, the class divisions now found even in Cherokee communities, is also difficult to conceptualize and to enact using Cherokee linguistic resources. A cousin is referred to using the word *talnedosdadanv:tsi*, 'my second brother,' in Cherokee. A friend is called *ogana:li*, meaning 'we are together.' This comes from the verb *gana:li*, meaning that one thing is lying across something else. Even the word for acquaintance, the most casual of these relationships, suggests closeness. It is *dostadohlgi*, 'we understand each other.' Almost anyone within a Cherokee community will fall within one of these categories with respect to another community member, if not within an even closer kinship category. Again, a conflict would arise between talking about people in these terms and failing to help them or to share resources with them. How can one person have great wealth and another have nothing if they truly 'understand each other'?

In a number of ways, Cherokee also expresses the connectedness between living people and their ancestors. Tom describes the sense of belonging Cherokees experience when they go through the gates of a stomp ground (a traditional ceremonial ground) and join the community of fellow worshipers. Much of this belonging is expressed or enacted linguistically. As we have seen above, Cherokee has a different pronominal structure from English, so that the English pronoun 'we' does not have an exact parallel. When Cherokees are in the physical context of a ceremonial ground, surrounded by relatives and other community members, the inclusive, plural form of 'we' indexes not only the connectedness among that living group, but also the continuity of the Cherokee community over time. Most stomp grounds have been in use for generations, and the dances, songs, and prayers performed at them certainly have. This means that 'we' has a bigger referential scope than the present group. It also comes to lend an indexical meaning to the stomp dance songs, even if their referential meaning is no longer understood. They signal the continuity of a group that has taught, learned, and sung the same songs across multiple generations.

Cherokee also expresses the connectedness between Cherokees and their homeland. There is a difference between being *from* a place and being *of* a place. When Tom was young, he learned this lesson on a trip to Los Angeles. He and some other youths were in the city for a summer seminar on Native American Studies. While in town, they ran into a man from the Omaha Tribe who wanted to show them something. He took them down to the bus station and pointed out three Diné men. When a bus was announced headed to Flagstaff, Arizona, the three men all got up and moved in the direction of the departing bus. Tom figured they were going home to Diné country. However, the man told the youths to follow the Diné men to the bus.

Watching, they saw the three men place their hands on the bus and hold them there. When they were finished, they walked off. They weren't returning home. They were connecting with home.

Cherokees have a similar sense of place, as illustrated by another experience Tom had. One evening, a Cherokee family from Oklahoma appeared at his door. They had driven all day and asked where they might find a place to spend the night as they wished to speak to him the next morning. The oldest member of the group, a grandmother, asked Tom if he knew of a certain place. She described the place, and he said yes, that he knew it. The place she described was the site of *Kituhwa*, a Cherokee mother town. The site, which has a mound in its center, was recently re-acquired by the Eastern Cherokees through purchase from a local farmer. The elder from Oklahoma asked Tom if he would take her there and he did. When she saw the place, she said that her father had described it to her when she was a little girl, telling her that it was a special place and that other (Eastern) Cherokees had stayed in the East to take care of it. Once she had seen and stood on the site, the grandmother was content, and she and her family headed immediately back to Oklahoma.

Tom notes that in order to take care of a place, you have to know what its name is. The Cherokee word for home place is *digalenvhv:ʔi*, 'where we rose up.' Notice once more that the inclusive plural 'we' cut across time and space to index the social and historic body of Cherokees as a whole. Describing *Kituhwa* this way makes it not a point of reference, but a point of origin.

For children who do not grow up speaking Cherokee, learning and using Cherokee can still produce in them that sense of community, that sense of being Cherokee. In Tom's experiences in Cherokee language education, he has seen young children in immersion settings correcting teachers who had intentionally made linguistic or spelling errors and helping each other to figure out the right answer in a language exercise. This practice has shown him that these students have really taken ownership of the language. Owning your own language, not because some external authority has told you it is yours, but because you have internalized it and treat it unhesitatingly as your own—this is linguistic sovereignty. These young Cherokee language learners are embodying linguistic sovereignty even though Cherokee is their second language. Tom has also observed a lack of discipline problems in these settings because the students themselves were making decisions about how to invest their time and where to direct their attention.

Tom was fortunate enough to meet some of the first group of high school students in the Native Hawaiian immersion program, probably the first Indigenous language immersion program in the United States. What seemed at first to be a cavalier attitude on the students' part turned out to be the pure, extreme confidence that comes from a lack of alienation from one's cultural and educational environment. These students were extremely polite and well-mannered, and eminently comfortable in their own cultural life ways. If students have ownership of what they are mastering, if they have a sense of control over it, then they will not be afraid of education and will excel.

Tom, whose first language is Cherokee, knows firsthand the sense of ownership that comes with Cherokee language ability. The power to name and describe things, not just for oneself, but for an existing community, is the power to imbue the world with meaning and to interact with it in a meaningful way. He remembers how, by the age of seven, he could play creatively with language, turning nouns into verbs, making contractions, and creating metaphors. Of course, Cherokee is not the only language in which one can develop these skills. However, it is the only language through which the development of those linguistic skills embodies and reflects the state of being Cherokee in a manner continuous across time and space. Tom points out that the imagery evoked by Cherokee can be very different from that evoked by English. In Cherokee, for example, one describes the weather as snowing *fast* rather than snowing *hard*. This adverbial difference then calls into being a whole set of different metaphors about snow. Tom remembers saying that the snow was like a thousand white trains hitting the ground. Tom by that time had also learned Cherokee discursive minimalism, a set of aesthetic norms and values that combine with Cherokee's efficient verbal structure to allow for the expression of precise and detailed meanings with few words. One time, he described the thick snow to his father simply by saying *hi?skwo:la uhsko:la?tsv?i*, 'your head faded.'[5]

Access to these kinds of cultural metaphors and conceptual categories is one of the important gifts that comes from studying the language associated with one's culture. For example, when learning Western Cherokee, children learn that the word for 'kangaroo' is *ju:tla:we:da*—literally, 'pockets.' This conceptual way of describing and thinking about animals will be extended by the children to other contexts. They will think of functional aspects of animals and other items as ways to characterize and name them. They will be able to predict the name for pants' pockets even before they learn it. This kind of productive ability speaks to ownership of a language and to the living status of a linguistic community.

Tom has seen that a new relationship to learning in general can emerge out of studying Cherokee for some children. Students who flourish in Cherokee language classes tend to also do well in other classes because they are more likely to take a questioning attitude toward what they are taught. Perhaps this is because of a critical flexibility associated with bilingualism. These Cherokee-speaking children also tend to recognize and know each other across classes and to build a sense of camaraderie based on their connection to the language.

There are many Cherokee values that are expressed linguistically and difficult to express and grasp without access to the Cherokee language. For example, there is a value in Cherokee culture placed on fullness, completeness, and maturity that comes out in many specific Cherokee words as well as in Cherokee discursive practices. The word *uyo:tlenv* describes a person who is pitiful, child-like, and incomplete, and it is used to refer to a person who is not socially mature. One common Cherokee word for an old man is *utvhsohnv?i*. This word may be translated as 'grown up,' but it means completely grown, like a plant that has reached its maximum growth. It implies the acquisition of comfort, gentleness, and confidence. The person, it is suggested, has reached completion. This pattern also links up with the formal Cherokee discursive style characteristic of traditional oratory—it must be morphologically complete and deliberate in pronunciation in order to be accepted and respected. In Cherokee, this morphological completeness adds precision (for example, through the addition of locative or aspectual morphemes that specify where or how an action takes place); it does not create flowery or padded speech.

Cultural values like respect, the importance of the community as a whole, and the connectedness of men and women are all reflected in the Cherokee language. The emphasis on respect can be seen in the high degree of specificity of Cherokee pronouns and in the evidential distinction discussed above. One can also see the value of Cherokee language ideology, in which addressing a person the proper way is important. In Cherokee author Robert Conley's book on the eighteenth-century Cherokee leader Dragging Canoe,[6] the author quotes Dragging Canoe as saying about Englishmen, "How can you trust people who can't even say your name?"

The importance of the community as a whole, of the group over the self, is reflected in the Cherokee word *gadu:gi*, recently used by Cherokee Nation Principal Chief Chad Smith to encourage togetherness and a sense of mutual obligation in the Cherokee Nation. The word, which is used most specifically to refer to the traditional Cherokee work cooperatives, means more broadly that everybody's heart is in the same place. It is because this word does not have a direct conceptual equivalent in English that the Cherokee word *gadu:gi* is so often used in ethnographic and historical accounts, and in political language as just described.

A culturally specific relationship between men and women is visible both lexically and in terms of discursive patterns in Cherokee. A lexical example comes from the Cherokee words for siblings, which differ according to sex, but not in the same way that English *brother* and *sister* differ. Sisters refer to each other using the word *vgi:lv?i*, and brothers refer to each other as *do?s:tadanv:tsi*. There is a special term for

siblings of the opposite sex, however: *vgi:do:?i*. This way of classifying sibling relationships acknowledges the special character of the cross-sex relationship. There is
also a particular discursive style that reflects the special relationship between men and
women. In a ceremonial stomp ground, the speech of male elders often has a com-
forting quality, partly because it is so complete and precise that it instills a sense of
security but also because, in this setting, the speech of elder men starts to approach
that of elder women.

The discursive styles associated with Cherokee enact culturally specific ways of
being in the world and of being with each other. Tom has described how he and a
childhood friend, reunited after many years, were able to catch up on decades of personal history in an extremely concentrated way at the beginning of their conversation.
The conversational pattern is like the one he observed as a child between his and her
friend's parents and grandparents. An English conversation would have taken days to
reach the same point of mutual understanding and would have involved many questions. The conversation began with Tom using the Cherokee phrase *hi?a nulastani-
dolvhi*, 'this is what happened,' but the literal meaning conveys that the speaker is
referring to a sequence of events, that the phrase has multiple referential objects. This
structure allows the hearer to understand that multiple events will be compressed in
the narrative. Tom went on to say *nvdagidi:tla wagilanvsi;tlv*, 'in the direction of Texas
I started a home.' The implication was that something specific happened that caused
him to move away, that he began another life for a short time. He continued, *nigohilv
agiluhisdi agwadulisgv?i*, 'for all the time I was living there, I wanted to come back
home.' Again, more is told by these words than seems to be on the surface. The
hearer understands that there were untoward reasons that the speaker left home and
that he had not wanted to do so. The implication was that sometimes things happen
that have unwanted consequences. The words indicated that the speaker was faced
with situations that were neither normal nor good, but that he had not lost track of
what was important. The words tell of a struggle, the kind of struggle that would
cause changes in a person's life, causing him to do things he did not want to do. Like
Jerome Tiger's paintings, these words painted the tragedy without actually painting
it. Tom's friend responded to these words by saying he had felt like that himself. He
and Tom were then on the same page, they knew that they had both had issues, things
had happened that they tried to fix, that they ultimately got back to their lives, and
that the problems were corrected. Tom's friend understood that there was a spiraling
out or getting away from normalcy or consensus, a taking apart from the whole that a
person was supposed to be. There was no need for them to discuss their exact experiences. This discursive pattern builds into it the protection of the speaker's dignity and
allows the hearer to treat him with respect. This conversational pattern allows the

participants to position and validate themselves at the outset, so that they then have a platform for bonding through the remainder of the conversation.

Why can't all this take place in English? Each language has vocabulary, grammatical categories, and patterns of use that make it unique. Beyond these elements, however, for Cherokees who speak Cherokee, it is just also the only real way to be. Speech is the sound of what, of who you are as a people. A cat might learn to bark, but once it does, it is no longer the same sort of cat. Tom remembers that when anthropologist Al Wahrhaftig asked Oklahoma Cherokee Andrew Dreadfulwater in the 1960s why he believed Cherokee language maintenance was so important, he answered, "Because I want my children to have a chance to *be* (that)." If you are not "that," i.e., the identity that you experience as your own, then you are incomplete, or you are something else, something other. For Cherokees who speak Cherokee, speech in English is a translation, not a straightforward expression, of thought. English-language speech in a traditional stomp ground comes across as commentary on the unfolding events, not participation in them. Speaking Cherokee embodies and expresses sovereignty directly; Cherokee speakers experience English language speech about Cherokee identity as being more an expression of opinion about sovereignty than an expression of sovereignty itself. Tom personally would not be Cherokee in the way he knows how if he could not speak Cherokee. He would all of a sudden suffer from a lack of understanding and have to have everything explained to him in the most important cultural settings.

It is not that Cherokee identity and culture are impossible without the Cherokee language, only that they constitute a new kind of identity and culture. However, those Cherokees who still speak Cherokee argue that the kind of identity and culture they are able to express through the Cherokee language is worth transmitting and keeping alive.

NOTES

1 In this chapter, when we use the first person plural "we," we are referring to authors Belt (a member of the Cherokee Nation) and Bender (not an enrolled member of an American Indian tribe and of largely Euro-American descent) or to humankind in general. When we talk about Cherokees in general, we use the third person plural "they," and when we talk about experiences that are uniquely Belt's, we use the third person singular (Tom or "he").

2 An easier way to phrase this might be: "sovereignty is about the radical right to be who one is." However, we like the fact that the given phrasing does not suggest an ontological break between the person and his or her manifestation.

3 A mode is a grammatical category that expresses the attitude of the speaker toward what is being said. Readers who have studied European languages are familiar with the subjunctive mood or mode, which expresses uncertainty of judgment on the part of the speaker.

4 Jack Frederick Kilpatrick and Ann Gritts Kilpatrick. *New Echota Letters of Samuel A. Worcester to the Cherokee Phoenix* (Dallas: Southern Methodist University, 1968).

5 This verbal minimalism is similar to the artistic minimalism of Cherokee artist Jerome Tiger, who is known for being able to paint cold and wind indirectly, through suggestion, on a nearly completely white canvas.

6 Robert J. Conley, *Cherokee Dragon: A Novel of the Real People* (New York: St. Martin's Press, 2000).

BIBLIOGRAPHY

Conley, Robert J. *Cherokee Dragon: A Novel of the Real People.* New York: St. Martin's Press, 2000.

Kilpatrick, Jack Frederick, and Ann Gritts Kilpatrick. *New Echota Letters of Samuel A. Worcester to the Cherokee Phoenix.* Dallas: Southern Methodist University, 1968.

11 PATHWAY TO AUTONOMY: WOMEN'S TESTIMONY OF THE CHIAPAS EXPERIENCE

Jeanne Simonelli, Josefa Hernandez Perez, and La Fomma

It was a chilly New Year's dawn when the world awakened to find an Indigenous uprising underway in Chiapas, Mexico's southernmost state. Coinciding with the signing of the North American Free Trade Agreement (NAFTA), the rebellion responded to long-standing patterns of exploitation and discrimination in this region of rich land and poor people. After ten days of fighting in 1994, a cease-fire led to stillborn peace accords in 1996. Since that time, the struggle has merged low intensity warfare with outright killing fields, exemplified by the massacre of forty-five women, children, and men in the highland village of Acteal in December 1997 and the violent break-up of four autonomous municipalities in 1998. Predating the actual rebellion, and imbedded in the history of Chiapas, patterns of state repression have been a critical part of official attempts to suppress all attempts at autonomy by Indigenous and mestizo campesinos. The spiritual and psychological resistance to the repression has been difficult to chronicle and to communicate beyond Chiapas. This essay attempts to build a bridge between Mayan voices and the Northern American hemisphere. It offers a historical context in the mode of western scholarship, but also provides for Indigenous voices to rise on their own terms. The author of this textual bridge, an Italian American academic trained in several disciplines, has worked and lived side by side with the Maya authors introduced below.

The reclamation of autonomy and sovereignty in the Americas is an undertaking that spans hundreds of years. As previous chapters detail, the North American struggle has been visible for over a century. In Mexico, Indigenous voices began to be widely heard only in the late 1960s, yet growing in strength and confidence with each ensuing decade, and finally culminating in the Zapatista rebellion. This essay introduces two Maya literary witnesses to Indigenous struggles for autonomy. The women of LA FOMMA (FORTALEZA DE LA MUJER MAYA) found their voice by forming a grassroots cooperative dedicated to women's health issues. LA FOMMA experimented with the genre of theater as an effective mechanism of education. The second Maya testimony is an autobiographical poetics of spiritual resistance and reclamation, written by a young Maya spiritual leader, Josefa Hernandez Perez. At the age of sixteen, Hernandez Perez chose to leave her highland community and joined MISED (Las Hermanas Misioneras Seglares Diocesana), a lay women's community under the jurisdiction of the Catholic diocese of San Cristóbal. Her vivid testimony, translated into English for the first time, blends Mayan and Catholic themes to evoke spiritual knowledge and the human heart as the basis for Maya autonomy.

ECCLESIASTICAL SUPPORT FOR THE STRUGGLE TO REGAIN AUTONOMY

In the years that led up to the Zapatista rebellion, the awakening of courage and consciousness grew from a number of separate seeds. Among these, the Roman Catholic Church has been a major facilitator in the expression of social conscience in Chiapas. The Church took shape under the tutelage of Bishop Samuel Ruíz García who arrived in the diocese of San Cristóbal de las Casas in 1960.[1] Comparable to other Latin American Catholic leaders of the time, who gained inspiration from the Second Vatican Council (1962–65) and the Latin American Bishops meeting in Medellín, Columbia (1968), Ruíz admits that he was born into belief, into the full flowering of faith, through the accompaniment of the poor and marginalized. This assessment reflects a basic insight of liberation theology, which notes that the poor hold a privileged place in God's plan.[2] According to Ruíz, their gift to First World countries is that they allow us to accompany them in their struggle.[3]

Though the change in the relationship between the Roman Catholic Church and the Indigenous and mestizos campesinos of Chiapas is often credited to the coming of Don Samuel, it has its roots in previous decades. As Presbyterian missionaries began to make inroads into Indigenous communities, the Church realized it was time to reconsider the model of evangelization derived from its priest centered, hierarchical form. In 1952, Samuel's predecessor made possible the participation of the first Indigenous lay practitioners, called *catequistas* (catechists), including both men and women. Finally, in 1962, two diocesan schools were established in San Cristóbal to provide training for a large cadre of these *catequistas,* who learned not just to interpret the Bible, but also Spanish and Western carpentry, horticulture, tailoring, and cooking, math, health, and sanitation.

Though dynamic in form, the school's teaching methods and content failed to take into consideration the particular cultural practices of the Maya pueblos. As a result, early catechists returned to their communities to work against the ancient beliefs and practices of their people. Evaluating their experience in 1968, these newly trained representatives of the Catholic Church criticized this and other limitations in their training, saying that "the Church and the Word of God have given us things to save our souls, but we don't know how to save our bodies."[4] Acting on this call to "embody the gospel" in the cultural and socioeconomic reality in which the Indigenous lived, the Church and its missionary teams began a process of theological reflection, based on the biblical story of Exodus.

The use of Exodus as a springboard for reflection made great sense in the context of increasing displacement and migration occurring in the highland Indigenous communities of Chiapas. Beginning particularly with the Tzeltal Maya speaking popula-tion,[5] pastoral agents grasped the opportunity to offer comparisons with the experi-ence of the ancient Hebrews. The Indigenous were an elected people, set free from the slavery and injustice of the land owning *patrones*. They had begun the road to the Promised Land of the jungle (*selva*), and this was the call to configure a new human experience, one that could transform the entire community of believers at the same time. In this light, many Chiapas clerics saw it as their opportunity to remedy the great missionary myopia of the sixteenth century, to wake up and become 'consci-ent'[6] alongside the Maya congregations. Thus, the migration to the jungle from the highlands became more than a move to a geographical location. It became a move-ment in social history and a setting for profound theological change.

Many of these new ideas were born in a Jesuit mission in the parish of Ocosingo which ministered to the Tzeltal speaking Maya, and was responsible for the majority of the Lacandon rainforest/jungle. In the early 1970s, the Ocosingo group held a meeting that invited the Tzeltal catechists to evaluate their work with the Church. Their key observation was that the people did not speak, did not participate because the Church representatives acted too much as lecturers. According to the Maya, the priests, brothers, and nuns needed to be facilitators rather than instructors.

A transition from instructor to facilitator among the priests and mestizo pastoral agents would have been of no consequence had it not been accompanied by a second transition, that of the metamorphosis of the Maya from colonial objects to autono-mous subjects of their lives in God and on earth. In the evolving theological model, the Tzeltal were the elected, called to announce the new age, not just receive the message of liberation. Encapsulating this idea, a three-part catechism was produced from the on-going reflections of the Tzeltal catechists in conjunction with the pastoral agents. This distinctly Maya version of a classic Catholic catechism explained:

1. The Thoughts of God from the beginning
2. How We Live in Oppression
3. Faith, Hope, and Charity.[7]

The second section of the catechism was revolutionary. It provided a concrete and unambiguous reflection on the situation of socioeconomic and cultural marginali-zation experienced by Indigenous communities, beginning in the experience of those who had moved from the highlands to the jungle. In this segment, and in the chapter concerning hope, the gospel's spiritual concepts became politicized, localized, and democratized. Gradually, the insights developing among this group spread to much of the diocese of San Cristóbal, including the highland villages surrounding that colonial city. The story of Exodus became a means of understanding and interpreting the on-going experience of all Maya.

It was firmly believed that the process of reflection on a verse of scripture encap-sulated a divine direction from God concerning Maya liberation and self-determination. In verses of the Bible, the Maya thus found passages that supported their cultural autonomy:

> Our culture is like a spring, and from it we have drunk that which we have, that which we know, that which we are. It is here where we have encountered God, because God speaks to us through the means of our own culture... And we are united because we have the same hope, the same struggle to arrive at a better life...The second commandment of God says this: Love your brother as you love yourself. God directs us that we love ourselves, that we love our race, our community, our family. We don't disparage or forget our race. He who disparages his race disparages his mother, as well as the work of God.[8]

Moreover, the Tzeltal proceeded with the understanding that they were elected to struggle for the liberation of all: "We want to say that our hope and our responsi-bility is to acquire through our work the new land that God gives us. When the land with her seeds is for all men, it will be the Promised Land."[9] Celebrating their ances-try and their land, Mayan activists Josefa Hernandez Perez and the women of La Fomma drank deeply from these wells.

THE OTHER ROAD: MOVING INTO THE POLITICAL ARENA
The Tzeltal emphasis on Indigenous autonomy and liberation received wider expo-sure during the First Indigenous Congress, held in 1974. Initiated by Chiapas gover-nor Dr. Manuel Velasco Suarez, the congress sought the assistance of the Church and Bishop Samuel Ruíz. The Congress marked the first time that Chiapas Maya would be able to meet and speak out in a public conference. The Bishop agreed to join Church with State, on the condition that the meeting not be turned into a folkloric perform-ance, but that the representatives of the Indigenous community would be allowed to give their true testimony in public after five hundred years of silence. In preparation for the Congress, meetings were held in Indigenous communities reflecting on the themes of land, commerce, education, and health. On October 13, over 1,230 Maya delegates, speaking four Maya languages, gathered to consider the themes under dis-cussion. At the conclusion of the Congress, Mayan participants agreed to unite to be able to rise out of the abyss of oppression and exploitation.[10]

Though the Congress was successful on many levels, it had not provided a forum for Indigenous peoples to discuss the theme of cultural identity and their feelings to-ward the institution of the Church at large. In response, in April 1975, Bishop Ruíz convened a meeting in a remote pueblo to hear and discuss the people's assessments of ecclesiastical structures. Stepping forward, Tzeltal catechist Domingo Gomez announced that, indeed, something important *was* lacking, and that was the opportunity for the people to hold in their hands the ingredients of the faith and to combine them as they saw fit. "Give us the Holy Spirit, and we will no longer blame you," he concluded.[11] Recognizing that the age-old structures of the church and the hierarchical pastoral model engendered continuing dependency, Ruíz vowed to enter onto a road that would let the new church grow from its Indigenous roots and its direction pass on to the people.

It was in these moments that Samuel Ruíz and the pastoral workers of the Diocese realized that the Catholic Church in Chiapas had to be an *iglesia autoctona,* an autochthonous body of believers and practice resurrected from Indigenous culture.

While many Maya were busy working for autonomy within the Church, other paths were also under construction in the highlands, canyons, and jungles of Chiapas. The January 1, 1994, Zapatista uprising in Chiapas constitutes a complex statement about a growing sense of the betrayal of the revolutionary and constitutional commitment to agrarian life and the nation's failure to protect the poor from internationally dictated structural adjustments to the logic of their economic system. Coinciding with the signing of NAFTA, the rebellion formulated a response to long-standing patterns of unjust interaction, exploitation, and discrimination.[12] NAFTA became a metaphor for betrayal not because of what it would do, but because of what it communicated politically: the demise of the Indigenous way of life.[13]

Contributing to this sense of betrayal was the reform of Article 27 of the Mexican Constitution, which allowed for the private sale of land held communally in *ejidos*. The notion of anti-Indigenous agrarian reform communicated in this change was an underlying cause of subsequent conflict, but not because there had been no history of agrarian reform in the state of Chiapas. By 1975, over three-quarters of the land in Chiapas was in the hands of the Indigenous agrarian population, in redistributive acts dating back to 1945, with much of the land concentrated in the jungle.[14] Absent from these figures, however, is the fact that the land was distributed in a fashion that replicated the elite system of patronage, thus reinforcing the colonial social structure. It was not so much that reform had not been attempted, but that the manner in which it occurred left many disenfranchised.

If the revolutionary failure is symbolized in complex land issues, it is also found in economic and social events.[15] The fall in the price of oil in 1982, the subsequent collapse of the peso, and the international financial bailout which followed laid the groundwork for a decline in living standards for the Indigenous and campesino peoples of Chiapas. As the Mexican government sought still more loans in the beginning of 1986, the removal of food subsidies and a retreat from social programs became a component of the economic reforms mandated for continued international funding.[16]

The timing of this decline parallels the escalation and expression of guerilla activity in the most marginal areas of the state of Chiapas. Outsiders who would eventually act as a catalyst in the formation of the Zapatista rebellion arrived in the jungle in the early 1980s, as genocidal violence in neighboring Guatemala brought tens of thousands of refugees into Chiapas. As described above, the Catholic Church was finding its own revolutionary route at the same time. In the heart of the jungle, independent peasant organizations were forming. Agro-ecological and production cooperatives became the social forces dealing with land reform, labor, commercialization, and credit. Sometimes allied, sometimes in competition, these groups established communication between distant locales, between jungle and highlands and canyon regions, and gave the campesinos a united voice.[17] The particular circumstances of the *selva* migration, the *conscientization* of the Church, and the need to organize for strength led to a serendipitous alliance between radical catechist campesinos, Marxist and Maoist intellectuals and agronomists, and incipient labor and trade unions.

The combination of all of these conditions fuelled a process of organization and change in some Chiapas communities. Community members formed committees and some became catechists. The formation of new structures was dynamic, and for many, faith and radical beliefs began to become alive in their daily lives. The young women and men, with their new families, began collective work, especially in health and education, thus providing for themselves what the government failed to provide. Where there were no medicines, they began herbal gardens, set up a community pharmacy, learned to be health *promotoras*. In some places, the women created their own systems of support and informal organization, which were facilitated by the Church and the *catequistas*.[18]

WOMEN OF COURAGE AND FORTITUDE

There was a great deal happening in the early 1990s: violence, changes in agrarian law, organizing. The Church had helped to open the road, but there were also other paths, and so a separation between groups began, the nonviolent route to autonomy proposed by the church, and the armed rebellion mounted by the Zapatistas.

Hearing the message of dignity and achievable human and Indigenous rights occurred for some through the church and some through the Ejercito Zapatista de Liberación Nacional (EZLN) uprising. In addition, through the space created by these two major forces, others crafted their own paths out of oppression. Women, especially, found the courage and fortitude to leave the communities in which they lived; the abusive and arranged marriages which were a by-product of an unholy alliance between Maya tradition and colonial oppression, and to seek new lives. Two exemplary choices are presented in the following pages, translated into English for the first time. They convey Mayan women's profound intellectual engagement with the historical forces that swept through Chiapas. They constitute responses of visionary clarity rooted in the sensibilities of Mayan women's spirituality and values.

1. DAUGHTER OF CHANGE: JOSEFA HERNANDEZ PEREZ

Josefa Hernandez Perez was sixteen years old when she came to the city of San Cristobál and joined MISED, having left her family home in Candelaria, one of the outlying Chamula Maya communities of the highlands of Chiapas. A Tzotzil Maya speaker, she defied her parents and went to dedicate her young life to the work of the church, the Iglesia Autoctona, that was forming in Chiapas. Within three months, Josefa Hernandez Perez had taught herself Spanish, and began working on MISED's social and religious outreach programs, providing invaluable help to the priests and other members of the diocese as they sought to refine the religious practice and sociopolitical commitment begun during the previous decades. Josefa Hernandez Perez heard both the Church and EZLN messages of autonomy and Indigenous rights and dignity resonating through the mountains and jungles of Chiapas. She chose to work through the religious path, but never lost sight of the revolutionary ideals of the Zapatistas as practiced in the communities where she led ceremonies, assisted in masses, and gave workshops in the areas of literacy, health, and human rights.

In October 2003, she traveled to the United States for the first time to present Maya perspectives on autonomy at a Wake Forest University symposium on sovereignty. In her spiritual reflections on the visit, especially the opening ceremony, Hernandez Perez echoes some of the profound spiritual and political sentiments felt by many symposium participants as they acknowledged their shared heritage as the Indigenous nations of the Americas. After the symposium, Hernandez Perez returned to Chiapas to share with the Maya people her life-changing knowledge that they were not alone, and that there was, indeed, hope alive and possible in the vast wasteland of the United States. Her extraordinary reflection on her visit to the United States is a window into the syncretism of worship and belief that is autonomous, Indigenous Catholicism in Chiapas. Her text is as follows.

Today I write my experience from which I have lived, I as an Indigenous Tzotzil woman of Chamula, a woman of Chiapas and a woman of Mexico, I, Josefa Hernandez Perez. I have seen, I have heard, I have experimented, I have shared, I have celebrated, living the fruits of our heart. Thanks to the Heart of Sky, Heart of Earth, I grew in your hands; thanks to my mother and my father who taught me to find you in the cold and the wind and the face of *Ajaw*; to the women of MISED for your help, and to my friends for assisting me through your great friendship. You are always with me.

Here on earth is the space that we are allowed to feel, breathe, contemplate, look at, walk in, know, and cross frontiers that the *Mundo* has created. For the Creator and Former there is no border, color, or language, except to hear all of the languages. The Heart of Sky, the Heart of Earth holds us all. In my Indigenous Tzotzil culture to be a woman, it is difficult to leave the house; in many areas of society, community, and in the family it is looked at badly to leave the house, to leave the home. For me, it has been a blessing, an adventure, and also a risk, though it has given me much pleasure, but only with the help of God, together with friends. To never leave [home] gives us much fear, insecurity to know and encounter another world, but you taught me to understand .... I have understood, I have accepted the differences of lives, as it is another border between the life of the Indigenous and the non Indigenous.

Here is the impression I had before the visit to the United States: only that it was an elaborate world, exploitative in many aspects, a world of much economic, political and social power. I only could see a world without need; also I had no idea that an Indigenous world existed there. On visiting, my expectations changed, I understood in my heart that there have been many people struggling with injustice, so that one day justice might exist with Indigenous, blacks, whites, and even people of my country, Mexico, having their rights. There have been many who have struggled for the truth. This I saw.

Always in my heart are these words that share the faith, the word ... even though many of them remain without expression of what my heart feels ... to share, to open to others, the most sacred aspects of our culture, to celebrate together with their hearts and mine mixed, to eat a meal that strengthens the friendships, the sharing, the caring, the acceptance, the love that you could touch, the solidarity, the generosity, the love of God with the people.

During the visit, I felt very well received, even better, welcomed ... I also lost my heart encountering my countrymen from Mexico, but it truly gave my heart joy to meet the Indigenous who carry the same blood as I. With those my heart overflowed with joy that I could only express with tears. Though we didn't understand each other's language, I felt a communication in the heart; that we didn't need to speak much, only with our looks.

In the [opening] ceremony there was a beauty that didn't have many words; it lived and it experimented, so that it was engraved in the mind and the Heart. When we entered the ceremony, I found it to be the same ritual that we have here in Chiapas: to ask permission to enter into the Sacred House that is the heart of each one of us, the *caracol* [conch shell that is blown to gather people together] that opens the door, the ceremonial prayer, the profound words of the heart that give us life, soul.

For me, the ceremony invited me to value my culture, to strengthen my heart, to give testimony to the *compañeras* [women comrades; gathered community] of my same blood, to say that we are many of the same dark skin that call out with the heart, saying:

Yes! We exist. *Yes!* We live. Here we are and we are many. Even though they would like to eat our fruits, cut our branches, burn our trunk, they cannot pull out our roots. We are alive. We celebrate our ceremonies, our rituals, we burn our candles, we offer incense to the heart of God, who listens to our silence. We sing, we dance with our regional music, we wear our ceremonial clothing. We welcome with the heart, we listen to the wind, we breathe the pure air, we listen to the sound of water and springs and it maintains us. We abandon ourselves to our Mother, nature, with the Heart of Sky, and Heart of Earth.

We spoke much of our autonomy: to not depend on anyone, that we are subjects of our history, we are power, we value, we struggle, we are valued, we are accepted, we live. We are all, with our culture, enriching the world, even though we suffer with hunger, thirst, with outcries, and pain, we struggle proudly as Indigenous, with autonomy. We struggle with a conscious right in our minds and hearts, awakened.

During the ceremony I led a prayer to the heart of knowledge of the community. It was as follows:

Fig. 2. Prayer Diagram for the Heart of Knowledge
as designed by Hernandez Perez

I was given a gift: a ceremonial necklace made of seeds, and my experience was so strong; it remains in my heart. He (Native Hawaiian ceremonial leader) gave me his necklace, a sign of the sacred. I value it. What is important is the person, that it represents our Indigenous race, it is a special gift that helps me enter into the depths of the heart of my culture. I promise, each time I pray I see it, it has in it the most sacred, and pushes me to work with my culture, as do the other gifts I received. I am grateful to Heart of Sky, Heart of Earth that recognizing us, they shared with us; that it was a gift for me, it changed my heart. Thanks to all of the friends, with your help, with your great friendship, you have given me a special gift for my life. This I say with fondness and love, to all who are united in our struggles. [End]

In July 2004, after her return from the United States, Josefa Hernandez Perez asked for a year's sabbatical from MISED to explore her future path, to determine what God and the world had in store for her. She dreamed of entering the Preparatoria or "Prepa," the equivalent of college preparatory high school. At the same time, she wanted to further investigate the spirituality that her Maya heritage and upbringing and Catholic training had produced. She continued to do the work that she was called to do, bringing health, education, and literacy workshops to Tzotzil speaking communities in conjunction with the Maya Catholic liturgy of the *iglesia autóctona* in Chiapas.

During the next two years, Hernandez Perez continued to work in each of these areas. She traveled to Guatemala to teach and take part in workshops concerning Maya spirituality. She visited the Jesuit mission outside of Ocosingo, as a retreat and a prayerful way of exploring her personal path. As part of her work with the Diocese of San Cristóbal, she wrote a new Holy Week liturgy, inspired by the wedding of Maya and Catholic cosmology and theology. She celebrated the liturgy with the people of her birth pueblo, Candelaria.[19] During the summer of 2006, Josefa returned to San Cristóbal and her spiritual base in MISED. Though she continues to travel to Guatemala to share her uniquely Maya understanding of how the spiritual and the practical travel together, she will also now pursue her goal of formal education.

2. DAUGHTERS OF CHANGE: LA FOMMA

LA FOMMA (FORTALEZA DE LA MUJER MAYA) was founded twelve years ago to offer a center for Indian women and children displaced from their communities and living in the mestizo city of San Cristóbal de las Casas in the state of Chiapas, Mexico.[20]

Fleeing social, political, and economic distress, they arrived in the city illiterate and monolingual, victims of a citizenry which disdained them. Their crippling fear and sense of worthlessness is a cycle FOMMA tried to arrest through an innovative model using workshops in bilingual education, job skills, classes in health and above all theatre.

The founders of LA FOMMA, Petrona de la Cruz Cruz and Isabel Juárez Espinosa, both came to San Cristóbal as children to work as servants. Through determination and good fortune, they attended elementary school, and as young adults they were hired by the Indian writers' cooperative, Sna Jtzi'bajom where they were trained in bilingual education and acting. They were the first Indian women to appear on stage in Chiapas. Scorned both in their own communities and in the city as alternately, "prostitutes" or "lesbians," they stimulated further animosity by writing plays depicting the lives of Indian women. After presenting scenes from their plays at the 4th International Women's Playwrights Conference in Toronto, they were heralded as Mexico's first Indian women playwrights.

They left Sna Jtzi'bajom soon after and spent a year giving workshops for children in the jungle area of Chiapas. Here, working together, the dream of a women and children's cooperative was born. With the help of friends they had made abroad and friends among the foreign community in San Cristóbal, they gathered funds to start a small center.

Their first production was Petrona's play, *La Mujer Desesparada*. Staged by the Women's Group of San Cristóbal on International Women's Day in 1993, it was an opening salvo. Never before had Indian women expressed their grievances publicly, and the play was received with extreme reactions—both approval and disapproval. The piece depicts a young woman whose stepfather demands to sleep with her as his rightful due for supporting her and her mother. Indian men said that such a thing would never occur in their villages, but it had the ring of truth, and is still cited both in San Cristóbal and internationally as a historical moment in Mexican theatre. The play appears in English in Diana Taylor's book *Holy Terrors: Latin American Women Perform.*[21]

The women who comprise the LA FOMMA troupe write plays both individually and collectively. The themes usually focus on social issues such as alcoholism, domestic violence, machismo, and migration to the city. They tour their plays in the Indigenous communities, throughout Mexico, and abroad when funding is available. Otherwise, they perform in San Cristóbal. They have written a radio serial in three languages on women's health. The program was aired in twenty-three regions throughout the state of Chiapas.

Over the years, the women have learned that literacy and theatre are powerful tools in building self-confidence and healing historical trauma. Not only do the women write their own plays, but by acting the parts of mestizo bosses and abusive husbands, they unmask the power plays of their abusers. It took courage to defy their modest upbringing and call attention to themselves by acting on stage. By daring to enact the part of men, they further defied traditional boundaries. Not only their communities, but their own families eventually disowned them.

In 2004, FOMMA was awarded a generous grant by the Hemispheric Institute of Politics and Performance to build a theatre in San Cristóbal, which was to be used by their theatre troupe as well as by other organizations participating in projects benefiting Chiapas Indians. Currently under construction, it will house a video room and photo archive as well as dressing rooms and bathrooms, a café and a small shop. The women continue to dream of the classes, workshops, and exhibitions they will offer to reach out to the community, and they look forward to performing as a repertory theatre as well as inviting other performers from Chiapas and other parts of the world.

FOMMA enjoys a reciprocal relationship with several institutions in the United States. The Maya Educational Foundation has relied on FOMMA to choose and guide many of its Indian student recipients of university scholarships. In return for this help, the students participate in "social service" at FOMMA, usually in the form of teaching the children in the bilingual reading classes. It is an opportunity for the women and children at FOMMA to share the companionship of some of the outstanding Indian students, and it is a reminder to the students of their roots and the importance of respecting their heritage.

Since FOMMA's founding, Cultural Survival has encouraged the group in various ways. They invited them on their first trip to the United States when they performed in Cambridge in 1996. Most recently, they have invited Isabel Juárez Espinosa to be a member of the program council for a series of conferences on Indigenous peoples. She traveled to New York in 2004 and to Boston in 2005 to participate in the meetings. In the spring of 2006, five members of the theatre traveled to Cambridge to perform two plays and participate in workshops at many of the universities in the Boston area.

FOMMA has remained small, but the impact of its theatre attracts attention far and wide. Using theatre as a tool for social change, the plays are written for the Indians of Chiapas, but their message carries a universality which enjoys an appeal abroad as well. Collectively or individually, the women have traveled to South America, Australia, and the United States.

In 2004, the five women in the theatre collective visited North Carolina for two weeks. They presented on-campus and community performances at numerous North Carolina venues. In addition, they worked with public school classes, creating improvisational pieces that reflected current and pertinent social issues in the lives of local communities. They also gave two interviews over the Latino radio station "Que Pasa," which broadcasts throughout the state. During this visit, and many others, the group was accompanied by Miriam Laughlin, who was implemental in founding FOMMA. She presently serves as their international coordinator.

FOMMA's theatre has blossomed over the last seven years under the directorship of Doris DiFarnecio. An actress, director and teacher from New York, Doris has come to FOMMA each summer for one to two months to work with the women in writing, improvisational dramatics, and to direct a new play. Keenly aware of cultural nuances and sensitivities, she has evolved a technique over the years, helping the women to elicit their pieces for the theatre collectively, through group conversations, improvisations, and interviews. For example, "*Crecí con el amor de mi madre*" was derived from conversations among the women about the difficulties of raising a family with an alcoholic husband. During these conversations, the women shared their own experiences, as well as those of family members and friends. They drew on this material to create improvisations from which they built the scenes and eventually the play.

Another work, "*Soledad y Esperanza*" was commissioned by the Hemispheric Institute of Politics and Performance for its conference in Belo Horizonte, Brazil, in 2004. Since only two actresses were invited, Doris worked with Isabel and Petrona. They agreed to create an autobiographical piece, and this time Doris used interviews with the two women to elicit the material. It was personally heart wrenching for one of the actresses, as it touched on a subject she had tried to erase from her mind and had never shared with her children. Despite this circumstance, and maybe even because of it, it resulted in one of the strongest performances either one of the women has ever presented, and served as a catharsis for the actresses.

A number of books and articles have appeared that include commentaries on FOMMA. The most recent publication is *La risa olvidada de mi madre: 10 años de Fortaleza de la Mujer Maya,* written by Anna Alabaldeja (Valencia, Spain, 2005).[22] The book includes interviews with the women and a play by Petrona and a play by Isabel, neither of which has yet been produced.

The women's theatre collective agrees that writing and acting in the plays they create about their lives is empowering, for not only does it express to the world the injustices they have suffered, but the process serves as therapy in helping them surmount their emotional suffering and dream a future beyond the lives they lead today. The play *Soledad y Esperanza* (Solitude and Hope) is translated below. Solitude and Hope are allegories, bringing into collective awareness women's and men's limited choices in a world not of one's own making, naming injustice and female trauma, and allowing the tensions inherent in moving between countryside and city, between Mexico and the United States, between men and women in colonialism to surface.

The play and Josefa Hernandez Perez's passionate invocation thus complement each other profoundly, providing both background and foreground for each other.

SOLEDAD AND ESPERANZA/SOLITUDE AND HOPE
A Play in Nine Scenes
Written by Petrona de la Cruz and Isabel Juarez (LA FOMMA)
Translated by Amy Gormley

Characters:
Soledad—sister, death, grandmother
Esperanza—child, woman, domestic worker
Angustias—mother, wife
Rosendo—father
Señora Esponda—Mestizo woman
Juan—gardener, boyfriend, Esperanza's husband
Dorotea—gossip 1
Pancha—gossip 2
Suegra—Juan's mother

Director: Doris DiFarnecio

*   *   *

The piece at the beginning: Music by Lila Downs #7
(Soledad appears talking to her little sister, Norma. At the same time, Esperanza appears from the other side observing her sister.)

SOLEDAD: Look how dirty your fingernails are. I'm going to have to cut them for you.
                Even though you'll cry. *(She seats herself to cut her nails and pick out any lice.)*
                Look, here you have a louse! Good grief! *(She realizes that Esperanza is present.)* Where did you take the child to play that she has so much dirt under her nails.

ESPERANZA: We play that we are making stuff. *(She continues chatting with the girl. She makes a hole in the ground with her fingers.)* I'm so bored. I wish I had a doll to play with.

SOLEDAD: You'll have one, but of flesh and blood.

ESPERANZA: Lend me your shawl so that I can make a doll.

SOLEDAD: No, because you'll get it dirty.

ESPERANZA: I won't get it dirty. I'm going to take care of it. (*She lies down on the ground and imagines playing marbles.*) Lend me the marbles that you took from me the other day.

SOLEDAD: No.

ESPERANZA: Come on, say yes. Lupita won the ones that I had left when I played with her.

SOLEDAD: (*She observes her for a moment.*) I'll lend them to you, but under one condition.

ESPERANZA: What?

SOLEDAD: That you cook the beans and blow on the fire.

ESPERANZA: Ok, I already started cooking the beans at five this morning.

SOLEDAD: Well, those are going to be done at dinnertime.

ESPERANZA: Ok. (*Soledad gives the marbles to Esperanza.*) Come on … Go in, Go in… I almost got it in the hole. If you get it in, I win. (*Upon   getting up, she realizes that she has bled through her pants. She cries and shouts.*) I'm bleeding.

SOLEDAD: (*Sitting*) What's wrong with you?

ESPERANZA: (*Crying*) I'm bleeding.

SOLEDAD: What's happening? It couldn't be that you hurt yourself when you climbed the mango tree, could it? (*She carries little Norma and goes to observe Esperanza.*) Let me see you. Does your head hurt?

ESPERANZA: No.

SOLEDAD: Do your insides hurt?

ESPERANZA: No.

SOLEDAD: Does your heart hurt?

ESPERANZA: No.

SOLEDAD: Does your back hurt?

ESPERANZA: No.

SOLEDAD: Does it hurt below your belly button?

ESPERANZA: Yes, a lot.

SOLEDAD: Your hips?

ESPERANZA: Them also.

SOLEDAD: And your breasts?

ESPERANZA: Yes.

SOLEDAD: Oh, don't be afraid, it's nothing serious. That's going to happen every month.

ESPERANZA: Liar! (*She goes to sit down in the chair, crying.*) I'm going to die, I'm going to die.

SOLEDAD: Why do you think so?

ESPERANZA: You bleed like this, too?

SOLEDAD: I already told you that it happens to all of us women.

ESPERANZA: And when is it going to go away?

SOLEDAD: It depends on how many days it lasts.

ESPERANZA: And if it doesn't go away, it will never stop? (*Sobbing*)

SOLEDAD: No because it only lasts two or three days or a little longer and later it stops. But now go change clothes, later put water on for coffee and blow on the fire; it won't be long until your father is home.

Esperanza leaves the stage, Soledad remains looking for money in her change purse.

SOLEDAD: I'm going to get corn. (*Soledad leaves.*)

ESPERANZA: Good. (*She appears on the stage. She blows on the fire with a blower.*) When my mother arrives with my little sister, I'm going to tell her what happened to me. And the little one, I'm going to name her Nichim, like the most beautiful flower that grows in my community.

ROSENDO: (*He shouts from behind the scene*) Angustias! (*He appears, half drunk, reclined at one side of the stage.*) Angustias!

ESPERANZA: I'm glad you've arrived, Father. I'm boiling the coffee so that we can eat.

ROSENDO: Angustias! (*He looks at Esperanza.*) Where is your mother?

ESPERANZA: She went to wait for my little sister who's coming from France in an airplane.

ROSENDO: Stop talking nonsense. I'm asking you! Where is your mother?

ESPERANZA: I already told you that she's coming flying in an airplane with my little sister. She's going to pass over the hills, Mexico, Chiapas, and will arrive at home. (*Making the blower fly like an airplane.*)

ROSENDO: Surely she must have gone with that big-mouth Juliana to the hospital. (*He looks at his daughter as if he were going to hit her.*) I said, where is your mother?!

ESPERANZA: (*Frightened*) Don't hit me. (*She runs to hide in a corner.*)

ROSENDO: Even though you're running away, you wretch… one way or another, I will find you. And I'm going to give you hell. (*He goes to his car.*) I'm going to go looking for you in my red Chevrolet that they brought me from the United States. (*He begins to drive.*)

Music from "Yoyomah" #3 begins.

Esperanza leaves, she transforms into Angustias. Angustias enters.

ANGUSTIAS: (*She knocks on the door. She almost cannot walk due to pain.*) Is Juliana here?… Where is she?… Tell her that I need her help. (*She turns around, rubbing her back while Rosendo speaks.*)

ROSENDO: (*Driving*): I remember when you asked me for the red silk shawl that you wanted so much… The white ribbons for you to show off in your hair…But what hurts me the most is seeing you walk in all of the shoe stores looking for shoes the color of honey so that the ribbons…(*He brakes and insults the old man.*)… Damn old moron! Why don't you pay attention to where you are going? (*He continues driving, thinking.*) She must have taken off with that damn bricklayer Paco Chávez.

ANGUSTIAS (*She gets up*): Juliana, he's coming right now. Bring me to Tuxtla. I don't want to return home, Rosendo is going to kill me.

The scene of the mother's absence.

ESPERANZA'S MONOLOGUE.

(Esperanza returns to being a child.)

ESPERANZA: My mother left in the spring. Now it's winter, I don't know anything about her. I don't know when my father left either, he took my little sister and I don't know anything about them. My sister Soledad and I stay here alone, the two of us working a lot, she sends me to the mountain to cut firewood, with a big and sharp machete, when it's really cold, my hand doesn't have any strength, because of this I have cut myself, here (she shows her arm) and on my foot. (She touches her foot.)

Music from "Lila Downs" # 6. Esperanza appears to be content.

Already death is going to come. Now, yes, I'm going to eat delicious food. Mmm, like meat, chicken, hot corn, bread, drinks, candy. Over there in the cemetery I play marbles with other children, but my sister says that I shouldn't play that, that it is only for little children. So I play secretly. Also, she says that I shouldn't play and that I ought to be very careful because they can grope me. (*Gesture*)

Death appears. It spins her; it takes her hands; it spins her; they continue dancing. The dead one shows his colors. Esperanza appears; she continues dancing; all of sudden she remembers about the firewood.

ESPERANZA: I forgot that I had to go to the mountain for firewood! (*Again, she takes the machete, motions as if she were cutting firewood three times. The third time she cuts her foot.*) Ouch, I cut my foot again. My sister is going to get angry. I'm going to put some dirt on it to stop the bleeding.

The snake begins to make noise. Esperanza reacts, looking all around.

CULEBRA: Don't be afraid. You are very pretty!

ESPERANZA   (Afraid): A viper.

CULEBRA: I love you. Don't be afraid. I won't bite you. *(While it speaks it coils its body.)* You are very beautiful, I love you. Come toward me. I'm going to ask your parents to marry you. *(It rises to disappear from the stage.)*

ESPERANZA: No! *(Frightened, she takes the firewood and the machete and crying, she arrives at the house, Soledad enters.)*

SOLEDAD: Why didn't you bring much firewood?

Esperanza doesn't answer, she continues crying.

SOLEDAD: Why are you crying?

ESPERANZA: I want to leave this place. I want to go to the city.

SOLEDAD: What flea bit you that you want to go?

ESPERANZA: I want to continue studying.

SOLEDAD: Studying? Well, I learned to work and not to study.

ESPERANZA: But I want to continue studying.

SOLEDAD: Studying… studying… studying?… Definitely not. You are going to go, but to work. I am going to give you a letter to take to Señora Esponda de Gutiérrez. She needs a girl.

ESPERANZA: It better be true because you always trick me.

SOLEDAD: Now you are going to see, wait for me here! *(Soledad goes to get the bag of clothing and a piece of paper to write the letter. She returns to sit in the chair.)* Señora Esponda, I am sending you my little sister, she says that she wants to work, but if she says that she wants to study, don't let her, so that she learns to work. Do not let her go out alone in the street even for one moment, she is not to look for a husband. She is going to work. I recommend her to you. Sincerely, Soledad, your preferred artisan. *(She looks at Esperanza.)* We're going.

ESPERANZA: I don't want to. (*She runs to hide.*)

SOLEDAD: (*Furious, she takes her by the hand.*) We are going! Didn't you say that
              you wanted to go! I'm going to send you in the last turkey truck that
              leaves! (*Esperanza clings to Soledad's hand.*) Climb up! She's in your
              hands, please take good care of her, señor. It's the first time that she's
              traveled, she's not familiar with the city. (*She looks at Esperanza.*) Be-
              have yourself. (*Soledad leaves.*)

Esperanza climbs into the truck and sleeps. Soon she wakes up.

ESPERANZA: Have we arrived, señor? (*She looks out the window.*) Oh! That old drunk
              is urinating and the same thing over there, the houses are very big.
              (*She looks upward.*) Yes, señor, I'll get off now.

ESPERANZA   (*In the street, she looks for the address, she reads the paper*):   Señora
              Esponda... (*She walks around behind the stage.*) Gu... ti... er... rez (*She
              rings the doorbell twice.*)

SRA ESPONDA (*Señora Esponda appears, she observes her for a moment:*) I have no
              money to give you now.

ESPERANZA: I don't want money, señora.

SRA ESPONDA: Are you hungry? Right now I'll bring you a plate of beans.

ESPERANZA: No, I don't want food, I brought you this paper.

SRA ESPONDA: (*The señora takes the paper, she examines it.*) Oh, you are Soledad's
              sister!

ESPERANZA: Yes.

SRA ESPONDA: Ok, come in. So you want to work?

ESPERANZA: Yes.

SRA ESPONDA: The work will be: to take care of the child that I love more than
              anything. You will bathe him, and careful that you don't get shampoo
              in his eyes, dry him well, put talc on him, give him milk, wash the
              baby bottles and boil them; if the child is sleeping, you will go to the
              kitchen, wash the utensils, wash the stove, mop, dry the utensils and
              put them in their place. Afterwards, you will go to the living room, if
              the child has already woken up, carry him, sweep, vacuum, mop,

clean the furniture, change the flowers, if the mailman comes by, pick up the mail, go to get tortillas, go to get the other child at school and never leave him alone for a moment, wash his clothes. Oh, and in the afternoon, you are going to be my lady companion, when I go to the dressmaker or the beauty salon. Now, see to washing yourself since you are so sweaty.

ESPERANZA: Where is the bathroom, señora?

SRA ESPONDA (*Gesturing*): The bathroom is there, but they just came to clean this morning, so wash up in the laundry room, with a bucket.

ESPERANZA: Where is the laundry room?

SRA ESPONDA: It's to the left of the door.

ESPERANZA: Señora, where am I going to sleep? (*Leaving*).

SRA ESPONDA: I'm going to make you a place in the storehouse.

SRA ESPONDA: (*Esperanza leaves and the chair converts into a cradle and the señora talks to her baby.*) Oh, what a beautiful baby! Now you are going to have a nanny, now you aren't going to be alone, right, baby? (*She calls Esperanza.*) Girl! Girl! Come.

ESPERANZA: (*From outside.*) I'm coming, señora. (*She appears, near the cradle.*) What a chubby-cheeked baby.

SRA ESPONDA: Look, he is Ivancito, the child that you are going to take care of; take good care of him, because I love him more than anything.

(*Esperanza begins to show the baby her colorful ribbons.*)

SRA ESPONDA: Don't give him dirty things. He has his own toys. And when you hold him, wash your hands well, because he could get sick. Now I'm trusting you to take very good care of him. I have to go to work. (*The señora leaves.*)

ESPERANZA: Your feet look like mine. Now child, what's bothering you? Did you poop? I'm going to change your diaper, yuck, you pooped a lot... Now you are ready, don't cry, I'm going to take you to the garden so that you can see the flowers. (*She lifts up the baby.*) Whew, you are heavy. (*She begins to sing and dance, showing flowers to the baby.*)

(Juan, the gardener, appears pruning flowers.)

JUAN: Hey, pretty girl, How are you? What's your name?

ESPERANZA: *(Strolling with the child, looking out of the corner of her eye.)* Esperanza.

JUAN: What a beautiful name. *(He smiles.)* Do you have a boyfriend?

Esperanza doesn't answer.

JUAN: Do you know how to speak Spanish?

ESPERANZA: Yes.

JUAN: Then why don't you answer me?

ESPERANZA: It's that I don't know you, I don't know who you are.

JUAN: I'm Juan, the gardener. Are you familiar with the city?

ESPERANZA: No, I'm not.

JUAN: Today, on Sunday, we can go for a walk and I'll show you around the city. What do you say, Lenchita?

ESPERANZA: Señora Esponda didn't tell me that I had Sunday free.

JUAN: Surely, she'll give it to you, if you want I can speak with her.

ESPERANZA: If you want.

(Esperanza leaves the stage to beautify herself. Juan remains on the stage, placing the chairs so that he can sit down, he looks at his watch with desperation that Esperanza does not arrive.)

JUAN: Get out of here doves, I didn't bring rice for you. *(He looks all around.)* Maybe she's not going to come?

(Esperanza appears running.)

JUAN: I thought that you weren't going to come!

ESPERANZA: I was late, because I went to buy Señora Esponda's stockings.

(Juan invites her to sit down.)

JUAN: Don't worry, the good thing is that you got here. (*He looks for his bag of candy.*) Do you like honey candy?

ESPERANZA: Yes.

JUAN: Take them, they are for you.

ESPERANZA: Ok... How many years have you worked in Señora Esponda's house?

JUAN: Phew...! I arrived at that house about seven years ago. Why do you think that I am telling you that they love me as if I were family?

ESPERANZA: And how old are you now?

JUAN: I'm twenty-four. And you, how old are you?

ESPERANZA: Fourteen.

JUAN: Fourteen! And already you are a lady! Could we be boyfriend and girlfriend? (*He takes Esperanza's hand...*).

ESPERANZA: (*She thinks for a moment if she should accept him or not.*) Ok. (*They move their chairs closer and she leans on his shoulder. Esperanza gets up, she takes the chairs and stays observing Juan.*)

Juan's Monologue:

JUAN: Here we are on my coffee plantation, Lenchita and I. We got married June 10th, the Day of the Body of Christ. I lost this land that belonged to me, but ever since I was a little orphaned child I worked as a waiter and gardener saving the little money I had in order to recover my land. Here people envy me and threaten me because I have the best coffee crops. They say that I am cocky and proud, but I don't pay attention to them. (*He sees that his friend is coming. He smiles.*) Already my friend has come! (*He is surprised to see more people.*) And these people! (*They shoot him for the first time, he sees the blood.*) You just shot me, idiot! (*He shoots him again. Esperanza comes closer and hugs him.*) You've killed me, you son of a bitch!

ESPERANZA: Stop killing him! (*She moves him slowly and takes him little by little off the stage to change into the gossip.*)

(*Two gossips dressed in black with masks appear.*)

DOROTEA: The food was delicious, I think that the deceased man had a lot of money. Oh! It's good that we went.

PANCHA: Poor guy…He was a hard-working man; he had many coffee plantations and had good crops.

DOROTEA: I don't believe it. I think that he had other dirty business.

PANCHA: Oh, Dorotea! What are you saying?

DOROTEA: Well that he might have trafficked drugs.

PANCHA: Did you see him do it?

DOROTEA: No, but we harvest enough coffee and never end being poor. Instead, he had that racy car, Texan hat, denim pants, boots, and even a pistol that he didn't have time to get to when they killed him. (*She smiles mockingly.*)

PANCHA: Oh, Dorotea! Now the deceased man is buried, paying for his sins. The one that's going to end up in purgatory for being a gossip is you.

DOROTEA   (*She crosses herself, and acts like she is not listening.*): Good afternoon Doña Queta, I hope you have a good day… (*To Pancha*) And you already know that the woman is going to cross the border into the United States?   Because they say that her lover was the one who killed her husband.

PANCHA: Yes, I know that she's going to go and that she is pregnant. But what are you saying, Dorotea? … Now it's late, I have to go.

Pancha leaves. Dorotea stays looking around for a minute. She turns around to remove her mask and transforms into the mother-in-law, and begins to blow the fire. Esperanza appears with a bag.

ESPERANZA: I'm going to go, mother-in-law.

SUEGRA: Where are you going to go?

ESPERANZA: I'm going to cross the border into the United States.

SUEGRA: How are you going to go?   Whom are you going to see there? Now I'm not going to see the birth of my grandson.

ESPERANZA: I'm going to bring him when he grows up.

SUEGRA: But you should stay and work here together.

ESPERANZA: I don't have anyone to work the land.

SUEGRA: Stay, don't go. Really think it over.

ESPERANZA: No, because if I stay, I'm going to die of sadness.

SUEGRA: Ok, if you've already thought about it a lot, may God bless you. I cannot stop you. (*She dries the tears in her eyes.*)

ESPERANZA: Yes, I've made up my mind about it.

SUEGRA: Then I hope all goes well for you, don't forget about me.

ESPERANZA: No, I won't forget you.

Music of "Lila Downs" #3.

Esperanza walks around, observing the town that she is leaving. Before leaving the stage, she looks intently at her mother-in-law. Then she leaves. The mother-in-law blows into the fire for a moment, afterwards she gets up slowly and transforms back into a young woman.

END

IN LIGHT OF A CONCLUSION

Both literary testimonies speak of Mayan women's need to build bridges of knowledge between the countryside and the city, between Earth and the human heart, between men and women, between the local and the global for transformation to take place. More than a decade after the 1994 uprising, Chiapas remains in a state of uneasy, but optimistic peace. Like the Zapatistas, Josefa Hernandez Perez and the women of LA FOMMA continue the struggle to bring autonomy, democracy, literacy, and human rights to the Indigenous peoples of Chiapas, in ways that work within the cultural logic of the Maya people. This essay, in multiple voices, constitutes both a tribute and a contribution to their on-going work.

NOTES

1 See Carlos Fazio, *Samuel Ruiz: El Caminante* (Mexico City: Espasa Calipe, 1994) and Jean Meyer, *Samuel Ruiz en San Cristóbal* (México City: Tusquets Editors, 2000).

2 See, among others, Gustavo Guiterrez, *The Density of the Present: Selected Writings* (Maryknoll, NY: Orbis Press, 1999).

3 Personal interview with Jeanne Simonelli, Jan. 25, 1999.

4 See Jan De Vos, *Una tierra para sembrar sueños* (México, DF: CIESAS, 2002), 221, 215–21. The bulk of the discussion of the role of the Church through the mid 70s derives from this excellent social history. See also Christine Kovic, *Walking with One Heart: Indigenous Rights and the Catholic Church in Highland Chiapas* (Austin: University of Texas Press, 2005).

5 There are six Maya languages spoken in Chiapas alone. The most common of these are Tzotzil and Tzeltal.

6 In Spanish, the term used for this awakening is *"tomar consciencia,"* a phrase with no direct translation in English.

7 Earle and Simonelli, *Uprising of Hope: Sharing the Zapatista Journey to Alternative Development*, 80.

8 De Vos, *Una tierra para sembrar sueños*, 227.

9 De Vos, *Una tierra para sembrar sueños*, 221–31.

10 Kovic, *Walking with One Heart: Indigenous Rights and the Catholic Church in Highland Chiapas.*

11 Quoted in De Vos, *Una tierra para sembrar sueños*, 215.

12 Cf. Thomas Benjamin, *A Rich Land for Poor People: Politics and Society in Modern Chiapas* (Albuquerque: University of New Mexico Press, 1996); George Collier and E. L. Quaratiello, *Basta! Land the Zapatista Rebellion in Chiapas* (Oakland, CA: Food First, 1994.)

13 Duncan Earle, "Indigenous Identity at the Margin," in *Cultural Survival* (Spring 1994), 28.

14 Federico Anaya Gallardo, "Making Peace in Chiapas: The Problem of State Reconstitution" (unpublished manuscript 1997), 7.

15 A. Gilly, "Chiapas and the Rebellion of the Enchanted World," in *Rural Revolt in Mexico: U.S. Intervention and the Domain of Subaltern Politics*, edited by D. Nugent (Durham: Duke University Press, 1998), 261–333.

16 Jeanne Simonelli, *Two Boys, A Girl, and Enough! Fertility and Economic Change on the Mexican Periphery* (Boulder, CO: Westview Press, 1986).

17 Collier and Quaratiello, *Basta! Land and the Zapatista Rebellion in Chiapas*, 69–81.

18 Simonelli and Earle, Fieldnotes, July 2000.

19 See Elizabeth Story, "Empowering Theology: The Transformation of Easter in Highland Chiapas" (Master's thesis, Department of Religion, Wake Forest University), May 2006.

20 This introductory text was written by Miriam Laughlin.

21 Diana Taylor, *Holy Terrors: Latin American Women Perform* (Durham, NC: Duke University Press, 2003).

22 Anna Alabaldeja, *La risa olvidada de mi madre: 10 años de Fortaleza de la Mujer Maya* (Valencia, Spain, 2005).

BIBLIOGRAPHY

Alabaldeja, Anna. *La risa olvidada de mi madre: 10 años de Fortaleza de la Mujer Maya.* Valencia, Spain, 2005.

Benjamin, Thomas. *A Rich Land for Poor People: Politics and Society in Modern Chiapas.* Albuquerque: University of New Mexico Press, 1996.

Collier, George, and E. L. Quaratiello, *Basta! Land the Zapatista Rebellion in Chiapas.* Oakland, CA: Food First, 1994.

De Vos, Jan. *Una tierra para sembrar sueños.* México, DF: CIESAS, 2002.

Earle, Duncan. "Indigenous Identity at the Margin," in *Cultural Survival* (Spring 1994), 26-30.

Earle, Duncan, and Jeanne Simonelli. *Uprising of Hope: Sharing the Zapatista Journey to Alternative Development.* Walnut Creek, CA: AltaMira Press, 2005.

Fazio, Carlos. *Samuel Ruiz: El Caminante.* Mexico City: Espasa Calipe, 1994.

Gallardo, Federico Anaya. "Making Peace in Chiapas: The Problem of State Reconstitution." Unpublished manuscript, 1997.

Gilly, A. "Chiapas and the Rebellion of the Enchanted World," in *Rural Revolt in Mexico: U.S. Intervention and the Domain of Subaltern Politics*, edited by D. Nugent. Durham: Duke University Press, 1998, 261-333.

Guiterrez, Gustavo. *The Density of the Present: Selected Writings.* Maryknoll, NY: Orbis Press, 1999.

Kovic, Christine. *Walking with One Heart: Indigenous Rights and the Catholic Church in Highland Chiapas.* Austin: University of Texas Press, 2005.

Meyer, Jean. *Samuel Ruiz en San Cristóbal.* México City: Tusquets Editors, 2000.

Simonelli, Jeanne. *Two Boys, A Girl, and Enough! Fertility and Economic Change on the Mexican Periphery.* Boulder, CO: Westview Press, 1986.

Story, Elizabeth. "Empowering Theology: The Transformation of Easter in Highland Chiapas." Master's thesis, Department of Religion, Wake Forest University, 2006.

Taylor, Diana. *Holy Terrors: Latin American Women Perform.* Durham, NC: Duke University Press, 2003.

12 CHALLENGING AUTHENTICITY: CONTEMPORARY ARTISTS' CONTRIBUTIONS TO AMERICAN INDIAN INTELLECTUAL SOVEREIGNTY

Eva Marie Garroutte

"He is of Maidu, Portuguese, and Hawaiian descent."
(Harry Fonseca)

"My art, my life experience, my tribal ties are totally enmeshed."
(Jaune Quick-to-See Smith)

"He grew up a stone's throw from the Cattaraugus reservation."
(Peter Jemison)

"For me, who has never been in a reservation situation, it would be foolish to try to do tribal art . . . . I do some traditional things, but it wasn't passed on to me."
(Rick Bartow)

"He calls himself an American artist who paints Indians, not an Indian artist. . . . He does not attempt to be authentic."
(John Nieto)

Like other creative professionals, American Indian artists are frequently the subjects of short biographies and interviews that accompany the work they display. The foregoing statements are excerpted from gallery brochures, art magazines, Internet sites, and exhibition catalogues.[1] The acknowledged purpose of such writings is to describe an individual, to locate his or her creative production in the context of a life history for the benefit of viewers and buyers. However, these statements also do more, pointing beyond the individual to the environment in which he moves. They reveal the larger social context in which racial-ethnic identities are never simply asserted, but negotiated. They instruct us about the role that artists play in the unfolding societal conversation regarding the right of American Indian people to name and define themselves.

The biographical statements of American Indian artists make clear that their subjects (like American Indian people in general) are not free simply to claim the racial-ethnic identity that they, or even their tribal communities, feel characterizes them best. Rather, they must submit their claim to the judgment of various audiences. Because artist statements are part of very delicate negotiations, they must be composed with exacting precision. Thus, the self-descriptions painstakingly lay out multiple ancestries and meticulously specify tribal ties and relationships to reservations (even, as in the Jemison description, offering a measure of physical distance separating the youthful artist from that legitimizing location). They also explicate the nature and specific provenance of any cultural knowledge that is said to underlie the work, establishing how the artists received it and from whom. The negotiated character of Indian identity claims also accounts for the difference with which artists describe tribal identity. Although all the artists identify Native ancestry, some qualify or even reject the title of "Indian artist."

It is neither right nor wrong that an audience might want to know the kind of details that regularly appear in Native artists' biographies, or that artists and their agents might want to share such facts. Such examples, though, invite us to consider the roots of one critic's claim that the visual arts function as "eloquent and forceful articulations of the contemporary politics of [American Indian] identity."[2] What are the strictures that claimants to an American Indian identity must confront? How have such artists used their work to challenge and subvert imposed ideas about racial-ethnic "authenticity"? What are the broader consequences of such challenges for the way that American Indian people understand, remember, and imagine themselves?

Subsequently, I will examine two of the many definitions that circumscribe claims to American Indian identity. Then, I will consider how many contemporary Native artists have moved from being passive subjects of such definitions to becoming active participants in the conversation about Indian-ness. These artists have used their work to assert a right to what Osage literary scholar Robert Warrior calls "intellectual sovereignty"—the right to create ideas and bodies of thought that break from imposed expectations, being instead infused by distinctly tribal values, experiences, knowledge, meanings, philosophies, paradigms, goals, and interests.[3]

In these tasks, I draw for illustration on specific works created by Native artists. I did not select these particular examples systematically—with the goal, for example, of representing a particular artistic school or revealing opinions that are supposedly shared among all Native artists. Rather, I have chosen works because they powerfully express ideas that I have repeatedly encountered as I move about, as an American Indian person, in tribal communities and in my professional work, which has focused to a large degree on issues of American Indian identity. I also chose these examples of artistic work simply because I like them. The resulting collection of images is not, accordingly, a basis for simplistic or broad generalizations. It illustrates, nevertheless, some important complexities of contemporary identity negotiations and allows us to explore the ways that artistic statements may both express and affect the realities and possibilities that impinge upon Indian lives.

LEGAL DEFINITIONS OF IDENTITY

I turn first to the task of examining particular definitions of American Indian identity, investigating both the ways that they function and the ways that artists have challenged them. Beginning with definitions grounded in law, it is immediately apparent that these highly formalized definitions have a considerable impact on Indian people. The federal government uses a wide array of distinct legal definitions to distinguish Indians from non-Indians. Such laws recognize that American Indians are much more than a racial minority; they are also a category of citizens with very particular rights and responsibilities in relation to the federal government. In historic negotiations, the federal government agreed to compensate tribes for the large amounts of lands and other resources that they surrendered, often by force.[4] This compensation includes certain benefits in the form of education, health care, and hunting and fishing rights. Legal definitions ensure that modern Indian people receive their inherited rights and prevent non-Indians from improperly gaining access to them.

A legal definition with particular consequences for American Indian artists is contained in the Indian Arts and Crafts Act of 1990. It specifies that only those individuals who are citizens of a state- or federally recognized tribe may market their work as "Indian-produced," and (unlike a related law passed in 1935) it attaches significant fines and prison sentences to its violation. The sculpture *Made in Japan*—a Japanese-style rice paper umbrella painted with designs recalling tribal creation myths—by Cattaraugus Seneca artist G. Peter Jemison (b. 1945) suggests one of the reasons that this legislation was created.

Many buyers consider artwork more valuable if it has been created by an Indian person. Consequently, a great deal of "Indian art" has been produced (often in Asian countries, but also domestically) and falsely labeled. In 1985, the Commerce Department estimated that specious "Indian art" imported from foreign countries created forty to eighty million dollars in lost income for genuine Indian artists every year, or between ten and twenty percent of annual Indian art sales.[5]

By regulating people's right to identify themselves as Indian in connection with their sale of artwork, the Indian Arts and Crafts Act thus protects many Native artists from unfair competition. At the same time, it may also contribute to the commodification of identity, reinforcing a situation in which the artists' racial or ethnic "authenticity" is marketable.[6] In addition, the Indian Arts and Crafts Act, like other legal definitions, seriously disadvantages many genuinely Indian people who are unable to satisfy the definition of "Indian" contained in it.[7]

There are many sound, historical reasons why some people of exclusive or substantial Indian ancestry are not citizens of governmentally recognized tribes. The situation is so complex that its discussion is well beyond the scope of this essay.[8]

However, one reason that some Indian people do not possess tribal citizenship is that a central criterion of enrollment in the majority of American Indian tribes is "blood quantum," or degree of Indian ancestry.[9] Given that Indian people have the highest rate of intermarriage of any American racial group,[10] it is not surprising that some mixed-race Indian people cannot meet the minimum blood quantum required by their tribe for citizenship. However, an individual with an objectively high blood quantum may also have difficulty establishing Indian identity because of how that measure is reckoned.

Initial calculation of blood quantum usually begins with a "base roll," a census listing of tribal membership and degree of ancestry in some particular year. Most base rolls were established in the late nineteenth or early twentieth centuries, and the Indian person's degree of ancestry was usually self-reported or estimated by a non-Indian agent of the federal government. These rolls allow one to calculate that the modern-day offspring of, say, a full-blood Navajo mother and a white father is one-half Navajo. If that half Navajo child in turn produces progeny with a Hopi person of one-quarter blood degree, those progeny will be judged to be one-quarter Navajo and one-eighth Hopi. As even this rather simple example shows, such calculations can, in time, become infinitesimally precise. A person's ancestry may be parsed into so many thirty-seconds, sixty-fourths, one-hundred-twenty-eighths, and so on. The final figure is authenticated by a Certificate of Degree of Indian Blood or CDIB, a document issued by the United States government. While individual tribes set their own criteria for citizenship, most rely on the federally calculated blood quantum figure at least in part, setting a minimum requirement that can vary from as high as one half in some tribes to as low as one thirty-second in others.[11]

In all cases even a small deviation in the calculation may make a modern descendant unable to meet his tribe's citizenship standard. A person's status can be affected by ancestors who eluded federal census takers, who spoke English poorly, who understated or underestimated their actual tribal blood degree, who refused to acknowledge a child's paternity, whose physical appearance contradicted some preconception of the census enumerator, or who were orphaned and consequently had incomplete knowledge of a parent's ancestry. It can also be substantially reduced by a forebear with mixed American Indian and African American ancestry, since such people were often treated quite differently by census takers than people of exclusively Indian ancestry, or of mixed American Indian and white ancestry.[12]

A Cherokee artist who often works in mixed media, Joe Cantrell (b. 1945) takes up the absurdity of American attempts to reduce racial complexities to tidy categorization schemes. He addresses the inherent unreliability of blood quantum records in his humorously imagined *Authentic Indian ID Card*, a computer-generated variant of the federal government's CDIB.

Cantrell's card explicitly purports to certify what the real document implicitly assumes that a person's ancestry really can be traced and recorded with complete accuracy over many generations. It assigns a blood quantum based on the sardonic promise that "every sexual encounter of all this person's ancestors since 1492 has been recorded and the heritage of all these folks was absolutely known."

Cantrell's piece also raises the significant issue of the federal government's shifting definitions of Indian-ness. The Indian Arts and Crafts Act is hardly the only piece of legislation to specify a particular definition of Native identity. The American government has crafted many distinct legal definitions, and still uses a range of definitions for different purposes: a 1978 congressional survey counted thirty-three definitions then in use, and more have been created since.[13] Some specify one or another minimum blood quantum requirement; some specify other criteria altogether. These variant definitions have often served particular governmental interests.

For instance, when land cessions required signatures from a certain percentage of tribal members, government agents in the latter decades of the nineteenth century often crafted lenient definitions of Indian identity that allowed mixed-race individuals to participate in the agreements. This was true to the extent that by 1892 President Benjamin Harrison's Commissioner of Indian Affairs, Thomas Jefferson Morgan, declared that "to decide at this time that . . . mixed bloods are not Indian . . . would unsettle or endanger the titles to much of the lands that have been relinquished by Indian tribes and patented to citizens of the United States."[14]

In other cases, however, as when mixed bloods were perceived to be fomenting tribal resistance to federal goals, the government formulated more restrictive definitions of who would be considered Indian. It often insisted on a standard of one-quarter, or even one-half, blood quantum before it would legally define individuals as Indians.[15]

The government's self-serving vacillations on the subject of American Indian identity continued in the twentieth century. For instance, in the late 1960s, the Department of Justice went to considerable lengths to exclude Alaska Native communities from the benefits of the 1946 Indian Claims Commission Act, a bill that created a special tribunal to hear tribal claims against the federal government for violations of treaties and agreements. The attempt ignored a long series of court decisions holding that any of the aboriginal peoples of the Americas, regardless of nomenclature, should be included under legislation written to apply to American Indians. Cantrell's identity card, which references the imaginary "Treaty of Hoaxalooser" and requires the holder to specify whether or not his tribe "has land worth taking," suggests that the American government's motives for drawing legal boundaries are not always disinterested.

Navajo/ Creek/ Seminole artist Hulleah J. Tsinhnahjinnie's (b. 1954) photo-installation *Nobody's Pet Indian*, which appeared at the San Francisco Art Institute's Walter McBean Gallery in 1993, made a similarly pointed criticism of the federal government's presumption of the right to legislate Indian identities (see fig.3).

Fig.3. Hulleah J. Tsinhnahjinnie, *Nobody's Pet Indian* (1993, Detail).

The installation, which surrounded photos of American Indian artists with their federal identification numbers and various imposed identity labels, fully confronted the Indian Arts and Crafts Act, drawing parallels between it and the racial tracking practices of Germany's Nazi government. The installation detail reproduced here shows an Indian person with identification number branded across the forehead, reducing the individual to a number after the fashion that cattle are branded or POWs dehumanized. Tsinhnahjinnie's piece dramatically summarizes a commentator's critique that "the Indian Arts and Crafts Act of 1990 . . . perpetuates the historical tendency to remove the 'Indian problem' by reducing the number of Indians."[16]

In another work, entitled *Grandchildren* (2003), Tsinhnahjinnie spotlights the related issue of people of mixed African and American Indian ancestry (fig.4). Many Americans are unaware that quite a few citizens of the Five Eastern Tribes that were forcibly relocated to Oklahoma in the nineteenth century—the Cherokee, Creek, Chickasaw, Choctaw, and Seminole—owned slaves before the Civil War. In addition, they are not aware that, after the Northern victory, those slaves received formal citizenship in tribal nations, or that these "freedmen" and their descendants often remained firmly connected to tribal life by speaking an Indian language, practicing traditional ceremonies, and even holding high offices in some tribal governments. Although intermarriage and racially mixed children have commonly resulted from the long-standing and close association of African and Indian people in some tribes, the conventional American norms for racial classification, along with governmental policies, have typically regarded them as strictly Black and denied them privileges of tribal citizenship available to those of mixed White and Indian ancestry.

Tsinhnahjinnie's *Grandchildren*, however, refuses Americans the opportunity to completely expunge historical realities. The photo honors the artist's own relatives among the Oklahoma Seminoles, a tribe with a significant number of families of similarly mixed ancestry.[17] Many such individuals may have been bureaucratically erased as Indian people, but Tsinhnahjinnie's work ensures that they do not become invisible.

 As all these artistic examples teach us, Indian-ness is hardly an unproblematic identity—one that individuals simply choose to claim—but one that must be carefully negotiated, often in legal contexts. However, whether or not they successfully endure the rigors of formal, legal identity definitions, American Indians today are often subject to still other, less formal standards of authenticity.

Fig.4. Hulleah J. Tsinhnahjinnie,
Grandchildren from "Portraits Against Amnesia Series", 2003.

CULTURAL DEFINITIONS OF INDIAN IDENTITY

Like other American Indian people, Native artists are also subject to identity definitions based on their cultural characteristics. Rather than grounding identity in legal fictions, cultural definitions hold out the promise of something observable and enduring. At first consideration, they appear to locate claims to identity in the distinctive lifeways and thoughtways that define "peoplehood." On the one hand, it is clear that historic Indian groups used cultural practice to distinguish their own from members of other groups, and most Indian people today continue to consider culture an important determinant of identity. It is tempting, perhaps, to conclude that these definitions are the true and self-evident foundation upon which Indian people may assert intellectual sovereignty in relation to matters of identity and self-definition. At the same time, even such an apparently sensible standard presents some puzzles and problems.

For one thing, the cultural definitions of identity that Indian people formulate for themselves are always in dialogue with, and often entirely overwhelmed by, definitions created by the dominant society—and the latter have often featured extremely odd requirements. In particular, non-Indians usually demand that "authentic" Indians be anachronisms. The mainstream image of Indians is frozen in a vividly imagined past memorialized, for example, in the paintings of the early, non-Indian painters of Indians such as George Catlin (b. 1796), Charles Russell (b. 1864), and Frederic Remington (b. 1861). Their American West was populated with mounted, buckskinned, painted, Indian warriors. They rode hard, led the charge, proudly displayed war trophies, brandished lances and rifles, crept up from behind large rocks, sent smoke signals, and carried out exotic ceremonies. Such images have become such a standard of the larger society's "knowledge" of American Indian cultures—the decorative stuff of an endless array of prints, posters, coffee mugs, T-shirts, note cards and similar household objects—that their reproduction here would be redundant. The continuing influence of such work—its pervasiveness and undying popularity—makes clear that American expectations about Indians are quite different from their expectations about other racial groups.

By way of illustrating this point, anthropologist Jack Forbes compares common assumptions about individuals of Indian ancestry with common assumptions about individuals of African ancestry. As he writes, "Africans always remain African (or black) even when they speak Spanish or English and serve as cabinet secretaries in the United States government or as trumpet players in a Cuban salsa group . . . ." Indians, on the other hand, "must remain [culturally] unchanged in order to be considered Indian."

This presumption prevails in much popular, and even scholarly, opinion. Forbes continues, "I am reminded of a Dutch book on 'The Last Indians' featuring pictures only of South American people still living a way of life which is stereotypically 'Indian.'" By contrast, "Blacks…are not seen only as traditional villagers in Africa. No one would dare to write a book on 'The Last Blacks,' with pictures of 'tribesmen' in ceremonial costumes. So the category of 'black' has a different quality than has that of 'Indian'. . . ."[18] The prevalent and powerful depictions of Indian cultural authenticity declare that an Indian who is not a historical relic is no Indian at all.

The significance of externally imposed expectations about Indian cultures is evident in the criteria of the Branch of Acknowledgment and Research (BAR), a subdivision within the federal Bureau of Indian Affairs that is responsible for evaluating the claims of groups to receive legal recognition as Indian tribes. Interestingly, this observation is based on facts, even though the definition the BAR uses to define Indian tribes into existence makes particular efforts to avoid stereotyped assumptions about culture. Thus, rather than assuming that the only "real" Indians are those who observe the life ways of the distant past, the BAR only requires successful petitioners to show that their community has been continuously identified as "in some way distinct from the wider society" since 1900.

However, it then goes on to name the individuals whose opinions or actions can be pointed to in order to establish this identification: parish or government officials, anthropologists, historians, authors, journalists, and so on. Identifications on the part of members of the petitioning group are specifically excluded. In other words, groups seeking federal recognition establish "distinctiveness" only by reference to the observations and opinions of outsiders. Given the long-standing linkage, in the minds of most Americans, between Indian-ness and ancient cultural practice, it seems likely that those who have been persistently recognized as Indians are, in fact, those whose cultural practices conformed to stereotypes of exotic primitivism.[19] In this way, the dominant society's definitions of Indian cultural authenticity, poorly informed as they often are, become central to the ability of Indian people to establish themselves as federally acknowledged tribes.

The frequently absurd romanticism of the dominant society's ideas about Indian cultures presents a challenge that American Indian artists have been unable to resist. Rick Bartow, for example, gently tweaks the stereotypes by giving his distinguished elder not only a feather headdress but also a pair of dapper, wire-rimmed spectacles. Are viewers surprised at this combination of the symbol of the exotic warrior with the hallmark of the gentle intellectual? The work's title, *Die Altersschwache* (German for an old woman weakened by the decay, decline, or infirmity as a result of old age) recalls the familiar motif of the "vanishing Indian"—but this subject does not seem threatened by his own imminent demise or "disappearance." He looks determinedly out of his portrait. He survives.

Cultural standards of American Indian identity can be treacherous even when they are rooted in informed understandings of tribal histories and lifeways. Just as legal definitions can exclude legitimately Indian people from recognition as such, cultural definitions also sometimes create debatable boundaries around Indian-ness. Many genuinely Indian people do not have access to the life experiences that others imagine for them. They may not know their language, their traditions, or even their tribe (as in the case of many infants who were adopted by non-Indians until the passage of the Indian Child Welfare Act of 1978 made this practice more difficult).

It is not that contemporary Indian peoples fail to maintain thriving, intact cultures. Somehow, with a persistence and resilience that almost defy the imagination, they do. Hopi people, for instance, still perform the ceremony for which John Nieto's *Snake Dance* is titled.

Others participate in the more recent but profoundly tribal cultural expression of the powwow, vividly depicted by artists such as L. David Eveningthunder (Doh-gwey Du-gwanee). However, not all Indian people remain connected to distinctive cultural practices. The reasons are painfully evident. Agents of the American government devoted hundreds of years and millions of dollars to separating Indian people from their cultures through policies such as warfare, missionary work, forcible relocation, land allotment, boarding schools, and the criminalization of American Indian religious practices. It would be very surprising if these efforts had not been widely effective in destroying language, spirituality, family and community relationships, geographic ties, and other elements of Native cultures. In fact, they have horribly damaged Indian communities and cut many Indian people adrift from their ethnic heritages.

The sad truth is that many Indian people have paid, and continue to pay, the economic, social, familial, personal, and other consequences of an Indian ancestry, but they have little "traditional culture" left to compensate them for it. It is a truth that Rosalie Favell, a Canadian Métis artist tells in an especially courageous photo. *All I Knew about my Indian Blood* shows a cheery group of children posed in front of a Christmas tree, one sporting a dime-store version of an Indian headdress.

Favell observes that, when she was growing up, the family was not allowed even to discuss her father's Native ancestry, laboring under an enforced silence that fed a profound sense of loss.[20] Her work reminds us that, in the words of Anishinaabe artist and teacher Kathleen Westcott, "while traditional cultures are still important in many Native people's lives, another part of 'The Indian Experience in America' is growing up White."[21] It reminds us that this situation is the result of intentional actions on the part of the dominant society. It reminds us that harshly enforcing cultural definitions of identity can impose an additional burden of shame upon just those American Indian people who have already suffered a profound loss.

CONTEMPORARY AMERICAN INDIAN ART AS INSTRUMENT OF INTELLECTUAL SOVEREIGNTY

I turn now to the task of considering the ways in which American Indian artists have used their work to speak back to definitions of racial-ethnic identity in ways that are relevant to the notion of "intellectual sovereignty," which I introduced at the beginning of this essay. The concept of sovereignty for American Indians originates in historic legal decisions, where it refers to the right of tribes, as semi-autonomous "domestic dependent nations" existing within the boundaries of the United States, to exercise governmental authority over their internal affairs.[22] It has proven a difficult concept to translate into practical application, but most commentators would agree that it is fundamentally about self-determination. "Tribal sovereignty," as legal scholar Charles Wilkinson has written, "is the lifeblood of an emerging Indian separatism that permits tribes to decide in the matters that really count . . . ."[23]

More recently, Osage academic Robert Warrior has coined the term "intellectual sovereignty" to extend the right of Indian self-determination into the realm of intellection and cultural expression.[24] Advocates of Indigenous intellectual sovereignty call for the creation of new ideas, perspectives, and bodies of thought by and about indigenous peoples, and for the benefit of their emancipation, growth, and survival as individuals, communities, and cultures.[25]

So far in this essay, I have shown how American Indian artists may be forced to negotiate their identity claims within both formal and informal standards and definitions that often have no counterparts in other American racial-ethnic groups. I have shown a few of the many ways that such artists have challenged and subverted the expectations of the larger society. In such efforts, they have made a powerful claim in service of American Indian intellectual sovereignty, and one that has a remarkable double aspect. That is, on the one hand, American Indian artists have succeeded wonderfully in drawing out the ambiguities, absurdities, and even cruelties of extant definitions of Indian-ness. At the same time, they do not typically then retreat to the position that anyone should therefore be able to make any identity claims he or she chooses. Somehow, Native artists seem to have been able to problematize existing meanings about racial-ethnic identity after the fashion of postmodernists, yet without invoking the relativistic collapse of all distinctions. They cling, in short, to a stubborn insistence that distinctions are possible and necessary.

Indian artists, it seems to me, have traversed the dangerous divide between stultifying order and uncritical relativism in regard to issues of American Indian identity by means of certain artistic strategies. These are certainly not unique to them, but are nevertheless deployed by them to considerable effect. One such strategy is the use of humor. My favorite example is a piece by Muriel Antoine, a Sicangu Lakota sculptor. She entitles her multimedia mask *I Dreamt I was an Aztec Goddess in my Maidenform Bra* (1994) and decorates it with Aztec and Northwest Coast style designs.

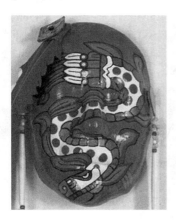

In Pacific Northwest cultural traditions, masks are often associated with the transformations of certain types of beings from one form into the other, and the artist observes that her piece is "inspired by the fact that everyone always says 'my grandmother was a Cherokee princess.'"[26] The droll title pokes fun at the arrogance implied by the fantasy, remarkably widespread even in segments of the general American population who have most clearly benefited from the destruction of the Indigenous inhabitants of this continent, that they somehow enjoy a special kinship with Indian people—are somehow themselves "really"

Fig. 5. Muriel Antoine, *I Dreamt I was an Aztec Goddess in my Maidenform Bra* (1994).

Indian—through their relationship with a mysterious and exotic (and naturally royal) Native forebear. By calling up a mental image of a woman luxuriating in picaresque fantasies, the title may hint at an additional point. This is a possible, sidelong reference to the speculation, prevalent in Native communities, that it is sexual attraction to Indian men that tempts non-Indian women to attempt such racial redefinition. Work such as Antoine's—humorous but with a sharp edge—makes clear that, for Indian artists, the habit of questioning regnant standards of classification does not simply throw wide the doors of racial-ethnic identification. It does not make all claims to Indian identity equally worthy of respect.

Another strategy that Indian artists have used to distinguish baby and bathwater in regard to American Indian identity claims is to draw attention to competing interpretations or perspectives simultaneously, while refusing to resolve them. For instance, Jaune Quick-to-See Smith's lithograph titled *Modern Times* (1993) offers a composite of images.

Fig.6. Jaune Quick-to-See Smith, *Modern Times* (1993).

It includes the split figure of a Native man framed by a pictograph on one side and a plant used in traditional medicine on the other. The figure sports both a Plains Indian-style headdress and an executive briefcase. The work seems, in part, a comment on the ability of Indian people to move between different and equally legitimate expressions of identity. At the same time, the piece incorporates reference to "apples," the slang term for Native people who have completely traversed the ethnic identity divide, being unchangeably "red on the outside" but nevertheless "white on the inside." Finally, the part of the image that dominates the picture by its use of color is a highly stylized advertising logo. Is the figure at the center of this image an individual who successfully embraces elements of two cultures? What do the pictograph, the traditional herbs, and the briefcase mean to the man, or to others? At what point does the ability to move comfortably between cultures become an act of selling one of them out? What does the larger society—the source, presumably, of the stereotyped and commercialized racial imagery—gain from answering that question in different ways? Viewers who study Smith's image may find themselves asking just such questions, even if they have little previous exposure to the complicated debates about American Indian identity. The artist puts different possible answers to those questions in dialogue with each other, but her refusal to provide a ready answer to them forces viewers to think them through for themselves.

A third strategy that some Native artists have used with particular skill is to incorporate layers of meaning into their cultural products, some of which speak differently to different audiences and may even deliberately draw attention to some viewers' inability to interpret certain subtleties. This strategy allows artists to simultaneously open up and close down communication. To borrow a phrase from anthropologist and art historian Charlotte Townsend-Gault, it is a strategy that allows artists to "control translatability, in respect for the final untranslatability of the essence of cultural difference."[27]

Cherokee artist Jimmie Durham, in a 1989 exhibition in New York entitled *The Bishop's Moose and the Pinkerton Men*, presses this strategy relentlessly. He repeatedly positions viewers who do not read and understand Cherokee in relation to those who do, forcing each person to acknowledge and experience the privileges and limitations of her specific perspective. Durham's interview with Jeannette Ingberman makes clear that his approach is intentional.

Ingberman:	The writing seems to be an integral part of the work if not the heart of the installation. You use words, especially in their hand drawn quality, as the visual body of the work....Obviously a lot of people who come in to see the show won't know the meaning of the Cherokee words.
Durham:	And I don't want them to know.
Ingberman:	That doesn't matter to you?
Durham:	What I want them to know is that they can't know that. That's what I want them to know. Here's a guy having his heart cut out with an obsidian knife and he's saying something in Cherokee and I don't want people that come into the gallery to know what he's saying.... The first text is the real thing, turquoise, words, gold, emeralds, obsidian and flint, the second text is the Cherokee counterpoint, and the third text is the fact that you don't know what the Cherokee means.[28]

Another piece, entitled *Six Authentic Things*, comments on the idea of "authenticity" by juxtaposing "real things," things similar to them, words describing them, and so on, in ways to which most viewers will be able to assign some meanings. At the same time, Durham's work forces them to acknowledge that there are truths about American Indian cultures, lives, and realities about which they are unable to form judgments because they simply lack the prerequisites to do so.

Through the use of all these strategies, American Indian artists have struck a blow for intellectual sovereignty. They have done so by refusing to allow the would-be interrogator of any individual's racial-ethnic authenticity to come to rest. They have done so by continually reminding us that some questions cannot be answered in the abstract, and by sensitizing anyone who proposes to judge identity claims, especially from outside Indian communities, to the complexity of the issue. These are lessons of which Harry Fonseca's *St. Coyote* might approve. As the trickster figure who scampers in and out of a number of Indian tribes' sacred stories, Coyote is as Indian as anyone gets. However, in Fonseca's rendering he appears as an urban renegade in leather and chains, looking distinctly unlike anyone who would fit either a legal or a cultural definition of Indian authenticity. Then again, why not? One of Coyote's customary jobs is to remind his audience that real life is never as orderly as the conceptual categories humans dream up. Reality always escapes the most concerted intellectual efforts to discipline it. Coyote always draws us back to the complexity, and the richness, at the core of all human experience, reminding us not to accept society's answers too easily. A fixture of traditional Native storytelling, he urges his viewers to remember that Indian-ness is a real thing, even if its location can move and is sometimes hard to pin down. Ubiquitous and indestructible, he also reminds Indian people that survival is possible, even for those who do not fit neatly into the available categories.

NOTES

1 An earlier, related version of this essay appears in Heather Fryer, ed., *Cowboys, Indians, and the Big Picture* (Chestnut Hill, MA: Charles S. and Isabella V. McMullen Museum of Art, Boston College, 2002).

2 The descriptions of the artists appear in the following sources: Margaret Archuleta, "Coyote: A Myth in the Making" (Fonseca exhibition brochure National History Museum Foundation, 1986); "Artist Profile: Jaune Quick-To-See Smith" (Washington, DC: National Museum of Women in the Arts, n. d.), available online at <http://www.nmwa.org/legacy/bios/bjqsmith.htm>; Michele Alaimo, "Peter Jemison: Native American Historian," available online at http://www.rit.edu/~paradigm/stories/seneca.htm; Margaret Dubin, "Talking Yurok: Painter/Sculptor Rick Bartow, *Indian Artist* 36 (winter 1999); "John Nieto: A New West Artist," *Art Life Arizona* (Tucson: The Stanbery Corporation, 1999–2000), available online at <http://www.artlifearizona.com/articles/nieto.html>.

3 Janet C. Berlo and Ruth B. Phillips, *Native North American Art* (Oxford: Oxford University Press, 1998), 3.

4 Robert Warrior, *Tribal Secrets: Recovering American Indian Intellectual Traditions* (Minneapolis: University of Minneapolis Press, 1995); Robert Warrior, "The Native American Scholar: Towards a New Intellectual Agenda," *Wicazo Sa Review: Journal of Native American Studies* 14.2 (1999): 46–55.

5 Wilcomb E. Washburn, *Red Man's Land/White Man's Law: A Study of the Past and Present Status of the American Indian* (New York: Charles Scribner's Sons, 1971).

6 H.R. 101–400, 101st Cong., 1st Sess., *Congressional Record* (1990): 4–5.

7 David W. Penney and Lisa Roberts, "America's Pueblo Artists: Encounters on the Borderlands", in *Native American Art in the Twentieth Century: Makers, Meanings, Histories*, ed. W. Jackson Rushing, III (New York: Routledge, 1999), 21–38; Bruce Bernstein, "Context of the Growth and Development of the Indian Art World in the 1960s and 1970s," in *Native American Art in the Twentieth Century: Makers, Histories,* ed. W. Jackson Rushing, III (New York: Routledge, 1999), 57–71. See also George Pierre Castile, "The Commodification of Indian Identity," *American Anthropologist* 98.4 (December 1996): 743–49.

8 See also Eva Garroutte, *Real Indians: Identity and the Survival of Native America* (Berkeley: University of California Press, 2003) and Gail K. Sheffield, *The Arbitrary Indian: The Indian Arts and Crafts Act of 1990* (Norman: University of Oklahoma Press, 1997).

9 Russell Thornton, "Tribal Membership Requirements and the Demography of 'Old' and 'New' Native Americans," *Population Research and Policy Review* 16 (1997): 37.

10 C. Matthew Snipp, *American Indians: The First of This Land* (New York: Russell Sage Foundation, 1989), 157.

11 Thornton, "Tribal Membership Requirements," 37.

12 Circe Sturm, *Blood Politics: Race, Culture and Identity in the Cherokee Nation of Oklahoma* (Berkeley: University of California Press, 2002); Kent Carter, *The Dawes Commission and the Allotment of the Five Civilized Tribes*, 1893–1914 (Orem, UT: Ancestry.com, 1999).

13 Sharon O'Brien, "Tribes and Indians: With Whom Does the United States Maintain a Relationship?" *Notre Dame Law Review* 66 (1991): 1481.

14 Thomas J. Morgan, *Annual Report* (Washington, DC: U.S. Government Printing Office, 1892), 30.

15 Washburn, *Red Man's Land,* 167. See also William T. Hagan, "Full Blood, Mixed Blood, Generic, and Ersatz: The Problem of Indian Identity," *Arizona and the West* 27 (1985): 121.

16 Charlotte Townsend-Gault, "Kinds of Knowing," in *Land Spirit Power: First Nations at the National Gallery of Canada* (Ottawa: National Gallery of Canada, 1992), 91, note 15.

17 Hulleah Tsinhnahjinnie, "Biography: Hulleah Tsinhnahjinnie," available online at <*http://www.andrewsmithgallery.com/exhibitions/hulleah/hulleah.htm*>.

18 Jack D. Forbes, "The Manipulation of Race, Caste, and Identity: Classifying AfroAmericans, Native Americans and Red-Black People," *Journal of Ethnic Studies* 17.4 (1990): 23–24.

19 Anne Merline McCulloch and David E. Wilkins, "Constructing Nations within States: The Quest for Federal Recognition by the Catawba and Lumbee Tribes," *American Indian Quarterly* 19.3 (Summer 1995): 369.

20 Rosalie Favell, quoted in W. Jackson Rushing, III, *Native American Art in the Twentieth Century,* 146.

21 Personal conversation, March 14, 2004.

22 Important court cases that first began to grapple with the meaning of tribal sovereignty are *Cherokee Nation v. Georgia* (1831) and, even more importantly, *Worcester v. Georgia* (1832). For a more detailed discussion of legal cases pertaining to tribal sovereignty, see Sharon O'Brien. *American Indian Tribal Governments* (Norman: University of Oklahoma Press, 1989).

23 Charles Wilkinson, *The Eagle Bird: Mapping a New West* (New York: Pantheon, 1992**)**.

24 Warrior, *Tribal Secrets* (1995).

25 Warrior, "The Native American Scholar" (1999). See further Taiaiake Alfred, *Peace, Power, Righteousness: An Indigenous Manifesto* (Don Mills, Ontario: Oxford University Press, 1999); Lester-Irabinna Rigner, "Internationalisation of an Indigenous Anti-Colonial Critique of Resarch Methodologies: A Guide to Indigenous Research Methodology and Its Priciples," *Wicazo Sa Review* 14.2 (1997): 109–25;

and Linda Tuhiwai Smith, *Decolonizing Methodologies: Research and Indigenous Peoples* (New York and London: Zed Books, 1999).

26 Muriel Antoine, exhibition catalogue for "Indian Humor" (American Indian Contemporary Arts, 1995), Sarah Bates, curator. Available online at <*http://www.nmai.si.edu/exhibitions/indian_humor/exhibit/3.htm*>.

27 Townsend-Gault, "Kinds of Knowing," 86.

28 "Conversation between Jimmie Durham and Jeannette Ingberman," in *The Bishop's Moose and the Pinkerton Men* (New York: Exit Art Gallery, 1990), 30–31.

BIBLIOGRAPHY

Alaimo, Michele. "Peter Jemison: Native American Historian." Available online at <*http://www.rit.edu/~paradigm/stories/_seneca.htm*>.

Alfred, Taiaiake. *Peace, Power, Righteousness: An Indigenous Manifesto.* Don Mills, Ontario: Oxford University Press, 1999.

Antoine, Muriel. Exhibition catalogue for "Indian Humor." American Indian Contemporary Arts, 1995. Sarah Bates, curator. Available online at <*http://www.nmai.si.edu/exhibitions/indian_humor/exhibit/3.htm*>.

Archuleta, Margaret. "Coyote: A Myth in the Making." Fonseca exhibition brochure, National History Museum Foundation, 1986.

"Artist Profile: Jaune Quick-To-See Smith." Washington, DC: National Museum of Women in the Arts. Available online at <*http://www.nmwa.org/legacy/bios/bjqsmith.htm*>.

Berlo, Janet C., and Ruth B. Phillips. *Native North American Art.* Oxford: Oxford University Press, 1998.

Bernstein, Bruce. "Contexts for the Growth and Development of the Indian Art World in the 1960s and 1970s." In *Native American Art in the Twentieth Century: Makers, Meanings, Histories,* edited by W. Jackson Rushing, III. New York: Routledge, 1999.

Carter, Kent. *The Dawes Commission and the Allotment of the Five Civilized Tribes, 1893–1914.* Orem, Utah: Ancestry.com, 1999.

Castile, George Pierre. "The Commodification of Indian Identity." *American Anthropologist* 98.4 (December, 1996).

"Conversation between Jimmie Durham and Jeannette Ingberman." In *The Bishop's Moose and the Pinkerton Men.* New York: Exit Art Gallery, 1990.

Dubin, Margaret. "Talking Yurok: Painter/Sculptor Rick Bartow." *Indian Artist* 36 (Winter 1999).

Forbes, Jack D. "The Manipulation of Race, Caste, and Identity: Classifying AfroAmericans, Native Americans and the Red-Black People." *Journal of Ethnic Studies* 17.4 (1990).

Garroutte, Eva. *Real Indians: Identity and the Survival of Native America*. Berkeley: University of California Press, 2003.

H.R. 101–400, 101ˢᵗ Cong., 1ˢᵗ Sess., *Congressional Record*, 1990, 4–5.

Hagan, William T. "Full Blood, Mixed Blood, Generic, and Ersatz: The Problem of Indian Identity." *Arizona and the West* 27 (1985).

"John Nieto: A New West Artist." *Art Life Arizona*. Tucson: The Stanbery Corporation, 1999–2000. Available online at *http://www.artlifearizona.com/articles/nieto.htm*.

McCulloch, Anne Merline and David E. Wilkins. "Constructing Nations within States: The Quest for Federal Recognition by the Catawba and Lumbee Tribes." *American Indian Quarterly* 19.3 (Summer 1995).

Morgan, Thomas J. *Annual Report*. Washington, DC: U.S. Government Printing Office, 1892.

O'Brien, Sharon. *American Indian Tribal Governments*. Norman: University of Oklahoma, 1989.

———. "Tribes and Indians: With Whom Does the United States Maintain a Relationship?" *Notre Dame Law Review* 66 (1991).

Penney, David W., and Lisa Roberts. "America's Pueblo Artists: Encounters on the Borderlands." In *Native American Art in the Twentieth Century: Makers, Meanings, Histories,* edited by W. Jackson Rushing, III. New York: Routledge, 1999.

Rigney, Lester-Irabinna. "Internationalisation of an Indigenous Anti-Colonial Critique of Research Methodologies: A Guide to Indigenous Research Methodology and Its Principles." *Wicazo Sa Review* 14.2 (1997).

Sheffield, Gail K. *The Arbitrary Indian: The Indian Arts and Crafts Act of 1990*. Norman: University of Oklahoma Press, 1997.

Smith, Linda Tuhiwai. *Decolonizing Methodologies: Research and Indigenous Peoples*. New York: Zed Books, 1999.

Snipp, C. Matthew. *American Indians: The First of This Land*. New York: Russell Sage Foundation, 1989.

Sturm, Circe. *Blood Politics: Race, Culture and Identity in the Cherokee Nation of Oklahoma*. Berkeley: University of California Press, 2002.

Thornton, Russell. "Tribal Membership Requirements and the Demography of 'Old' and 'New' Native Americans." *Population Research and Policy Review* 16 (1997).

Townsend-Gault, Charlotte. "Kinds of Knowing." In *Land Spirit Power: First Nations at the National Gallery of Canada*. Ottawa: National Gallery of Canada, 1992.

Tsinhnahjinnie, Hulleah. "Biography: Hulleah Tsinhnahjinnie." Available online at <http://www.andrewsmithgallery.com/exhibitions/hulleah/hulleah.htm>.

Warrior, Robert. *Tribal Secrets: Recovering American Indian Intellectual Traditions*. Minneapolis: University of Minneapolis Press, 1995.

————. "The Native American Scholar: Towards a New Intellectual Agenda." *Wicazo Sa Review: Journal of Native American Studies* 14.2 (1999).

Washburn, Wilcomb E. *Red Man's Land/White Man's Law: A Study of the Past and Present Status of the American Indian*. New York: Charles Scribner's Sons, 1971.

Wilkinson, Charles. *The Eagle Bird: Mapping a New West*. New York: Pantheon, 1992.

CONTRIBUTORS

Thomas Belt is a fluent native speaker of Cherokee and has been teaching the Cherokee language since 1993. Belt started teaching in the Cherokee Central Schools on the Eastern Cherokee reservation, but he is currently an Elder-in-Residence at Western Carolina University. He is the co-author of a series of Cherokee language textbooks for grades three through six. He is respected in Cherokee communities and beyond, not only as a speaker, but also as someone who is knowledgeable about Cherokee culture. On numerous occasions, he has been called upon to give public presentations, including at UNC-Chapel Hill, Virginia Tech, and Wake Forest University, to name a few.

Margaret Bender, Ph.D, is a linguistic and cultural anthropologist who has studied the relationship between language and culture in a variety of contexts—from political rhetoric in Iran to family literacy education in Chicago. The author of *Signs of Cherokee Culture: Sequoyah's Syllabary in Eastern Cherokee Life* (2007), her most recent research and publications have explored language use and gender among Native Americans and linguistic diversity in the U.S. South. Since 1993, she has served several times as a linguistic consultant to the Eastern Band of Cherokee Indians. Dr. Bender is also currently engaged in a study of contemporary fatherhood and masculinity among the Kiowas, Comanches, Fort Sill Apaches, and Chickasaws of Oklahoma and in a linguistic analysis of Cherokee texts.

Thomas J. Blumer, Ph.D., served as senior editor, European Law Division, of the U.S. Library of Congress in Washington, DC. He has published, among others, *A Bibliography of the Catawba* (1987), *Catawba Pottery: Survival of a Folk Tradition* (2004), and *Catawba Nation: Treasures in History* (2007). Blumer received his B.A. and M.A. in English from the University of Mississippi and his Ph.D. from the University of South Carolina. Blumer's passion has been an ongoing relationship with the Catawba Nation, which began in 1976 while he was serving as curator for a pottery exhibit at Winthrop University. In 1979 the Native American Rights Fund asked him to be its official Catawba history consultant, and he was later asked by the Catawba to serve as their official tribal historian, a position which he has held for almost thirty years.

Harry Charger is a community educator, a certified Lakota language instructor, and a ceremonial leader. Charger has taught as a community college instructor on several Lakota reservations in South Dakota. He has lectured widely to students K through 12, civic groups, and veteran organizations, and in correctional facilities. His speaking engagements include Portland State University, Portland University, Mt. Hood Community College, the University of Minnesota, Wake Forest University, and Winston-Salem State University.

Kauila Clark is vice chair of the Waianae Coast Comprehensive Health Center and a community educator and ceremonial leader. His distinguished career includes positions as executive director of the Community Mentoring Program at Nanakuli Intermediate School, president and CEO of the Employment and Training Program in the Kapolei Region, director of the Waianae RAP Center, and national facilitator and curriculum developer for Hawaiian Cultural Activities with the U.S. Office of Substance Abuse Prevention, Washington, DC.

Petrona de la Cruz, co-founder of LA FOMMA with Isabel Juarez Espinosa, grew up in the Mayan community of Zinacantán, Chiapas. She was a servant in the mestizo city of San Cristóbal de Las Casas and a librarian in Zinacantán when she joined the Indian writers' group, Sna Jtz'ibajom. She was trained in puppetry and theatre by Amy Trompetter of Barnard College and Ralph Lee of the Mettawee River Theatre Company of New York. One of Mexico's first two Indigenous women playwrights, she received the Premio Chiapas Prize for Literature. Several of her plays have been produced by LA FOMMA, both at home and abroad. Her first play, *La mujer desesperada,* has recently been translated into English. Her life was threatened while she served as the first Indian member of the human rights commission of Chiapas.

Isabel Juarez Espinosa, co-founder of LA FOMMA with Petrona de la Cruz, grew up in the Mayan village of Aguacatenango in Chiapas. She first arrived in San Cristóbal de Las Casas at the age of eight to work as a nursemaid for a mestizo family. Despite obstacles, she was able to attend school through 12th grade and became a receptionist in a café. During the 1980s, she assisted Guatemalan refugees living in the Chiapas jungle. In terms of her literary achievements, she was the first woman to join the writers' group Sna Jtz'ibajom and was instrumental in establishing a program in women's health as well as a literacy program in Tzeltal and Spanish. The author of many plays, a book of her collected works was published by SEP (a government educational press) and was reissued in 2002 to be distributed in public schools.

J. T. Garrett, Ed.D., is the health director of Carteret County, North Carolina, and the author of *Meditations with the Cherokee* (2001) and *The Cherokee Herbal* (2003) and co-author, with his son Michael, of *Medicine of the Cherokee* (1996), *Native American Faith in America* (with J.Gordon Melton, 2003), and *The Cherokee Full Circle* (2002). As a student and teacher of Cherokee medicine for over thirty-five years, he draws on the wisdom of his medicine elders on the Cherokee Lands of the Great Smoky Mountains. His dedication to community health issues includes thirty years in hospital administration, environmental and occupational safety, and public health administration.

Eva Marie Garroutte, Ph.D., is associate professor in the Department of Sociology at Boston College. Her areas of research include Native American Studies with a special interest in the arts, health and aging, and the sociology of culture with an emphasis on religion, science, and the construction of knowledge. She is the author of *Real Indians: Identity and the Survival of Native America* (2003). One of her current research projects, funded by the National Institute on Aging and Boston College, examines doctor-patient communication in tribal clinics.

Matthew D. Herman, Ph.D., is an assistant professor in the Native American Studies Department at Montana State University, Bozeman. He has presented and published on Native American literature and culture, western American regionalism, and composition pedagogy. His current book project examines intersections of nationalism, cosmopolitanism, and tribal sovereignty in contemporary Native American literature.

LeAnne Howe is an author of short stories, two novels, a book prose and poems, plays, and screenplays. She is a citizen of the Choctaw Nation of Oklahoma. During the 2006–2007 school year, she was the John and Renée Grisham Writer in Residence at the University of Mississippi at Oxford. She was also the screenwriter for *Indian Country Diaries: Spiral of Fire,* a 90-minute PBS documentary released in November 2006. Howe's fiction appears in *Fiction International, Story, Callaloo, Yalobusha Review*, and numerous other journals and literary magazines. Currently, Howe is the Interim Director for American Indian Studies at the University of Illinois, Urbana-Champaign, and she teaches in the MFA program in English. She divides her time between her home in Ada, Oklahoma, and Urbana, Illinois.

Malinda M. Maynor, Ph.D., is an assistant professor in the Department of History at Harvard University. She has an M.A. in Documentary Film and Video Production (Stanford, 1997) and is a film producer/director/editor. Among other projects, she co-produced the widely acclaimed documentary *In the Light of Reverence* and produced, directed, and edited *Sounds of Faith* and *Real Indian*. Her publications and research focus on Lumbee history, particularly on the intersection of Lumbee and African American church music.

Josefa Hernandez Perez is a member of the order of Las Hermanas Misioneras Seglares Diocesana, San Cristóbal de Las Casas, Chamula, Chiapas, Mexico, and a ceremonial leader and community educator. Her work is dedicated to the well-being of her Mayan brothers and sisters, including lobbying for children's schooling, being active in the implementation of women's cooperatives, and supporting the Fray Bartolomé de Las Casas Center for Human Rights in Chiapas.

Ione V. Quigley is the chair person of the Lakota Studies Program at Sinte Gleska University, South Dakota. Her areas of specialization include Lakota Language Studies, ethnogeography, Lakota botany, and field reconnaissance archeological surveys. Among other community initiatives, she has been instrumental in producing surveys for the Mni Wiconi Project to provide water for the Rosebud Sioux Tribe and for the Environmental Health Services of the Indian Health Service.

E. Fred Sanders served as Assistant Chief to the Catawba Nation in the early nineties, and has lectured widely on Catawba history and culture. He currently serves as Councilman for the Catawba Nation.

Lawrence Shorty is Director of Public Health Programs at the National Indian Health Board and an activist researcher in the field of public health. His expertise is in Indigenous tobacco control, and he has worked and collaborated with others in that area throughout the world. Along with Professor Joseph Winter, he helped establish an innovative seed bank and educational program and *Nicotiana* seed bank at the University of New Mexico. His contributions to the field of tobacco control include the development of Indigenous knowledge frameworks, media development and literacy, curriculum development, policy advocacy, and the incorporation of Indigenous studies topics into public health.

Jeanne Simonelli, Ph.D., is an anthropologist and writer, and former chairperson of the Anthropology Department at Wake Forest University. Her field experiences are united by the broad theme of change and choice in difficult situations. Her principal publications include *Crossing Between Worlds: The Navajos of Canyon de Chelly* (1997), *Too Wet to Plow: The Family Farm in Transition* (1992) and *Two Boys, a Girl, and Enough!* (1986). She is currently doing fieldwork concerning development and conflict resolution in Chiapas, Mexico. She received the 2000 prize for poetry from the Society for

Humanistic Anthropology. Simonelli is the editor of the journal *Practicing Anthropology* and is co-director of the Maya Study Program, which teaches undergraduates to conduct field research. She has co-authored several monographs concerning Chiapas. These include *Help Without Hurt* (Urban Anthropology, 2000), *Meeting Resistance* (Qualitative Inquiry, 2003) and *Disencumbering Development* (2002), and "The Scent of Change in Chiapas," a book chapter published in 2002.

David Kekaulike Sing, Ph.D., is Director of the Center for Gifted and Talented Native Hawaiian Children at the University of Hawai'i at Hilo. In addition, he is active in the preservation and revitalization of Hawaiian culture and philosophy through education reform and development.

Ulrike Wiethaus, Ph.D., teaches interdisciplinary studies in the Humanities Program at Wake Forest University. Her research is focused on the history, politics, and psychology of Christian spirituality with a special interest in women, gender, and power. She combines scholarship, documentary film making, and community engagement through Wake Forest University's numerous community partnership initiatives.

David E. Wilkins, Ph.D., is professor of American Indian Studies and adjunct professor of Political Science, Law, and American Studies at the University of Minnesota, Twin Cities. One of the leading experts on First Nations' sovereignty, he has written several seminal books and articles dealing with the political and legal relationship between indigenous nations and the federal and state governments. His most recent book-length studies are *On the Drafting of Tribal Constitutions* (with Felix S. Cohen and Lindsay Gordon, 2007), *American Indian Politics and the American Political System* (2006), and *Uneven Ground: American Indian Sovereignty and Federal Law* (with Tsianina Lomawaima, 2002).

INDEX